MAINE
Ingredients

Fresh & Fabulous Recipes

from

The Junior League of Portland, Maine, Inc.

MAINE
Ingredients

The Junior League of Portland, Maine, Inc., is an organization of women committed to promoting voluntarism and to improving the community through the effective action and leadership of trained volunteers. Its purpose is exclusively educational and charitable.

The Junior League of Portland reaches out to women of all races, religions and national origins who demonstrate an interest in and commitment to voluntarism.

Profits realized from the sale of *Maine Ingredients* will be used to support community projects and services of the Junior League of Portland, Maine, Inc., including those involving the prevention, intervention and treatment of child abuse and neglect.

Copyright © 1995
First Printing 11,500 May, 1995
Second Printing 10,000 March, 1996
Third Printing 10,000 April, 1997

Illustrations by Dawn Peterson

ISBN 0-9644691-0-3
Library of Congress catalogue card number 95-75247

For additional copies, use the order forms in the back of this book or send a check for $19.95 plus $4.50 shipping and handling (Maine residents add 6% sales tax) to:

Maine Ingredients
Junior League of Portland, Maine, Inc.
107 Elm Street, Suite 100R
Portland, Maine 04101
207-874-9756

Printed in the USA by

WIMMER
The Wimmer Companies, Inc.
Memphis

Table of Contents

Maine Ingredients is the result of three years of dedication and thousands of volunteer hours. This cookbook became a reality through the collaborative efforts and individual "ingredients" of the following committee members and their families.

The Committee

Editor-in-Chief
Carol I. Austin

Art Director & Design
Carolyn T. Cianchette

Coordinating Chair 1994-95
Lucy L. Tucker

Chair 1993-94, Marketing Chair 1994-95
Ann V. Perrino

Ex-Officio
Shelly Paules

1993-95
Nan Corcoran
Lesley P. Craig
Elaine Graef
Mary Gresge
Margaret C. Hewes
Julie Lake
Susan E. Leach
Sonya A. Messer
Hope Mitchell
Sally Nichols
Laurie J. Piasio
Janet G. Rivard
Elisabeth H. Sears
Linda S. Schrader
Joan McClure Smith
Victoria W. Wright

Past Committee Members
Lee Wilson, *Chair 1992-93*
Pamela S. Bates
Anne W. Bosworth
Lisa W. Gregoire
Judy Jurevic
Linda LeBlond
Ann Mason
Karen D. McMann
Lucia Orefice
Janet Tunis

1995-96
Chairs
Suzy Andrews
Kim Joyce
Heidi Kingman
Victoria Wright
Anita Zidow

Committee
Tammy Acker
Debbie Beauregard
Patricia Berry
Renee Forbes
Janet Gibson
Pam Higgins
Sharon Jordan
Katie Keith
Julie Lake
Kim Levandoski
Dorothy MacDiarmid
Margaret Mixon
Sally Nichols
Regis Park
Janet Rivard
Linda Shraeder
Joan Smith

1996-97
Chairs
Suzy Andrews
Jane Parker
Courtney Spencer

Committee
Lyndsay Alexander
Ann Marie Beaudette
Patricia Berry
Michele Broderick
Lori-Hill Burns
Catherine Cloudman
Jennifer Kameisha
Dorothy MacDiarmid
Mary Martin
Sylvie Montello
Lisa Morris
Stacy Ryan
Kate Snyder
Cathy Steele
Vicki Wahrer

*f*rom the knife's edge of Mt. Katahdin to the endless
flatlands and potato fields of Aroostook County;
from the sparkling lakes of the Sebago Region to the treacherous
crests of the Allagash; and from the snow-capped mountains to the
jagged rockbound coast, Maine conjures up contrasting images.

*m*aine was "Land of the Dawn", to the Abenaki Indians.
To the Europeans, it was Norumbega, a mythical city of gold-plated
roofs, crystal gates and lapis lazuli pillars. Today, Maine is a vision of
"the way life should be." It offers a peaceful escape from the crowded
cities; a place where neither the beauties of nature nor the
pace of life has been spoiled by over development.

*m*aine *Ingredients* recognizes Maine's changing faces
and images while emphasizing the importance of its natural delicacies.
The goodness of these fine ingredients, the lobster, shellfish,
sweet corn, wild blueberries, apples, potatoes and other indigenous
resources lives on in new combinations. They blend the freshest
ingredients with a splash of zest and a pinch of savvy seasoning
to create a whole new recipe for Maine cooking.

*m*aine's most valuable and precious ingredient,
and the inspiration for this book, is its children. They need nurturing
that is often unavailable in our modern world. They are often
abused and exploited. They are often underprivileged and defenseless.
In an effort to protect these children, and ensure their future,
the Junior League of Portland dedicates the proceeds of this book
to the prevention of child abuse and neglect.

*W*e thank you for your support in our efforts,
and hope you will enjoy your journey through the many ingredients,
images and flavors of Maine.

Traveling & Tasting
MAINE
Vacation Guide with Menus

m any Mainers enjoy visitors "from away" throughout the year, or take time to enjoy Vacation-land themselves. Whether you have guests or are vacationing with your family, Maine's seasons provide ample opportunity to savor abundant *"Maine Ingredients"* in beautiful settings.

This travel and menu guide is full of easy and delicious make-ahead meals using fresh ingredients that allow you to enjoy your guests and all Maine has to offer. Maine has been referred to as "the way life should be." Come visit with us and see why.

We hope you enjoy traveling with us on a journey throughout the seasons and flavors of Maine. We're sure you will use this cookbook time and time again to measure the goodness of our *Maine Ingredients*!

Come Visit this Summer

*L*ong sunny, blue sky days and wonderful, warm evenings entice many to explore Maine in the summer. We've tried to capture a few highlights just to get you started.

Strolling the Old Port

A satisfying brunch on the patio will ease your guests into the vacation mode.

Get Reacquainted Brunch

Maine Blueberry Muffins • Sunshine Yogurt Cups with Yogurt Bar
Crab Meat Tart • Cheesy Shredded Potatoes

After brunch, visit Portland's revitalized "Old Port." Specialty shops and Portland's finest restaurants fill the picturesque cobblestone streets in this historic section of town.

A Farmer's Market occurs midweek in Monument Square at the top of the Old Port. Browse through the wide selection of local fare including an abundance of seasonal fruits, vegetables, herbs, spices, and fresh or dried flowers.

After the Farmer's Market head to Portland's bustling harbor on Commercial Street. Its wooden piers, seagoing vessels, seafood vendors, ferry rides and restaurants combine to create the timeless aura of a New England port. Here lobsters and clams can be purchased for this evening's "Shore Dinner."

Maine Shore Dinner

Kettle Cove Clams • Effortless French Bread • Herbed Fish Chowder
Fresh Grilled Lobster • Grilled Sweet Corn • Glazed Truffle Cake • Ginger Almond Iced Tea

Discover Down East

Northeasterly winds dominate Maine's rocky coast. Sailors traveling in this direction navigated "down wind," hence the coastal area in Northern Maine was nicknamed "Down East." A trip "Down East" can include a visit to gems like Camden, Owl's Head or Deer Isle. Enjoy breathtaking ocean vistas as you travel up the coast to any of these charming harbor towns. Acadia National Park is also located Down East, but a day is only long enough to whet one's appetite.

Cruising the Coast

Fresh Mozzarella & Tomato Salad • Blissful Herb Potato Salad
Pack-a-Picnic Sandwich • Doubly Decadent Raspberry Brownies • Cranberry Citrus Iced Tea

Leaf Peeping Weekend in the Fall

*f*all is a wonderful season to enjoy Maine and entertain guests. Bountiful harvests and colorful foliage complement traditional Vacationland hospitality. Autumn's vibrant colors invite many to take advantage of Maine's celebrated beauty.

Leaf Peeping

Travel along coastal routes or inland along more mountainous regions to peep at the fiery red, golden orange, and bright yellow foliage. For an incredible treat, soar high above the picture perfect countryside in a hot air balloon.

In the afternoon, enjoy the crisp, fresh air of October at one of Maine's numerous orchards. After harvesting a bushel of apples with friends, bring the party home to the kitchen and put the fruits of your labor to good use. Sip warm mulled cider by the fire as the sweet aroma of apple pie fills the house.

Fireside Harvest Supper

Autumn Brie • Hearty Harvest Ratatouille • Fall Harvest Veal Cutlets
Down East Dinner Rolls • Oven Roasted Potatoes • Apple Cranberry Pear Pie • Mulled Apple Cider

Fresh Air Fun

Maine has beautiful parks and trails sure to please all levels of outdoor enthusiasts, from the leisurely hiker to the adventurous climber. Pull on a sweater and take a brisk walk. Hear the leaves crunch under foot. A simple hike up Bradbury Mountain in Pownal can be enjoyed by the whole family.

Non-hikers may enjoy a scenic foliage tour around Moosehead Lake on the cruise ship, "Katahdin," or try a bicycle ride on a favorite route. Capture the flavors of autumn with this satisfying lunch.

Fall Bounty Luncheon

Apple Walnut Vinaigrette Salad • Carrot Dill Pesto Soup
Zucchini Apple Harvest Bread

Winter Wonderland Retreat

*m*aine is known for its long winters and abundance of snow. Winter in Maine is the time to enjoy numerous outdoor activities and savor the flavor of warm winter delicacies.

We're Off!

After packing up the car with skis, sleds and outdoor gear, head northwest to one of Maine's premier ski resorts. Snow covered slopes, a crackling fire, and this warm, enticing meal will confirm that you are truly in a winter wonderland. Be sure to turn in early so you will have plenty of energy for a full day of skiing tomorrow!

Winter Weekend Warm-Up
Berry Good Eggnog • Shrimp & Pork Treasures
Herbed Focaccia • Skiers' Stew • Mocha Madness

Ski Extravaganza

Start your day of winter sports with this energizing breakfast.

Get Crackin' Breakfast
Get Crackin' Eggs • Hearty Potato Pancakes • Pear Hazelnut Muffins

Experience the thrill of downhill on hundreds of challenging trails, ride a gondola to the summit and pause at the top to take in the incredible view. Enjoy the scenic splendor of miles of countryside decorated with frozen lakes and forests blanketed with snow.

If cross-country skiing is more your style, spend the day exploring well-groomed trails. Glide under canopies of pine trees weighted down by new-fallen snow or traverse vast open fields. You may even sneak a peek at a moose!

More Fun in the Snow

Bundle up and choose your sport. Winter's clear, crisp magic draws you outdoors for skating or sledding. Return to your home base rosy-cheeked for a hearty lunch.

Homeward Bound
Savory Tomato Soup • Turkey Tortilla Wrap
Nubble Light Nut Bars • Brown Sugar Hot Chocolate

Appetizers

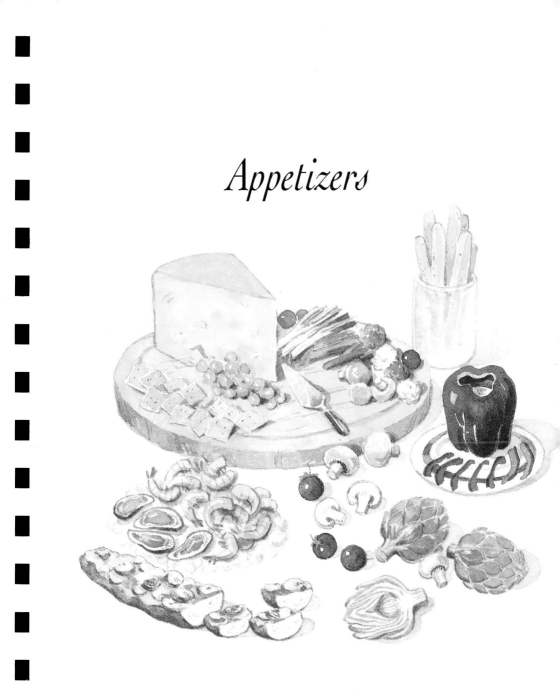

MAINE
Ingredients

Clams & Quahogs

Clams can readily be found along Maine's extensive coastline. Great shell heaps are scattered from Kittery to Quoddy Head. The largest of these can still be found near Damariscotta where the Indians gathered after the corn harvest. They feasted on shellfish and dried the clams in the sun for winter use. Three acres of shells, in mounds as deep as thirty feet, remain along the river's edge.

To Mainers there are many well known hybrids of clams. The most popular soft shell is the steamer. More than two million pounds of this long-necked bivalve are harvested annually by commercial fisherman. This does not include the uncounted thousands of pounds dug from clam flats by natives and visitors.

The hard-shell, short-necked varieties range in size from the smallest, the littleneck, to the mid-sized cherrystone, followed by the largest, the quahog (pronounced Kwô-hog).

Quahogs, a Mainer's favorite, are dense and thick and ideal for simmering in chowder!

Kettle Cove Clams

24 Littleneck clams on the half shell

2 tablespoons butter,
    at room temperature

5 dashes Tabasco sauce

3 scallions, chopped

1 tablespoon minced garlic

1 tablespoon finely chopped shallots

1/4 teaspoon salt

2 tablespoons lemon juice

1 tablespoon Dijon mustard

2 ounces Cognac (optional)

freshly ground pepper to taste

4 slices bacon

1/2 cup cracker crumbs

1/2 cup melted butter

paprika and parsley for garnish

• Preheat oven to 425°.

• Loosen clam in its shell. Arrange clams, shell down, on a rack or baking dish.

• Combine the soft butter with the Tabasco, scallions, garlic, shallots, salt, lemon juice, mustard, Cognac and pepper. Spread an equal portion of the mixture on top of each clam.

• Put the bacon in a saucepan and add water to cover. Bring to a boil and drain. Pat dry. Cut the bacon into small rectangles and cover each clam with a portion of it. Sprinkle with cracker crumbs and pour the melted butter over all. Sprinkle with paprika and parsley. Bake for 20 minutes.

Yields 24 baked clams

Blazing Shrimp Brochettes

forty-eight 8-inch wooden skewers

1 clove garlic

¹/₂ teaspoon salt

2 tablespoons vegetable oil

12-ounce jar jalapeno peppers

1 pound large uncooked shrimp

• In a shallow dish, let the skewers soak in water to cover for 1 hour. On a cutting board, mince and mash the garlic to a paste with salt. In a bowl, combine the garlic paste, the oil and 1 of the jalapeno peppers, drained seeded and minced. Mix well. Peel, devein, rinse and drain shrimp and toss them until they are coated with the marinade and let them marinate for 30 minutes.

• Cut the remaining jalapeno peppers cross-wise into forty-eight ¹/₄-inch slices and thread 1 shrimp around 1 jalapeno slice on each skewer. The brochettes may be prepared up to this point 2 hours in advance and kept covered and chilled.

• Grill the brochettes on a rack set about 4 inches over glowing coals, turning them once, for 2 to 3 minutes or until the shrimp are pink and firm. Alternatively, the brochettes can be broiled on racks set in jelly-roll pans under a preheated broiler about 4 inches from the heat, turning them once, for 2 to 3 minutes or until the shrimp are pink and just firm.

Yields 48 hors d'oeuvres

Shrimp & Pork Treasures

Pastry:

1 cup unsalted butter, softened

8 ounces cream cheese, softened

2 cups flour

Filling:

1 pound lean ground pork, cooked
  but not well done

1/2 cup cooked shrimp, minced

2 teaspoons salt

1/4 cup chopped scallions

1/4 cup water chestnuts, chopped

1/2 teaspoon ground ginger

1 tablespoon soy sauce

1 egg

1/2 cup dry bread crumbs

Egg wash:

1 egg

1 teaspoon milk

• Combine pastry ingredients until a stiff dough forms. Refrigerate 1 hour or longer.

• In a large bowl, mix filling ingredients. May be stored up to 3 days in refrigerator, adding shrimp when ready to use.

• Divide pastry dough into 4 sections. Roll each to a 9x12 rectangle and cut in half to form two 4 1/2 x 12-inch pieces. Spread each with 1/8 of filling. Roll up from long side, jelly-roll style. Moisten edges with water and press to seal. Place seam side down on an ungreased baking sheet. Chill 1 hour or longer.

• May be frozen at this point. Defrost in refrigerator before baking.

• Preheat oven to 375°. Brush each roll with egg wash. Bake for 30 to 35 minutes or until golden brown. Cool slightly and cut diagonally into 1-inch slices. May serve warm or cold.

Yields 8 rolls or 8 dozen slices

Lobster Bundles

1 scallion

8 ounces cooked lobster meat

¹/4 cup crumbled feta cheese

1 tablespoon Dijon mustard

4 ounces cream cheese, softened

salt and pepper to taste

1 tablespoon chopped fresh tarragon

1 tablespoon white wine

24 wonton wrappers (3x3)

vegetable cooking spray

• Trim and slice scallion, using green part only. In a medium bowl, toss lobster with scallion and feta. Mix with mustard, cream cheese, salt, pepper, tarragon and wine.

• Spray mini-muffin tins with vegetable cooking spray. Place one wonton wrapper in each cup and gently press down. Place a heaping teaspoon of lobster mixture in each cup. Fold sides on top to seal or twist to enclose. Spray each bundle with cooking spray. (May be prepared without mini-muffin tins. Simply fill each wonton the same as above and pull up and twist sides together to seal. Place on cookie sheets sprayed with cooking spray and spray each wonton).

• Bake at 375° for 12 to 15 minutes or until lightly brown. Serve immediately.

Yields 2 dozen

Lobster Stuffed Mushrooms

1 pound large mushrooms, washed, stems removed

6 tablespoons butter

2 cloves garlic, minced

1/4 teaspoon pepper

2 tablespoons olive oil

1/4 cup dry sherry

1/4 cup toasted bread crumbs

3/4 cup shredded Gruyere or Parmesan cheese

1/2 to 1 pound cooked lobster meat, finely chopped

- Preheat oven to 400°.

- Finely chop mushroom stems. In a small skillet, melt the butter over medium heat and sauté the mushroom stems and garlic. In a small bowl, combine sautéed mushroom stems and garlic with pepper, olive oil, sherry, bread crumbs and cheese, adding more bread crumbs if too moist or more sherry if too dry. Fold in lobster meat. Stuff mushroom caps with the lobster filling.

- Pour just enough water into a 9x13 jelly roll or shallow baking pan to cover the bottom. Put mushrooms in pan and bake for 15 to 20 minutes.

Yields approximately 2 dozen

Hollandaise sauce:

6 tablespoons butter

4 egg yolks

juice of 1 lemon

salt and pepper to taste

- In a small saucepan, heat butter until it just starts to smoke but not to burn. In blender or food processor, combine egg yolks, lemon, salt and pepper. With the motor running, slowly pour the hot butter into the egg yolk mixture. If mixture curdles, add a few drops of water. Pour sauce into sauce pan and cook over medium heat, stirring constantly, until egg starts to cook to sides of pan. Pour back into blender or food processor to smooth out.

- Pour Hollandaise sauce over stuffed mushrooms and serve.

Scallop Canapés

6 dozen 1-inch bread rounds

1 ¹/₂ tablespoons butter

¹/₂ pound scallops, chopped

2 teaspoons minced lemon zest

2 cloves garlic, minced

¹/₈ cup chopped fresh dill

1 cup grated Swiss or Gruyere cheese

¹/₂ to ³/₄ cup mayonnaise

freshly ground pepper to taste

paprika

lemon slices and dill sprigs
     for garnish

• Cut 1-inch bread rounds with cookie cutter and lightly toast. Melt the butter in a medium skillet. Add the scallops, lemon zest and garlic. Cook, stirring constantly, until the scallops are just barely cooked through, 2 to 3 minutes. Add the dill and cook 30 seconds longer. Let cool.

• Add the cheese, mayonnaise and pepper to the scallop mixture and stir to combine well.

• Preheat the broiler. Place the toast rounds ¹/₂ inch apart on baking sheets. Top each toast round with a heaping teaspoon of the scallop mixture and sprinkle lightly with paprika.

• Broil the canapés 5 inches from the heat until puffed and golden, 2 to 3 minutes. Transfer the canapés to platters and garnish with lemon slices and dill sprigs. Serve hot.

Yields 6 dozen

Bacon Banded Scallops

10 slices bacon

20 large sea scallops

1 cup whipping cream

2 tablespoons Dijon mustard

2 tablespoons maple syrup

• Preheat oven to 350°. Arrange bacon on baking sheet and bake until golden (approximately 8 minutes). Cut each slice in half. Drain and cool.

• Wrap each slice of bacon around a scallop. Secure with toothpick. Preheat oven to 400°. Place scallops on baking sheet and bake until cooked through (8 to 10 minutes).

• Meanwhile, boil cream in heavy skillet until reduced to $^3/_4$ cup (approximately 3 minutes). Add mustard and syrup and boil until sauce has a thick consistency (approximately 3 minutes). Place sauce on platter. Arrange scallops on sauce. Keep warm.

Yields 20 hors d'oeuvres

Seasoned Steamed Mussels

5 scallions, chopped
including green tops

2 cloves garlic, finely chopped

1 tablespoon olive oil

¹/4 cup white wine

2 pounds cultivated mussels

3 tablespoons parsley, chopped
1 tablespoon reserved

2 plum tomatoes

hot sauce, to taste

1 tablespoon butter

loaf of French bread

- Sauté scallions and garlic in oil until translucent — about 3 minutes. Add wine, mussels, parsley, tomato and favorite hot sauce. Stir to coat and cover.

- Cook until mussels open — about 7-8 minutes. Remove mussels to platter when done with slotted spoon. Discard any unopened mussels.

- Turn heat to high, reduce juices and whisk in butter. Continue stirring to a boil and reduce.

- Pour reduced liquid over mussels. Garnish with reserved tablespoon of parsley. Serve with French bread to absorb juices.

Serves 4

Debearding Mussels

Inside a mussel is a whisker like substance which must be removed. If the musssel shell is not closed too tightly it is possible to remove the beard prior to cooking. Firmly grasp the whisker and pull loose from the shell, being careful not to remove any of the mussel meat. Mussels which are tightly closed before cooking may be debearded after they have been steamed opened.

Devilicious Shrimp

6 tablespoons unsalted butter

4 anchovy fillets

2 large cloves garlic

1 1/2 teaspoons Dijon mustard

1 teaspoon Tabasco

1 1/2 teaspoons Worcestershire sauce

1 pound uncooked shrimp

1/4 cup minced fresh flat leaf parsley

• Let butter warm to room temperature. Drain and mince anchovy. Peel and devein shrimp with tails left intact. Using back of spoon, mash first 6 ingredients in small bowl. (Can be made 3 days ahead. Cover; chill. Bring to room temperature before using).

• Preheat broiler. Place shrimp in single layer in large broiler-proof baking dish. Smear butter mixture over shrimp. Broil shrimp without turning until cooked through, about 5 minutes. Sprinkle with parsley.

Serves 8

Petite Stuffed Potatoes

2 pints bite size new potatoes, red or white

1/2 pound bacon or caviar

8 ounces sour cream

1 bunch chives, minced

2-3 parsley sprigs, for garnish

• Wash and drain potatoes. In boiling water, cook potatoes for 20 minutes, until tender. Rinse under cold water and let cool.
• Cook bacon until crisp, drain on paper towels. Crumble into small bits.
• Carefully, cut tops off potatoes and scoop out middle with melon baller. Mix sour cream with chives. Stuff mixture into potatoes. Sprinkle top with crumbled bacon or caviar. Garnish with parsley. Serve chilled.

Serves 4-8

Crab Island Spread

6 ounces fresh crabmeat

¼ cup light mayonnaise

⅛ cup chopped fresh chives

1 tablespoon minced fresh tarragon
   or fresh dill

salt and pepper to taste

• Mix crabmeat and mayonnaise together until mixture is fine. Add remaining ingredients.

• Serve with delicate crackers for best flavor.

Yields ¾ cup

Any fresh herb can be added for variety. If chives are not available, use scallions.

> ### Recipe Alternative
>
> Excellent for stuffing cherry tomatoes. Wash and cut top part off each tomato. Hollow out inside of tomato with a small melon scoop. Fill with crab spread. To keep tomatoes from rolling around platter, cut the bottom leaving the stem end as a flat and secure base.

The Great Crab Caper

1 pound crabmeat

1 tablespoon horseradish

2 tablespoons capers, rinsed

2 cups mayonnaise

1 teaspoon lemon rind, grated

½ teaspoon garlic powder

2 dashes Tabasco

1 teaspoon Worcestershire sauce

• Preheat oven to 350°.

• Gently toss all ingredients together.

• Pour into a greased 2-quart casserole. Bake 20 to 30 minutes.

• Serve directly from oven or from a chafing dish with assorted crackers.

Yields approximately 3 cups

Apple Jack Spread

8 ounces cream cheese, softened

4 ounces Monterey Jack cheese, shredded

2 teaspoons Dijon mustard

1 large Granny Smith Apple, shredded

2 tablespoons chopped chives

½ cup finely chopped pecans

• In a food processor or by hand, combine cheeses and mustard, blending until smooth. Remove to a medium bowl. Add apples and chives and gently combine mixture. Sprinkle with pecans.

• Chill and serve with crackers.

Yields 2 cups

Autumn Brie

1 small Macintosh or Cortland apple

⅓ cup golden raisins

1 cup apple cider

4-inch round of Brie

chopped pecans for garnish

loaf of french bread

• Preheat oven to 350°.

• Core and chop apples. Cook apple and raisins in cider, on top of stove, until apples are tender but not mushy (approximately ½ to 2 minutes). Put brie in ovenproof dish slightly larger than the brie. Strain liquid from apple/raisin mixture and put cooked apple and raisins on top of brie. Garnish with chopped pecans and bake at 350° for 15 to 20 minutes.

• Serve with sliced French bread.

Serves 4

Savory Blue Cheese Cake

¹/₃ cup fine bread crumbs

¹/₄ cup grated Parmesan cheese

¹/₂ pound bacon

28 ounces cream cheese

4 eggs

¹/₂ cup heavy cream

1 medium onion, finely chopped

¹/₂ pound blue cheese

salt and freshly ground pepper to taste

2 to 3 drops Tabasco

This savory appetizer freezes well. For a smaller crowd prepare half the recipe. Roquefort, Stilton or Gorgonzola type blue cheese are best suited for this recipe.

• Sprinkle bread crumbs and Parmesan cheese in a buttered, water-tight 8-inch round springform pan. Set aside.

• Cook and finely chop bacon, reserving 1 tablespoon drippings. Combine cream cheese, eggs and cream in mixer. Sauté onion in reserved 1 tablespoon bacon drippings until transparent. Add onion, bacon, crumbled blue cheese, salt and pepper and Tabasco to cream cheese mixture. Mix well. Pour into prepared pan. Set pan inside a larger one; pour boiling water 2 inches deep into larger pan.

• Bake 1 hour and 40 minutes at 300°. Turn off oven and let "cake" set for 1 hour in oven. Remove pan from water and cool 2 hours.

• Serve on a bed of leafy greens with an assortment of crackers.

Yields 50 servings

Roquefort & Pistachio Purses

1 pound (24 sheets) phyllo dough

1/2 pound unsalted butter, melted

1/4 pound Roquefort cheese

1/4 pound cream cheese

1 egg

2/3 cup pistachio nuts, coarsely chopped

1/8 teaspoon nutmeg

freshly ground pepper to taste

- Preheat oven to 350°.

- Bring cheeses to room temperature. Mix cheeses together. Add the egg and stir in pistachios. Season with nutmeg and pepper.

- Once phyllo dough is completely thawed, take one sheet and brush with melted butter. Stack a second sheet on top and brush that with butter also. Cut the buttered phyllo dough sheets into fifths. Place a teaspoon of filling in the center of first strip about 1 inch from the top. Fold a corner across the filling and then continue to fold like folding a flag. Repeat this process for remaining sheets and filling.

- Place all triangles on a buttered baking sheet and brush with butter. Bake for about 25 minutes or until golden brown.

Yields 40 triangles

Freezing Phyllo Purses

These can be refrigerated up to 24 hours or can be frozen. Do not thaw before baking. Brush with butter and bake for 35-40 minutes at 350°.

Sizzling Chicken Skewers

3 whole boneless chicken breasts

1 cup crunchy peanut butter

$^{1}/_{3}$ cup chopped cilantro

$^{3}/_{4}$ cup salsa (see recipe on page 209)

$^{1}/_{4}$ cup brown sugar

$^{1}/_{2}$ cup soy sauce

1 tablespoon salt

$^{1}/_{4}$ cup lemon juice

$^{1}/_{2}$ teaspoon cayenne pepper

$^{1}/_{2}$ teaspoon pepper

3 tablespoons minced garlic

1 bunch scallions, chopped

2 peppers (red, green or yellow),
   cubed

• Slice chicken lengthwise into long strips. In a bowl, combine all remaining ingredients except peppers. Add chicken strips, stir well. Let marinate at least 4 hours.

• Soak long bamboo skewers in water for 1 hour, so they do not burn. Thread chicken onto skewers like a snake, and in between each loop add a cube of bell pepper. Grill skewers, turning once, over charcoal for 4 to 6 minutes, or broil, just until browned and cooked through.

Yields 12 appetizer servings

Mozzarella Tomato Crostini

1 loaf Italian or French bread

¹/₂ to 1 cup extra virgin olive oil

2 fresh mozzarella balls, sliced*

Italian Salsa (recipe follows)

*available at specialty shops

• Preheat oven to 350°. Slice bread into ¹/₂-inch slices. Place slices on cookie sheets and brush with oil, then top with cheese. Bake until cheese is lightly golden.

• Serve on platter with *Italian Salsa* for spreading on top.

Serves 6

Italian Salsa

3 ripe tomatoes, chopped

1 small onion, chopped

2 dill pickles, finely chopped

¹/₃ cup extra virgin olive oil

¹/₄ cup fresh basil, chopped

salt and pepper to taste

• Mix all ingredients in a small bowl.

• Serve with *Mozzarella Tomato Crostini.*

Yields 2 cups

Pork & Scallion Wraps

¹/₂ pound pork tenderloin

6 scallions

1 clove garlic, crushed

1 tablespoon soy sauce

1 tablespoon honey

1 tablespoon oil

1 tablespoon hoisin sauce*

1 teaspoon grated fresh ginger root

*available in the Oriental section at the supermarket

- Preheat oven to 400°.

- Trim any excess fat from pork, then cut into 20 round slices.

- Flatten meat slices with a knife or mallet. Trim roots and any wilted leaves from scallions, then cut each scallion into 3 or 4 pieces.

- Place scallion on a meat slice and roll up. (There is no need to fasten rolls closed - moisture in the meat will keep them from coming open). In a shallow baking dish, stir together garlic, soy sauce, honey, oil, hoisin sauce and ginger root. Place pork rolls in soy mixture seam side down and turn to coat. If preparing ahead, cover and refrigerate.

- Bake, uncovered, 10 to 15 minutes or until meat is no longer pink in center; cut to test. During baking, baste rolls frequently with sauce. Serve hot or warm.

Yields 20

Mini-Meatballs
with Spicy Marinara Sauce

1 1/2 pounds ground meat
   (combination of pork and beef)

5 spinach leaves, finely chopped

1 egg, beaten

3/4 cup red wine

1/2 cup Italian bread crumbs

2 cloves garlic, chopped

2 tablespoons chopped pine nuts

1/2 cup grated Parmesan cheese

1/2 cup chopped sun-dried tomatoes

salt and pepper to taste

• In a large bowl, mix all ingredients until well blended. Form into mini meatballs.

• In a large non-stick fry pan, cook meatballs until golden brown and crispy all around. Turn meatballs frequently and do not overcrowd in pan.

• Serve with *Spicy Marinara Sauce* for dipping.

Serves 6

May be frozen.

Spicy Marinara Sauce:

1 tablespoon olive oil

2 cloves garlic, chopped

16-ounce can whole tomatoes

1/4 cup red wine

1/2 teaspoon salt

1 tablespoon fresh ground pepper

1 1/2 tablespoons Italian seasoning

1/2 teaspoon onion powder

dash of red pepper flakes

• In a saucepan, sauté oil and garlic for 1 minute on medium heat.

• Break up tomatoes (including liquid) and add these to oil and garlic. Add wine and spices.

• Reduce heat to low and cook for 20 minutes.

Yields 2 cups

Freezes well.

Artichoke & Pepper Clusters

13 ³/4 ounce can artichoke hearts

3 red peppers

3 yellow peppers

2 tablespoons butter

1 bunch scallions, minced

2 cloves garlic, minced

3 ounces thinly sliced prosciutto, minced

3 tablespoons chopped fresh basil

¹/2 cup grated Parmesan cheese

¹/2 cup grated Jarlsberg or Gruyere cheese

1 tablespoon fresh lemon juice

¹/2 cup mayonnaise

¹/4 cup olive oil

2 tablespoons balsamic vinegar

salt and pepper to taste

- Drain and dice artichoke hearts. Prepare peppers by seeding and cut into 2 x 2¹/2-inch squares. Melt the butter in a small skillet over medium-high heat. Add the scallions and garlic and cook, stirring frequently, until softened, 2 to 3 minutes. Transfer to a bowl.

- Add the artichokes, prosciutto, basil and both cheeses to the scallions and toss to combine. Sprinkle with the lemon juice. Toss with the mayonnaise and refrigerate at least 1 hour.

- Preheat the oven to 400°. Place the peppers in a single layer in a large, shallow baking dish. Drizzle with the olive oil and vinegar and sprinkle with salt and pepper. Roast the peppers 15 minutes, stirring once halfway through the cooking time.

- When ready to serve, preheat the broiler. Mound about 2 teaspoons of the artichoke mixture onto each pepper. Broil 3 to 4 - inches from the heat until bubbly (2 to 3 minutes). Serve immediately.

Yields approximately 2 ¹/2 dozen

Eggplant Tapenade

2 extra large eggplants

1 tablespoon extra virgin olive oil

2 cups drained canned chick peas

³/4 cup stuffed olives

1 teaspoon finely chopped garlic

2 tablespoons lemon juice

¹/2 cup light olive oil

2 tablespoons chopped flat leaf parsley

freshly ground pepper to taste

3 ounces diced pimiento, optional

• Coat whole eggplant with extra virgin olive oil. Bake in 400° oven for 60 minutes or 10 minutes in microwave oven, until soft. Cool. Scoop out seeds and discard. Remove flesh to bowl and chop coarsely. In food processor, chop chick peas, olives, garlic, lemon juice, olive oil, parsley and pepper until mixture has a part smooth, part chunky texture. Add to eggplant, mix well. Chill for at least 1 hour.

• Serve at room temperature. Garnish with pimiento. Serve with assorted crackers.

Serves 6

Tomato Basil Phyllo Pinwheels

1 cup sun-dried tomatoes

1/2 cup grated Parmesan cheese

1/2 pound grated Mozzarella cheese

8 ounces cream cheese, softened

2 eggs

1 cup fresh basil, minced

2 cloves garlic, crushed

salt and pepper to taste

1 pound phyllo dough, thawed

1/2 cup unsalted butter, melted

- Soak sun-dried tomatoes in hot water to soften, drain and squeeze dry.

- Combine all ingredients except phyllo and butter. Lay phyllo flat and cover with waxed paper weighted with a damp towel.

- Remove 1 sheet of phyllo and place on waxed paper. Brush with butter. Remove two additional sheets, one at a time, brush each with butter and place over the first. Spread 1/8 tomato mixture evenly along one long edge of phyllo or spread thin layer over entire sheet. Roll lengthwise, turning ends as you roll. Brush rolls with butter and refrigerate or freeze until ready to use.

- Repeat with remaining dough, making 8 rolls.

- Preheat oven to 350°. Bake for 20 minutes if refrigerated or for 30 minutes if frozen.

- Slice into pinwheels and serve immediately.

Yields 4-5 dozen pinwheels

Making your own sun-dried tomatoes

Start with the ripest tomatoes, slice and arrange on cookie sheets. For a gas oven, no heat is needed. Simply place the tomatoes in the oven and the pilot light will dry the tomatoes in approximately 8-12 hours. For an electric oven, turn the temperature to the lowest setting and dry for approximately 8-12 hours. Monitor carefully, as oven temperatures vary.

Stuffed Mushroom Caps

1 pound mushrooms, approximately 24

3 cloves garlic, minced

¹/₂ cup finely chopped onion

¹/₄ cup olive oil

¹/₂ cup finely chopped prosciutto (3 ounces)

¹/₄ cup dry bread crumbs

3 tablespoons minced flat leaf parsley

1 cup freshly grated Parmesan cheese

1 egg, lightly beaten

salt and pepper to taste

• Preheat oven to 400°. Clean mushrooms with damp paper towel, removing and finely chopping stems.

• In a skillet sauté stems, garlic and onion in 2 tablespoons of the oil over moderate heat, stirring, for 8 minutes or until the stems are very tender. Add the prosciutto, the bread crumbs, parsley, ³/₄ cup of Parmesan, egg and salt and pepper. Stir the mixture until it is well combined.

• Divide the mixture among the mushroom caps and arrange the mushrooms in one layer in a lightly greased shallow baking dish. Sprinkle the mushrooms with the remaining ¹/₄ cup Parmesan and drizzle with the remaining 2 tablespoons oil. Bake them in the middle of oven for 12 to 15 minutes or until they are heated through and lightly golden.

Yields 24 hors d'oeuvres

Cleaning mushrooms

To clean mushrooms, wipe with a damp towel or damp cloth. Mushrooms retain water, therefore they should never be rinsed.

Pesto Bruschetta

1 loaf Italian bread

¹/₂ cup basil pesto
 (see recipe on page 101)

6 plum tomatoes, sliced thin

2 cups shredded mozzarella

¹/₂ to 1 cup grated Romano cheese

• Preheat oven to 400°. Cut bread in half
lengthwise. Place bread on a cookie sheet.
Toast until golden. Spread pesto onto bread,
top with tomato slices and sprinkle with
cheeses.

• Bake 8 to 10 minutes or until cheese is melted
and bubbly.

Serves 8

Sun-dried Tomato Pesto

3 ounces sun-dried tomatoes

³/₄ to 1 cup olive oil

3 cloves garlic, crushed

1 cup minced pine nuts or walnuts

1 teaspoon salt

dash of pepper

1 cup grated Parmesan cheese

• Soften sun-dried tomatoes by soaking in hot
water and squeeze dry. Blend all ingredients
in a blender. Serve as a spread.

Yields approximately 3 cups

Freezes well.

Roasted Red Pepper Dip

3 ounces sun-dried tomatoes

12-ounce jar roasted red peppers, drained

2 teaspoons chopped garlic

1 tablespoon fresh lemon juice

2 tablespoons chopped flat leaf parsley

3-ounce package light or non-fat cream cheese

¹/₂ cup low or non-fat sour cream

salt and pepper to taste

• Soak sun-dried tomatoes in hot water and squeeze dry. Purée all ingredients in a food processor until smooth. Garnish with extra parsley. Serve with crackers.

Yields approximately 2 ¹/₂ cups

Roasting Red Peppers

Set oven to highest temperature and preheat for 20 minutes. Place red peppers directly on middle rack. Line the lower rack with a large cookie sheet or aluminum foil to catch drippings of peppers. Roast peppers until the skin blisters and starts to crack, approximately 20 minutes. Remove from oven and place in an airtight container. This allows the peppers to cool and makes skin removal easier. Once they have cooled, remove the charred skin, stem and seeds. Slice into strips and serve or store in oil in refrigerator for 3-4 days.

Breakfast & Brunch

MAINE
Ingredients
Wild Maine Blueberries

*O*ne quarter-million to one half-million pounds of wild blueberries are harvested annually in Maine. This accounts for ninety percent of the total wild blueberry crop in the United States. Maine blueberries are one of only three fruits native to North America. The wild blueberry may appear similar to the cultivated berry, but in fact it is smaller, deeper in color, and has a distinctive taste.

To the native Indian tribes, the wild blueberry was not only a staple of their diet, but also a thing of myth. They believed that the tiny star atop each berry was a sign, and therefore held the berries in religious awe. During hard times it was believed these "star berries" were sent by the Great Spirit to feed his hungry children. When the early settlers arrived, the Indians taught them how to burn the fields to encourage plant growth. Puritans found many new uses for blueberries, including medicinal purposes. The juice was used for cough remedies and a pungent blueberry tea was served as an anti-spasmodic.

Since blueberries are still harvested by hand, many Mainers leave their jobs for the summer to rake the wild berries. The blueberry harvest begins in late July and may last through the end of August.

We've found some wonderful uses for Maine's wild blueberries, and while they may not cure the common cold, they will satisfy the senses.

Maine Blueberry Muffins

½ cup plus 2 tablespoons unsalted butter

1 ¾ cups sugar

3 eggs

¼ cup plus 1 tablespoon half and half

¾ teaspoon vanilla

2 ½ cups flour

1 ½ teaspoons baking powder

½ teaspoon salt

1 ½ cups blueberries

• Preheat oven to 425°. Grease muffin tins.

• In a large bowl, cream butter and sugar. Add eggs, half and half and vanilla. Add remaining dry ingredients. Mix well. Batter will be stiff. Fold in blueberries. Distribute evenly among greased tins. Bake for 23 to 25 minutes.

Yields 12 muffins

Molasses Ginger Scones

2 cups flour

2 tablespoons sugar plus
  additional for garnish

1 tablespoon baking powder

1/2 teaspoon ground ginger

pinch of salt

1/2 cup unsalted butter, chilled

2 ounces candied ginger, chopped

1 egg

3 tablespoons molasses

1/4 cup heavy cream

1 beaten egg, for wash

• Preheat oven to 400°.

• Lightly butter a baking sheet and set aside.
  Twice sift together flour, sugar, baking
  powder, ground ginger and salt. Cut in
  butter by hand or with a pastry blender until
  mixture resembles coarse meal. Stir in
  chopped candied ginger.

• Beat together egg, molasses and cream.
  Make a well in the center of the dry ingredients and pour in egg mixture. Stir lightly
  with a fork just until dough comes together.
  Turn out onto a lightly floured surface and
  knead a few times to mix well but do not
  overwork dough.

• Pat dough into a rectangle or circle about 3/4
  inch thick. Cut into 2 1/2-inch triangles with a
  floured knife or into shapes with floured
  cookie cutters.

• Transfer to prepared baking sheet. Brush
  scone tops with beaten egg and sprinkle with
  sugar. Bake 12 to 15 minutes or until an even
  golden brown. Cool on wire racks.

Yields 10 to 12

Tri-berry Muffins

3 cups unbleached flour

1 ¹/₂ cups sugar plus ¹/₂ cup

1 tablespoon baking powder

¹/₂ teaspoon baking soda

¹/₂ teaspoon salt

3-4 teaspoons ground cinnamon,
   or to taste

1 ¹/₄ cups milk

2 large eggs

1 cup unsalted butter, melted

1 cup blueberries

¹/₂ cup diced strawberries

¹/₂ cup raspberries

• Preheat the oven to 375°. Place paper liners in 20 muffin cups or grease.

• Combine the flour, 1¹/₂ cups sugar, baking powder, baking soda, salt and cinnamon in a large bowl. Make a well in the center of the flour mixture. Mix together the milk and eggs and pour into well along with the butter. Stir quickly just to combine. Gently fold in berries.

• Spoon the batter into the cups, filling each cup almost to the top. Sprinkle remaining ¹/₂ cup sugar on top of each muffin. Bake until brown and crusty, about 20 minutes.

Yields 20 muffins

Cranberry Island Muffins

2 cups flour

¹/₂ cup firmly packed light brown sugar

¹/₂ cup wheat germ

2 teaspoons baking powder

¹/₂ teaspoon baking soda

1 cup coarsely chopped fresh cranberries or frozen, thawed and drained

¹/₃ cup granulated sugar

³/₄ cup orange juice

¹/₃ cup vegetable oil

1 egg, lightly beaten

1 ¹/₂ teaspoons grated orange peel

1 teaspoon vanilla

¹/₂ cup chopped pecans

- Preheat oven to 400°. Grease twelve muffin cups.

- In large bowl, stir together flour, brown sugar, wheat germ, baking powder and baking soda. In small bowl, combine cranberries and granulated sugar; let stand 2 minutes.

- In medium bowl, stir together orange juice, oil, egg, orange peel and vanilla until blended.

- Make a well in the center of dry ingredients; add cranberry mixture and orange juice mixture and stir just to combine. Stir in pecans. Spoon batter into muffin cups. Bake 15 to 20 minutes or until a cake tester inserted in center of muffin comes out clean.

- Cool 5 minutes on a wire rack before removing from muffin cups.

Yields 12 muffins

Freezes well.

Bursting Berries

¹/₄ cup maple syrup
¹/₂ cup fresh cranberries
- In a saucepan, heat maple syrup with cranberries over medium-high heat about 5 minutes or until berries begin to pop.

Pear Hazelnut Muffins

¹/₃ cup roasted and peeled hazelnuts

³/₄ cup sugar

2 ¹/₄ cups flour

1 teaspoon baking soda

¹/₂ teaspoon baking powder

¹/₂ teaspoon salt

¹/₂ teaspoon cinnamon

1 ¹/₄ cups buttermilk

1 egg

1 ¹/₂ firm, ripe pears

¹/₂ cup unsalted butter, melted

finely chopped zest of 1 lemon

1 ³/₄ teaspoons sugar

¹/₄ teaspoon cinnamon

- Preheat oven to 375°.

- In food processor, mix nuts with sugar until nuts are chopped but not finely ground. Transfer to a bowl and mix in flour, baking soda, baking powder, salt and cinnamon.

- Beat buttermilk and egg together in separate bowl. Peel, core and chop pear into pieces about the size of a pea.

- Make a well in the center of dry ingredients; add egg mixture, butter and zest. Stir until just combined. Fold in pears. Pour into 12 paper lined muffin tins. Combine the 1³/₄ teaspoons sugar and cinnamon. Sprinkle on top of muffins. Bake for 30 to 35 minutes or until golden.

Yields 12 muffins

Roasting Hazelnuts

Shell the nuts and roast in a 375° oven for 12 minutes. Place them in a brown paper bag and shake to help loosen the skins. Leave nuts in bag for 10 minutes to further steam the skins, then peel away the skins with help of a terrycloth towel.

Blushing Muffins

2 cups flour

1/2 teaspoon cinnamon

1/2 teaspoon baking soda

2 eggs, beaten

1 cup sugar

3/4 cup mashed strawberries

3/4 cup mashed banana

1/4 cup vegetable oil

1 teaspoon grated orange peel

1 cup chopped walnuts

• Preheat oven to 350°.

• Sift together flour, cinnamon and baking soda. Set aside. Stir together eggs, sugar, strawberries, banana, oil and orange peel. Add flour mixture, stirring just until combined. Stir in nuts. Pour into paper lined or greased muffin cups. Bake 30 minutes.

Yields 12 muffins

*These muffins freeze well.

Berry Butters

1 cup fresh berries (blueberries, raspberries or strawberries)

3 tablespoons light corn syrup

1 cup butter, softened

• In blender or food processor, purée berries. Press through strainer to remove seeds. In small bowl, beat butter until light and fluffy, about 1 to 2 minutes. Add berry purée and corn syrup to butter. Beat at medium speed until well mixed, about 1 minute.

• Cover. Store refrigerated. Let stand at room temperature 30 minutes before serving.

Yields approximately 2 cups

Blueberries in a Jam

Blueberry Jam

2 cups fresh blueberries

¹/₃ cup sugar

2 teaspoons grated orange rind

1 envelope unflavored gelatin

1 cup water

- In a medium saucepan, combine blueberries and sugar. Crush berries slightly. Bring to a boil then boil rapidly, stirring constantly for 3 minutes. Stir in orange rind.

- In a small bowl, sprinkle gelatin over water; let stand 1 minute. Add to berries; stir over low heat until gelatin is dissolved, about 5 minutes. Ladle into small jars, cover and cool slightly before refrigerating.

Yields approximately 1 pint

Blueberry Jam with a kick

blueberry jam (see above)

1 to 2 tablespoons raspberry liqueur

- In a medium bowl, combine the jam and liqueur. Return to the jar, cover and refrigerate at least one day to allow the flavors to blend.

Yields approximately 1 ¹/₂ cups

Adding liqueur

The addition of the liqueur gives the jam a sauce-like consistency. Not only does this make toast and English muffins extra special, but it can also be used to fill cake layers and cookie sandwiches.

Blueberry Coffee Cake

2 cups flour

1 1/2 cups sugar

2 teaspoons baking powder

1 teaspoon salt

1/3 cup butter

2 eggs

1 cup milk

2 cups blueberries

1/2 cup sugar

1 teaspoon cinnamon

• Preheat oven to 350°.

• Mix flour, sugar, baking powder and salt. Cut in butter. Add eggs and milk and beat until smooth.

• Pour into greased 13x9 inch pan. Top with blueberries. Combine the 1/2 cup sugar and cinnamon and sprinkle over blueberries.

• Bake 35 to 40 minutes.

• Cool pan on a wire rack for 20 minutes.

Serves 12

Wild Blueberry Pancakes

1 cup sifted flour

1/4 teaspoon salt

1/2 teaspoon baking soda

2 tablespoons melted butter

1 egg, slightly beaten

1 cup buttermilk

3/4 cup fresh blueberries or thawed frozen blueberries

• Sift together the flour, salt and soda. Combine the butter, egg and buttermilk. Pour into the flour mixture and stir just enough to moisten the dry ingredients. Fold in blueberries.

• Heat a griddle or skillet, grease if necessary, and drop the batter by spoonfuls onto it. When bubbles break on top of the cakes, turn and cook on the other side until lightly golden.

Serves 4

Sand Dollar Pancakes

2 eggs

¹/₃ cup cottage cheese

1 cup sour cream

¹/₂ cup flour

1 teaspoon salt

1 teaspoon sugar

¹/₂ teaspoon baking soda

1 teaspoon baking powder

2 tablespoons butter

• Beat eggs then add cottage cheese and sour cream. Add dry ingredients and mix well. Let stand 10 minutes.

• Melt butter in skillet over medium-high heat. Place medium spoonful of batter for small delicate pancake, into skillet. Cook until lightly golden on each side. Serve immediately.

Serves 4 to 6

Breakfast Cloud Popover

¹/₂ cup milk

¹/₂ cup flour

3 eggs

¹/₄ teaspoon salt

2 tablespoons butter

• Preheat oven to 450°. Combine the milk, flour, eggs and salt and blend at low speed. Melt the butter in a 10 to 12-inch cast iron skillet. Pour the batter evenly in the hot skillet. Bake in oven 10 to 12 minutes, until puffed and golden brown.

• Serve with topping for an easy breakfast treat. Suggested toppings: berries and whipped cream or lemon juice and confectioners sugar.

Serves 2

Cinnamon Baked French Toast

1 loaf raisin bread

6 eggs

1 1/2 cups milk

1 cup light cream or half and half

1 teaspoon vanilla

1/4 teaspoon cinnamon

1/4 teaspoon nutmeg

1/4 cup soft butter

1/2 cup firmly packed brown sugar

1/2 cup chopped walnuts

1 tablespoon corn syrup

maple syrup

• Butter a baking pan. Arrange bread slices, overlapping and fill pan completely. Mix next 6 ingredients and pour over slices. Refrigerate over night.

• The next day, preheat oven to 350°. Combine butter, sugar, walnuts and corn syrup and spread over bread. Bake 40 minutes or until puffed and golden. Serve with maple syrup.

Serves 4 to 6

Maple syrup

The sugar maple, also found in Vermont and Canada, is a native Maine tree. In Maine's northern woods, particularly along the St. John River, sugar maples are tapped extensively for their rich syrup.

Hearty Potato Pancakes

5 to 6 medium potatoes

1/2 medium onion, coarsely grated

1 egg

3 to 6 tablespoons flour

6 tablespoons milk

1/2 teaspoon salt

1/8 teaspoon pepper

1/4 cup vegetable oil

sour cream

fresh chives, chopped

• Peel potatoes and coarsely grate. Combine with next 6 ingredients, mixing well and using enough flour to absorb moisture.

• Preheat oil in a large non-stick skillet. When oil is hot but not smoking, add large spoonfuls of potato mixture, one at a time, flattening slightly to form a pancake shape. Fry 3 to 4 minutes until golden brown; turn and continue to cook until other side is brown and crisp.

• Remove and drain on paper towels. Serve immediately or keep warm in a 200° oven until entire batch is done. Serve individually with a dollop of sour cream and sprinkling of fresh chives.

Serves 6

Eggemoggin Eggs Florentine

two 10-ounce packages frozen chopped spinach

1 pound mushrooms, sliced

2 tablespoons butter

1/2 cup white wine

2 cloves garlic, minced

1/4 teaspoon pepper

8 eggs

3/4 cup grated Cheddar cheese

• Preheat oven to 350°.

• Cook spinach and squeeze dry. Sauté mushrooms in butter, wine and garlic. Add pepper. Combine spinach and mushroom mixture.

• Spray 8 ramekins with cooking spray. Divide the spinach-mushroom mixture among the ramekins. Drop 1 egg in each ramekin then top with cheese.

• Bake for 20 minutes or until cheese is browned and eggs are fully set. This can be made the day before and refrigerated. It can also be made in a casserole.

Serves 8

What is a ramekin?

A ramekin is a small round ceramic baking dish made for custards, crème brulées and cheese dishes. Used for individual servings, they are ideal for entertaining.

Asparagus & Egg Creation

1 pound thin asparagus spears,
    cooked or 2 cans asparagus
    spears, drained

5 hard cooked eggs, sliced

salt and pepper to taste

8 ounces Cheddar cheese, grated

2 cups medium white sauce
    (see recipe on page 251)

1/2 cup bread crumbs

2 tablespoons butter, melted

paprika

• Preheat oven to 350°.

• Arrange the asparagus in bottom of a 2-quart casserole. Top with egg slices, sprinkle with salt and pepper and cheese. Spoon the white sauce over eggs and cheese. Mix bread crumbs and butter. Sprinkle over top. Dust with paprika.

• Bake for 30 minutes. Let stand to firm before serving.

Serves 6

Fiesta Egg Cups

2 cups grated sharp Cheddar cheese

6 eggs

4 teaspoons chopped onion

5 slices cooked bacon, crumbled

6 tablespoons mild chunky salsa
    or more to taste

cooking spray

• Preheat oven to 350°.

• Spray bottoms of 6 ramekins with cooking spray. Divide 1 cup of the cheese among the ramekins. Crack 1 egg into each ramekin. Sprinkle onion and bacon on each then put 1 tablespoon or more salsa on top of each one. Sprinkle the remaining cheese on top.

• Bake for about 25 minutes until eggs are set and the top is slightly brown.

Serves 6

Break 'o Day Egg Bake

3 cups shredded Cheddar cheese

3 cups shredded Mozzarella cheese

1/4 cup butter

4.5-ounce can sliced mushrooms, drained or 1/4 pound fresh mushrooms, sliced

1/3 cup sliced scallions

1/2 red bell pepper, chopped

8 ounces cooked ham, cut in fine strips

1/2 cup flour

1 3/4 cups milk

2 tablespoons chopped fresh parsley

8 eggs

red pepper and parsley, for garnish

• Preheat oven to 350°.

• In large bowl, lightly toss cheeses together. Sprinkle 1/2 of the cheese in an ungreased 13x9-inch baking dish.

• In medium skillet, melt butter and sauté mushrooms, scallions and red pepper until tender. Arrange cooked vegetables over cheese. Arrange ham over vegetables and sprinkle remaining cheese over ham.

• In large bowl, using a wire whisk, blend flour, milk, parsley and eggs; pour over cheeses, vegetables and ham. Bake for 35 to 40 minutes or until set and top is lightly browned.

• Let stand about 10 minutes. Cut into squares. Garnish with red pepper and parsley if desired.

Serves 12

Potato & Egg Scramble

¹/₂ pound bacon, chopped

3 medium onions, chopped

¹/₂ cup bacon fat or butter

*3 pounds potatoes, cooked and
diced with skins*

salt and pepper to taste

6 eggs, beaten

• Cook bacon until crisp. Add onions and cook until tender. Set aside.

• Brown potatoes in fat. Add salt and pepper to taste. Drain fat. Stir in bacon, onions and eggs. Mix and cook until eggs are set, stirring constantly. Serve immediately.

Serves 6

Get Crackin' Eggs

8 to 10 eggs

1 teaspoon dill

3 tablespoons Parmesan cheese

2 tablespoons heavy cream

1 teaspoon butter

• In a large bowl, lightly beat the eggs. Add remaining ingredients except butter and combine well.

• Melt butter in skillet over medium heat. Pour in egg mixture and scramble until done. Do not over cook. Serve with buttered toast and jam.

Serves 4 to 5

Wild Mushroom & Gruyere Omelette

2 tablespoons butter

4 ounces fresh shiitake or portobello mushrooms, sliced

2 shallots, chopped

2 cloves garlic, chopped

salt and pepper to taste

6 eggs

1/4 cup chopped fresh parsley

3/4 cup grated Gruyere cheese

fresh parsley, for garnish

The Perfect Omelette

Heat an 8-inch nonstick skillet to medium-high heat. Add 1 tablespoon butter and melt until butter bubbles. Pour in egg mixture prepared according to recipe, cook slowly. Turn a spatula around the edges, gently lifting up to allow the uncooked portion to flow underneath. When the egg is almost completely set, add filling ingredients. Fold over once, tilt pan and slide omelette directly onto serving plate.

• Melt 1 tablespoon butter in heavy small skillet over medium heat. Add mushrooms, shallots and garlic and sauté until tender, about 3 minutes. Season to taste with salt and pepper. Set aside.

• Combine eggs, 1/4 cup chopped fresh parsley and 1/4 cup cheese in medium bowl. Season with salt and pepper. Beat to blend.

• Heat medium omelet pan or skillet over medium-high heat. Add 1/2 tablespoon butter; heat until butter melts and foam begins to subside. Add half of egg mixture. Stir with fork until eggs begin to set. Cook until omelet is set, lifting edge with spatula to let uncooked egg flow under. Top with 1/4 cup cheese and half of mushroom mixture. Fold omelet into thirds and turn out onto plate.

• Repeat with remaining 1/2 tablespoon butter, egg mixture, 1/4 cup grated cheese and mushrooms. Sprinkle omelets with additional chopped fresh parsley.

Serves 2

Sunshine Yogurt Cups

1 to 2 oranges, halved

2 small containers vanilla yogurt

1 tablespoon honey

$^1/_2$ tablespoon orange zest

mint sprigs, optional

• Scoop out orange halves, removing all pulp, to make cups. Mix next 3 ingredients and fill cups. Garnish with mint if desired.

Serves 2 to 4

Yogurt Bar

For a fresh and healthy way to start your day, set up a "yogurt bar"! Start with a pot of piping hot coffee, freshly squeezed orange juice and warm-from-the-oven *Tri-berry Muffins*. Next, put out a large container of low-fat vanilla yogurt, then in small bowls arrange the following toppings to fill the Sunshine Yogurt Cups: Granola, fresh berries, sliced bananas, pecan or walnut pieces, wheat germ and for a garnish, a sprinkling of brown sugar. Your guests will be delighted by this quick, easy and tasty morning treat.

Appledore Scalloped Apples

4 cooking apples, pared and
    thinly sliced

$^1/_2$ cup golden raisins

1 teaspoon cinnamon

1 $^1/_2$ tablespoons flour

3 tablespoons sugar

1 tablespoon butter, diced

- Preheat oven to 350°.

- Arrange apple slices in a greased 1-quart casserole. Top with raisins. Mix cinnamon, flour and sugar in a small bowl. Sprinkle over apples and raisins. Put butter on top of mixture.

- Bake for 50 to 55 minutes.

Serves 4

Glazed Green Grapes

5 cups seedless green and red grapes

$^1/_4$ cup firmly packed
    light brown sugar

$^1/_2$ cup sour cream

almonds to garnish

- Wash grapes and remove stems. Combine brown sugar and sour cream in large mixing bowl. Stir in grapes.

- Chill several hours. Spoon into individual serving dishes. Garnish with almonds.

Serves 6 to 8

Spring Asparagus Tart

9-inch pie crust dough

1 teaspoon flour

1 pound asparagus, trimmed

²/₃ cup half and half

2 eggs

¹/₂ cup freshly grated
   Parmesan cheese

1 tablespoon chopped fresh tarragon
   or 1 teaspoon dried

¹/₂ teaspoon salt

freshly ground pepper to taste

• Preheat oven to 450°. Roll out dough and rub with flour. Arrange dough, flour side down, in 9-inch tart pan with removable bottom. Press dough into pan. Fold excess dough border over to form double-thick sides. Pierce dough all over with fork. Bake until golden, about 15 minutes. Cool on rack. Reduce oven temperature to 375°.

• Cook asparagus in pot of boiling salted water until just crisp-tender, about 4 minutes. Drain well. Place on paper towels.

• Mix half and half, eggs, cheese, tarragon and salt in bowl. Season with pepper. Arrange asparagus in spoke-of-wheel fashion in crust, tips toward edge and ends meeting in center. Pour custard over.

• Bake until tart puffs and top browns, about 35 minutes. Cool slightly.

Serves 4

Quoddy Head Quiche

Pastry:

1 ½ cups sifted flour

pinch of salt

8 tablespoons unsalted butter

1 large egg yolk

2 or 3 tablespoons ice water

• Put all the ingredients for the pastry, except the water, in the bowl of a food processor and blend for 5 seconds (or mix by hand with a large whisk). Add the water and blend just until the pastry pulls away from the sides of the bowl and begins to form a ball.

• Flour a flat surface. Using a rolling pin, roll out the dough into a circle about 13 inches in diameter and ¼ inch thick. Pick up the dough by rolling it onto the pin and then unroll it over a tart or quiche pan (preferably made of black steel). Work the dough into the pan with your fingers, crimping it against the walls to make the sides of the quiche thicker than the bottom. Refrigerate the pastry-lined pan for 10 to 15 minutes to relax the dough.

• Preheat the oven to 375°.

• Line the shell with waxed paper and weight it down with aluminum pellets or dried beans. Bake for 10 minutes. Remove the paper and beans and bake again for about 5 minutes. Remove the shell from the oven and let it cool on a wire rack.

Filling:

2 tablespoons unsalted butter

4 tablespoons finely chopped shallots

2 tablespoons cream sherry

4 tablespoons finely chopped fresh dill or parsley

1 1/2 cups cooked seafood combination of shrimp, lobster or scallops

3 large eggs

1 cup heavy cream

1/2 cup milk

freshly grated nutmeg to taste

salt and freshly ground white pepper to taste

1/2 cup grated Swiss or Gruyere cheese

• Meanwhile, make the filling. In a saucepan, melt the butter and sauté the chopped shallots over medium-high heat. Cook briefly, do not allow them to brown; add the sherry, dill and seafood. Cook, stirring, for about 2 minutes. Remove from the heat.

• In a mixing bowl, beat together the eggs, cream, milk, nutmeg, salt and pepper and 1/4 cup of the grated cheese. Combine this with the seafood mixture.

• Pour the mixture into the partially baked pastry shell and sprinkle with the remaining cheese. Bake for about 35 minutes or until golden brown and firm.

Serves 6 to 8

Crabmeat Tart

8 large eggs

2 cups half-and-half

1/2 cup finely chopped scallions

1 cup diced bell pepper

6 ounces fresh crabmeat,
   torn in shreds

1 cup shredded Swiss cheese

1 cup shredded Cheddar cheese

1 teaspoon salt

1/2 teaspoon pepper

1 cup fresh bread crumbs
   (from white bread)

• Heat oven to 350°. Grease a 10-inch quiche
  pan or shallow 2-quart baking dish.

• Whisk eggs until blended. Add remaining
  ingredients and stir to mix well. Pour into
  prepared pan.

• Bake 45 minutes or until set and knife
  inserted near center comes out clean. Let
  stand about 10 minutes before serving.

Serves 8

Northeast Ham Crepes

1 medium onion, chopped

1/3 pound mushrooms, chopped

4 tablespoons butter

1/4 cup flour

2 cups milk

1/2 teaspoon salt

freshly ground white pepper to taste

3 cups julienned cooked ham

12 crepes

2 cups medium white sauce
 (see recipe on page 251)

2 tablespoons dry white wine

1/4 cup freshly grated
 Parmesan cheese

• Preheat oven to 325°.

• Sauté onion and mushrooms in butter until soft. Add flour. Stir well and cook for 3 minutes, gradually adding milk. Stir until thickened. Add salt, pepper and ham.

•Put 3 to 4 tablespoons of filling on each crepe and roll. Arrange in a buttered shallow oven-proof serving dish, rolled edge down.

• Combine white sauce and wine, heat, and add cheese. Stir to melt cheese. Pour over crepes and bake for 20 minutes, until heated through and bubbly.

Serves 6

Crepes

1 1/2 cups flour

1/4 teaspoon salt

2 cups milk

3 eggs

2 tablespoons melted butter

1 tablespoon oil

• Combine flour, salt, milk, eggs and melted butter in a blender or mixer. Chill 1 hour.

• Rub oil in a small nonstick skillet over medium heat. Pour scant 1/4 cup batter in center of pan, tilting pan to cover bottom of skillet in a thin layer. Crepes should be quite thin. When crepe is dry on top and golden on bottom, remove from skillet.

Yields 1 dozen crepes

Dilled Lobster Rolls

1 pound cooked lobster meat, cut into
   bite size pieces

1 small cucumber, peeled and diced

1/2 cup shredded carrots

1/2 cup mayonnaise

2 tablespoons Dijon mustard

1 teaspoon fresh or dried dill

freshly ground pepper to taste

4 rolls, lightly toasted

paprika for garnish

• In a medium bowl, gently toss lobster,
cucumber and carrots. In a small bowl, mix
mayonnaise, mustard, dill and pepper.
Combine mayonnaise mixture with lobster.

• Serve in toasted rolls. Lightly sprinkle with
paprika.

Serves 4

Turkey Tortilla Wraps

1/3 cup shredded Cheddar cheese

2 tablespoons chopped fresh chives

2 teaspoons Dijon mustard

8-ounces cream cheese, softened

six 8-inch flour tortillas

12 thin slices cooked turkey breast

12 spinach or Romaine leaves

24 slices cucumber

• Combine cheese, chives, mustard and cream
cheese in a bowl; mix well. Spread 3
tablespoons cheese mixture over each tortilla.
Top each with 2 slices turkey, 2 spinach or
Romaine leaves and 4 cucumber slices; roll
up.

Serves 6

Open Deck Shrimp Sandwich

¹/2 cup mayonnaise

¹/2 cup chopped fresh dill

4 teaspoons Dijon mustard

2 teaspoons fresh lemon juice

salt and pepper to taste

4 crusty sourdough bread slices

*1 pound cooked Maine or
    medium-sized shrimp*

4 red leaf lettuce leaves

¹/2 medium cucumber, thinly sliced

4 thin lemon slices

• Combine first 4 ingredients in medium bowl. Season with salt and pepper. Toast bread. Spread 1 tablespoon dressing over each bread slice. Mix shrimp into remaining dressing.

• Place 1 lettuce leaf on each bread slice, pressing to adhere. Arrange 6 cucumber slices atop lettuce on each slice. Arrange shrimp mixture atop cucumbers. Garnish with lemon slice.

Serves 4

Pack-a-Picnic Sandwich

*1 large round Tuscan or peasant
    bread*

*2 cups Italian salsa (see recipe
    on page 25)*

1 pound sliced provolone cheese

*1 ¹/2 pounds thinly sliced deli meats
    (any combination of prosciutto,
    salami, capacola, mortadella)*

12-ounce jar roasted peppers

• Carefully cut top off bread and save. Scoop out inside of bread (reserve for making croutons or bread crumbs). Spread ¹/4 of salsa on bottom of bread then, starting with cheese, make alternating layers of all ingredients. Place bread top back on, wrap in aluminum foil and refrigerate for 1 hour. Slice like a pie.

Serves 6 to 8

Soups & Breads

MAINE
Ingredients
Fiddlehead Ferns

*T*he fiddlehead fern, or more correctly, the ostrich fern, is Maine's first native green of the season. Its annual appearance along the banks of rivers, streams and other marshy spots begins about the second week of May and lasts approximately three weeks. During this period, the fiddlehead is tender, young and juicy. Its slightly bitter flavor resembles a cross between an asparagus and an artichoke. If allowed to grow to maturity without being picked, the fiddlehead unrolls its scroll-like tip, quickly becoming stringy and inedible.

The tightly curled shoots of the fiddlehead fern are one of Maine's springtime delights. Micmac Indians introduced fiddleheads to the early settlers of Maine. The annual harvesting of spring greens was once a common rite throughout America. Today, Mainers continue this ritual each spring as they go "greening" to gather fiddleheads and dandelions for the table.

Fiddlehead Fern Soup

4 cups fresh, cleaned fiddleheads

2 tablespoons unsalted butter

1 small onion, minced

2 cups chicken stock

2 cups milk or cream

1/2 teaspoon lemon zest

salt and freshly ground pepper

paprika

• Bring a large pot of salted water to a boil over high heat. Add the fiddleheads, return to a boil and cook until they are almost tender and turn pale green, 5 to 8 minutes. Drain and rinse with cold water. Coarsely chop and reserve.

• Melt the butter in a saucepan over medium heat. Add the onion and cook, stirring occasionally, until they become translucent, about 5 minutes. Add the fiddleheads and chicken stock. Stir, increase the heat to medium-high and bring to a gentle boil. Cover and cook until the fiddleheads are thoroughly tender, about 5 minutes. Add the milk, reduce the heat to medium, and heat until nearly boiling. Do not let the soup boil or the milk will curdle.

• Stir in the lemon zest and season the soup to taste with salt and pepper. Divide the soup into four bowls, garnish with paprika and serve immediately.

Serves 4

Pumpkin Black Bean Soup

1 pound dried black beans

2 tablespoons olive oil

1 1/2 cups finely chopped onions

3 large cloves garlic, finely minced

*1 cup canned, drained plum
    tomatoes*

1 tablespoon ground cumin

4 tablespoons sherry vinegar

1 cup fresh or canned pumpkin purée

*6 ounces boiled ham, cut into
    1/8-inch cubes*

2 1/2 cups beef stock

salt and pepper to taste

3/4 cup dry sherry

- Wash and pick over beans. Place beans into heavy pot and cover with boiling water to about 2 inches above beans. Simmer until tender, about 2 hours. Add more water if beans become dry. Leave extra liquid with beans when puréeing.

- Meanwhile, heat oil in a heavy skillet. Add onions and garlic and sauté until tender and lightly colored.

- When beans are tender, add tomatoes, onion, garlic, cumin and vinegar and coarsely chop in food processor. Return to pot and add pumpkin, ham and beef stock. Add salt and pepper to taste. Simmer uncovered 20 to 25 minutes. Stir in sherry.

- Serve immediately or cool and refrigerate. Flavor increases overnight.

Serves 6 to 8

Pumpkin Bowls

To add flair to your fall harvest table, serve this pumpkin soup in a hollowed out pumpkin — either one big one to serve from or small individual pumpkins placed on dinner plates. To prepare, cut the top off the pumpkin and remove all seeds as well as most of the flesh, leaving a half inch wall. Fill with soup and serve.

Roquefort & Walnut Butternut Soup

2 tablespoons butter

1 ¹/₂ cups chopped onion

2 ¹/₂ cups peeled butternut squash, cubed

1 teaspoon dried sage

1 teaspoon dried thyme

4 cups chicken broth

pinch of cayenne pepper

2 ounces Roquefort cheese, crumbled

¹/₂ cup chopped walnuts

• Melt butter in heavy large saucepan over medium heat. Add onion and sauté 10 minutes. Add sage, thyme, broth and squash and bring to boil. Reduce heat and simmer until squash is tender, about 20 to 30 minutes.

• Transfer soup to blender or food processor and purée until smooth. Season to taste with cayenne pepper.

• Rewarm soup over medium heat. Sprinkle with Roquefort cheese and walnuts and serve.

Serves 4

Fresh Carrot Soup with Dill Pesto

Soup:

1 pound carrots

4 tablespoons unsalted butter

1 large onion, chopped

1 ¼ teaspoons dill weed

4 cups chicken broth

Dill pesto:

1 cup packed coarsely chopped
    fresh dill

3 tablespoons pine nuts

2 tablespoons grated Parmesan
    cheese

3 tablespoons olive oil

- Peel carrots and thinly slice. Melt butter in heavy large saucepan over medium heat. Add carrots, onion and dill and sauté until onion is translucent and tender, about 10 minutes. Add broth and bring to boil. Reduce heat and simmer until carrots are very tender, about 35 minutes. Transfer soup to blender in batches and purée. Thin with more broth if desired. Season to taste with salt and pepper.

- Combine dill, pine nuts and Parmesan cheese in processor and chop finely using on/off turns. With processor running, slowly add oil and process until well blended. Season to taste with salt and pepper. (Soup and Pesto can be prepared 1 day ahead. Cover separately and refrigerate).

- Rewarm soup and ladle into bowls. Drop a small teaspoon of pesto into each bowl.

Serves 4 to 6

Peas to Please Soup

¹/₂ cup split peas

¹/₂ cup lentils

5 cups chicken or vegetable broth

³/₄ cup sliced carrot

³/₄ cup sliced celery

¹/₂ medium red sweet pepper, chopped

1 onion, chopped

1 bay leaf

1 teaspoon ground cumin

¹/₄ teaspoon pepper

• Rinse and drain split peas and lentils.

• In a Dutch oven, combine peas, lentils, broth, carrot, celery, red pepper, onion, bay leaf, cumin and pepper. Bring mixture to a boil on range top. Reduce heat and simmer, covered, for 1 hour or until peas are tender. Remove bay leaf and serve.

Serves 4 as a main dish

Savory Tomato Soup

¹/4 cup olive oil

2 leeks, minced

2 carrots, peeled and minced

1 small red onion

2 cloves garlic, minced

grated zest of ¹/2 orange

1 ¹/2 teaspoons dried thyme

¹/2 teaspoon fennel seeds

*¹/2 teaspoon saffron threads
    (available in specialty shops as
    well as some super markets)*

6 large, ripe tomatoes

*two 28-ounce cans Italian plum
    tomatoes, undrained*

4 cups chicken stock

¹/2 cup orange juice

*salt and freshly ground pepper,
    to taste*

³/4 cup chopped fresh basil

*¹/4 cup goat cheese, for garnish
    (optional)*

• Heat the oil in a large stockpot over high heat. Add the leeks, carrots, onion and garlic and cook, stirring frequently, for 15 minutes.

• Add the orange zest, thyme, fennel seeds and saffron; cook, stirring frequently, for 3 minutes. Peel, seed and dice tomatoes. Add the fresh and canned tomatoes, chicken stock and orange juice and stir to combine. Simmer the soup, uncovered, over medium heat, for 30 minutes.

• Remove from the heat and purée in batches in a blender or food processor fitted with a steel blade. Season to taste with salt and pepper.

• Return the soup to the pot and bring just to a simmer. Just before serving, stir in the basil. Garnish each serving with a sprinkle of crumbled goat cheese.

Yields 2 quarts

Signs of Spring Asparagus Soup

¹/₂ cup unsalted butter

2 large yellow onions, coarsely chopped

5 cloves garlic, chopped

6 cups chicken stock

3 pounds asparagus

2 carrots

1 teaspoon dried basil

1 tablespoon dried tarragon

1 teaspoon salt

1 teaspoon freshly ground pepper

pinch cayenne pepper

1 cup sour cream, for garnish

1 large tomato, seeded and diced, for garnish

fresh parsley, for garnish

• Melt butter in a heavy large saucepan over low heat. Add the onions and garlic. Cook, uncovered, until onions are softened, about 20 minutes. Add chicken stock and heat to boiling.

• Trim the woody ends from the asparagus and cut stalks into 1-inch pieces, reserving the tips. Peel carrots and cut into chunks.

• Add the asparagus pieces, carrots, basil, tarragon, salt, pepper and cayenne pepper to the stock. Reduce to medium-low and simmer, covered, until vegetables are tender, about 50 minutes.

• Remove the soup from the heat and let cool. Process the soup in batches in a food processor, fitted with a steel blade, or blender, until smooth. Strain the soup through a medium-sized sieve to remove the woody fibers.

• Return the strained soup to pan. Add asparagus tips and simmer over medium heat until the tips are tender, about 10 minutes.

• Ladle the soup into bowls. Serve with a dollop of sour cream and sprinkle with diced tomatoes and fresh parsley.

Serves 6

Lemon Basil Squash Soup

2 tablespoons olive oil

1 large sweet onion, chopped

1 clove garlic, chopped

4 cups chicken stock or canned broth

3 medium zucchini, coarsely
   shredded

3 medium summer squash, coarsely
   shredded

1 medium carrot, peeled and coarsely
   shredded

3 tablespoons coarsely shredded
   fresh basil

grated rind of 1 lemon

salt and freshly ground black pepper
   to taste

• In a large saucepan, warm the oil over low
heat. Add the onion and garlic and sauté
until the onion is translucent.

• Add the chicken broth, zucchini, summer
squash, carrot, basil and lemon rind. Cook
for five to eight minutes, until the vegetables
are tender but still firm. Season to taste with
salt and pepper.

Serves 6 to 8

Great for a food processor. The vegetables shred uniformly.

Chicken Bean Soup

*1 pound package mixed soup beans
or any combination of your
favorite beans*

1 can plum tomatoes

*1 large Vidalia or Spanish onion,
chopped*

6 to 8 small boiling onions, halved

juice of 1 lemon

1 pound boneless chicken, cubed

1 bay leaf

1 cup chicken broth

2 cloves garlic, minced

salt and pepper to taste

• Soak beans overnight.

• Rinse beans and place in large pot on stove.
Add 2 quarts of water. Bring to a boil.
Reduce to a simmer and add all remaining
ingredients. Simmer on stove 2$^1/_2$ to 3 hours.

Serves 6 to 8

Recipe Variation

This is a very healthy, hearty
meal and wonderful on a
chilly day. For variations
add rice, barley or pasta.
Substitute chicken with ham
or sausage. Add your
favorite spices — be
creative! Common soup
beans: aduki, black, black
eye, garbonzo, great
northern split, lentil, pinto,
kidney and yellow eye.

Curried Turkey Soup

6 cups turkey stock

1 cup peeled and chopped apples

1 large onion, chopped

1/2 teaspoon salt

2 teaspoons curry powder

1/4 teaspoon garlic powder

1 cup buttermilk

1 cup cooked diced turkey

- Simmer stock, apples, onion, salt and curry for 30 minutes.

- Purée in blender. Add garlic powder, buttermilk and meat to the stock. Heat just to the boiling point, but do not allow to come to a full boil.

Serves 6

If desired, rice may be added.

Mussel Chablis Soup

2 pounds mussels

1 tablespoon olive oil

3 cloves garlic, minced

2 cups chicken stock

2 cups Chablis wine

freshly ground pepper to taste

2 tablespoons butter

2 tablespoons chopped fresh parsley

- Discard opened mussels. Clean and debeard mussels, removing any debris. Rinse well.

- In a large pot, heat oil and sauté garlic for 1 minute over medium heat. Add stock, wine, pepper and mussels. Cover. Lower heat to medium low and cook for 20 minutes. Add butter. Discard any unopened mussels.

- Divide mussels evenly among two bowls and pour broth over mussels. Sprinkle with parsley. Use a mussel shell as a spoon!

Serves 2

Sausage Vegetable Soup

1 1/2 pounds sweet Italian sausage

1 tablespoon fennel seeds (optional)

2 cloves garlic, minced

1 large onion, chopped

28-ounce can whole plum tomatoes

three 14-ounce cans beef broth

1 1/2 cups dry red wine

1 teaspoon salt

1 teaspoon basil

3 tablespoons parsley

1/2 pound fresh mushrooms,
    thickly sliced

1 medium red pepper, chopped

2 medium zucchini, chopped

1 cup uncooked small bowtie pasta

grated Parmesan cheese, for garnish

• Remove sausage from casing and crumble. In a large stockpot, brown sausage and fennel. With a slotted spoon, remove sausage.

• To stockpot, add garlic and onion. Sauté 2 to 3 minutes. Add tomatoes and their juice, breaking up tomatoes. Add broth, wine, herbs, vegetables and sausage. Simmer 1 hour.

• Add pasta to pot and continue cooking for 8 to 10 minutes or until tender.

• Serve in bowls or mugs with a dusting of grated Parmesan cheese.

Serves 6

Lobster Bisque

1 ¹/4 to 1 ¹/2 pound lobster, cooked

1 ¹/4 cups water

8-ounce bottle clam juice

1 clove

2 bay leaves

1 tablespoon butter

1 small onion, finely chopped

¹/4 cup finely chopped celery

3 tablespoons flour

2 cups milk

3 tablespoons tomato paste

¹/4 teaspoon salt

dash of freshly ground pepper

2 tablespoons dry sherry

3 tablespoons fresh parsley

• Remove the meat from the lobster, chop and set aside. Place lobster shell in a large pot with water, clam juice, clove and bay leaves. Cook over medium-low heat for 30 minutes. Strain the mixture and reserve stock.

• Melt butter in large saucepan. Add onion and celery and sauté for 3 minutes. Sprinkle flour over onions and cook for 1 minute, stirring frequently.

• Add the stock, milk, tomato paste, salt and pepper and cook on medium for 10 minutes to thicken, stirring constantly. Add lobster meat. Remove from heat, add sherry and stir.

• Garnish with parsley.

Yields 4 cups

Lobsterman's Stew

four 1 ¹/₂-pound lobsters
(soft shell), cooked

tomalley (green lobster liver,
found in the body)

10 tablespoons butter, divided

¹/₂ cup onion

10 cloves garlic, minced

pepper to taste

2 cups plus 2 tablespoons Madeira

6 cups heavy cream

3 cups light cream

cheese cloth

• Scoop tomalley from lobster body. Set aside.
Remove lobster meat from shells. Set shells
aside.

• In a large saucepan, melt 6 tablespoons of the
butter over medium heat. Add tomalley,
onion, garlic, pepper, 2 tablespoons of
Madeira and sauté until onion is soft.

• Add remaining 4 tablespoons butter, heavy
cream, light cream and remaining Madeira.
Stir to combine ingredients. Add lobster
meat.

• Tie lobster shells in a cheesecloth and let soak
in stew. Simmer stew on low heat for 3 to 5
hours or longer if time allows. The longer it
simmers, the more flavorful.

Serves 4

Soft Shell Lobster

Soft shell lobsters are found
in the summer months after
the lobsters molt. Soft shells
are not as meaty as hard
shells because their new
shell is larger than the
molted one. Soft shells are
extremely fragile and are
known for their tenderness
and sweet meat.

Chicken Vegetable Stew

2 tablespoons butter

3 1/2 to 4 pounds chicken

salt and freshly ground pepper

2 yellow onions, thinly sliced

2 green peppers, finely chopped

4 to 6 cloves garlic, finely minced

1/4 to 1/2 teaspoon red pepper flakes

2 bay leaves

1/2 cup coarsely chopped parsley

3 cups water

2 tomatoes, peeled and chopped

4 ears of corn or 10-ounce package
    frozen whole kernel corn

2 large potatoes, peeled and cubed

1/2 tablespoon Worcestershire sauce

• Heat the butter in a large pot. Cut chicken into serving pieces. Sprinkle the chicken pieces with salt and pepper and brown on all sides, over medium heat. Remove chicken. Add onions, peppers and garlic to pot. Cook until vegetables give up their juices. Continue to cook until liquid evaporates and vegetables begin to turn brown, about 7 to 10 minutes. Return chicken to pot and add pepper flakes, bay leaves, parsley, water and tomatoes. Cover and cook 15 minutes.

• Meanwhile, bring 2 quarts of water to a boil. Drop ears of corn into boiling water. Cook for 3 to 5 minutes, until corn is tender. Drain and let cool. Scrape the kernels from the cob. If using frozen, cook according to package directions. Drain.

• Add potatoes to the stew and cook, covered, for additional 20 minutes. Uncover and continue cooking 10 minutes or until potatoes are tender. Add corn to the stew. Add salt and pepper to taste. Stir in Worcestershire sauce and serve.

Serves 6 to 8

Skiers' Stew

2 pounds stew beef

2 tablespoons vegetable oil

1 cup chopped onion

4-ounce can mushrooms

16-ounce can whole tomatoes

6-ounce can tomato paste

2 ³/4 cups hot water

1 tablespoon sugar

1 ¹/2 teaspoons salt

¹/4 teaspoon pepper

1 bay leaf

¹/2 teaspoon dried thyme

¹/4 teaspoon dried marjoram

1 cup thinly sliced carrots

1 cup diced celery

¹/4 cup cold water

2 tablespoons flour

• Cut stew beef into 1-inch pieces. Heat oil in Dutch oven. Add beef and onion. Cook and stir until beef is brown.

• Stir in mushrooms, (with liquid), tomatoes (with liquid), tomato paste, hot water, sugar, salt and pepper. Heat to boiling, stirring occasionally; reduce heat. Cover and simmer, stirring occasionally, until beef is almost tender, about 1¹/2 hours.

• Add bay leaf, thyme, marjoram, carrots and celery. Cover and simmer 30 minutes. In a small bowl, mix cold water and flour until smooth; gradually stir into stew and serve immediately.

Serves 4

Top It Off!

Add a bottle of robust Chianti wine, and a loaf of hot crusty bread to warm you on a cold, snowy night.

Moosehead Lake Stew

6 pounds venison stew meat
  marinade (recipe follows)

6 tablespoons vegetable oil

¹/4 cup flour

¹/4 cup cognac (optional)

1 ³/4 cup water

24 pearl onions, peeled

¹/2 pound salt pork

12 ounces mushrooms, halved

freshly ground pepper to taste

3 tablespoons red currant jelly

• Cut stew meat into 2-inch cubes and marinate. Remove the venison from the marinade
and place it in a colander to drain. Strain the
marinade into a bowl. Reserve marinade,
herbs and vegetables. Tie herbs and vegetables in cheesecloth.

• Brown the venison over high heat in four
batches, using 1 tablespoon oil for each
batch. Transfer the meat, as it is cooked, with
a slotted spoon to a cast-iron Dutch oven.

• Preheat the oven to 350°.

• When all the venison is in the Dutch oven,
sprinkle the flour over the meat and stir well
over high heat. Add the cognac, 7 cups
marinade and the water. Stir well and place
the cheesecloth bundle in the pot. Bring to a
boil, scraping the bottom of the Dutch oven.
Cover and place in the oven. Cook for 1 hour
and 45 minutes or until the meat is tender.
Remove the cheesecloth bundle. Squeeze
the bundle to return the juice to the pot.
Discard the bundle.

• Meanwhile, place the onions in a saucepan
and cover with cold water. Bring to a boil
and blanch for 5 minutes. Drain and remove.
Cut salt pork into ¹/4-inch strips and put in
the saucepan. Cover with water. Bring to a
boil and blanch for 1 minute. Drain.

Marinade:

2 cups onion chunks

1 1/2 cups leek green chunks

1 1/2 cups celery chunks

1 1/2 cups carrot chunks

3 cloves garlic, peeled and halved

2 bay leaves

*4 sprigs fresh thyme or 1 teaspoon
dried thyme*

4 whole cloves

*1 tablespoon chopped fresh rosemary
or 2 teaspoons dried rosemary*

*1 tablespoon chopped fresh sage
or 1 teaspoon dried sage*

1 teaspoon coriander seeds

*1 tablespoon chopped fresh marjoram
or 2 teaspoons dried marjoram*

6 whole allspice

1 teaspoon black peppercorns

6 parsley sprigs

1/2 cup red-wine vinegar

6 cups dry red wine

salt to taste

• Add remaining 2 tablespoons of vegetable oil to a sauté pan over medium-high heat and cook the salt pork 1 minute longer. Add the mushrooms and onions. Season with pepper. Sauté for 2 to 3 minutes or until the onions are lightly browned. Drain. When the stew is cooked, add the salt-pork mixture.

• Put 3/4 cup of the cooking liquid in a small saucepan. Add the jelly and cook over medium heat until it is melted. Add the mixture to the stew. Simmer for several minutes, stirring well. Taste for seasoning and serve.

Serves 10

For the marinade:
• Combine all the ingredients in a large bowl or pot and stir well. Use it to marinate venison, covered, for 4 to 5 days.

Yields 10 to 12 cups

New England Clam Chowder

4 small potatoes

1/4 pound butter

1/2 cup chopped onions

1/2 cup chopped celery

1/3 cup chopped leek

2 scallions, chopped

2/3 cup flour

four 8-ounce bottles clam juice

4 cups half and half

1 cup dry white wine

2 pounds fresh clam meat

1 teaspoon dried tarragon

1/2 teaspoon dried thyme

salt and freshly ground black pepper,
    to taste

chopped fresh parsley or fresh dill,
    for garnish

• Boil potatoes, cool, peel, dice and set aside. Melt butter in a large pot over medium-high heat. Stirring constantly, sauté chopped onion, celery, leek and scallions 3 to 4 minutes until vegetables soften. Add the flour and cook, stirring, 2 minutes longer, watching to see that the roux does not brown.

• Reduce heat. Stirring constantly, slowly pour in the clam juice. Simmer the soup base 5 to 10 minutes. After simmering, stir in the half and half and white wine. Chop the clams and add along with diced potatoes, tarragon and thyme.

• Gently simmer the soup, without allowing it to boil, an additional 8 to 10 minutes. Season with salt and pepper. Serve garnished with chopped fresh parsley or fresh dill.

Makes about 2 1/2 quarts

Herbed Fish Chowder

³/₄ pound haddock or
  other firm fish fillet

3 ounces salt pork, diced

1 onion, chopped

4 scallions, chopped

³/₄ pound potatoes, peeled and diced

2 cups fish stock or 1 cup bottled
  clam juice

³/₄ teaspoon dried marjoram

¹/₄ teaspoon dried oregano

pinch of nutmeg

2 cups light cream

salt and pepper to taste

2 tablespoons minced chives,
  for garnish

2 tablespoons butter

- Cut the fish into approximately 1-inch pieces.

- In a large, heavy saucepan, sauté the salt pork over low heat until crisp and the fat is rendered, about 10 minutes. Remove with a slotted spoon. Pour off all but 3 tablespoons of drippings from the pan. Add the onion and scallions and sauté over low heat until softened, about 3 minutes.

- Add the potatoes, fish stock plus 1 cup water (or clam juice plus 2 cups water), marjoram, oregano and nutmeg. Bring to a boil, lower heat, cover, and cook until the potatoes are tender, about 8 minutes.

- Add the fish and 1 cup of the cream. Cook over low heat until the fish is just cooked, about 2 to 3 minutes. Add the remaining cream and heat through without boiling.

- Season to taste with salt and pepper. Stir in the chives and butter.

Serves 4

Garden Fresh Corn Chowder

2 tablespoons unsalted butter

1 cup chopped onions

1/2 cup minced celery

4 small new potatoes, diced

1 cup water

4 cups fresh sweet corn (4 to 5 cobs)

1 red pepper, minced

freshly ground pepper

1/4 teaspoon dried thyme

1/2 teaspoon dried basil

1 cup evaporated milk

salt to taste

• In a medium saucepan, melt butter over medium-low heat. Cook onions for about 3 to 5 minutes. Add celery and cook for 5 more minutes. To the same pan, add the potatoes and water. Cover and simmer for 15 minutes. Add corn, peppers and spices. Cover and simmer 10 more minutes.

• Using a food processor or blender, puree half of the solids with some of the soups own liquid. Return to pan. Add the milk and gently heat. Do not allow to boil. Salt to taste.

Serves 4

Vegetarian Chili

2 cups tomato juice

1/2 cup bulgar wheat

1 onion, chopped

1 carrot, chopped

1/2 green pepper, chopped

2 tablespoons olive oil

1 to 1 1/2 tablespoons chili powder

1/4 teaspoon dried oregano

1/4 teaspoon garlic powder

1/4 teaspoon ground red pepper

1/4 teaspoon ground black pepper

1 teaspoon honey

14 ounce can tomatoes, coarsely chopped

2 cups cooked kidney beans

2 ounces mild canned chili peppers, chopped (optional)

• In a 1-quart saucepan, over medium heat, bring the tomato juice to a boil. Stir in the bulgar wheat. Cover pan, remove from heat and set aside.

• Sauté the onion, carrot and green pepper in the oil for about 5 minutes or until tender, using a 3-quart saucepan. Add the spices and honey. Stir over heat for 1 minute. Stir in the tomatoes (with their juice), kidney beans and if desired, the chili peppers.

• Fluff the bulgar wheat with a fork. Add to the pan. Bring to a boil then reduce the heat and simmer for 20 minutes.

Serves 6 to 8

Spicy Crab Gazpacho

5 large ripe tomatoes, quartered

2 to 3 large cloves garlic

1 medium red onion, quartered

1/2 sweet red pepper, halved

2 tablespoons red wine vinegar

3 tablespoons olive oil

1 tablespoon fresh lime juice

Tabasco to taste

salt and pepper to taste

6 tablespoons chopped fresh parsley

6 ounce package crab meat

1 1/2 cups peeled, seeded and cubed
   cucumber, for garnish

fresh cilantro, for garnish

• Combine all of the ingredients (except the garnishes and crab) in a food processor or blender and blend until desired texture. Pour into bowl and chill until cold.

• When ready to serve, mix in the crab meat. Garnish each bowl with cucumbers and fresh cilantro.

Serves 6

Fresh Watercress Soup

2 tablespoons unsalted butter

1 large onion, chopped

3 cloves garlic, chopped

4 cups chicken stock or canned
  low-salt broth

1 large russet potato, peeled
  and diced

4 cups packed trimmed watercress

1/3 cup whipping cream

additional whipping cream,
  for garnish

4 watercress leaves

• Melt butter in heavy large saucepan over medium-low heat. Add onion and garlic and sauté until tender, about 10 minutes. Mix in stock and potato. Cover and simmer until potato is very tender, about 15 minutes.

• Add 4 cups watercress and simmer just until wilted and tender, about 4 minutes. Remove from heat. Stir in cream.

• Purée soup in blender in batches until smooth. Return purée to saucepan. Season to taste with salt and pepper. (Can be prepared 1 day ahead. Cover and refrigerate).

• Bring soup to simmer if serving hot. Ladle into bowls. Drizzle with cream and garnish with watercress leaves. Note: Can also be served cold.

Serves 4

Wild Berry Summer Soup

1 cup blueberries

1 cup raspberries

4 cups strawberries, hulled

1/2 cup Port wine

1 teaspoon minced gingerroot

1/4 cup light cream

1 tablespoon chopped fresh mint

2 tablespoons sugar

1 to 2 tablespoons raspberry vinegar
   or white wine vinegar

fresh mint sprigs

lemon zest

orange zest

- Put blueberries in a blender or bowl of food processor fitted with a steel blade. Blend until smooth; strain. Set aside. Process raspberries and then strawberries. Strain and set aside.

- In a 1-quart saucepan, bring wine and ginger to boiling. Reduce heat and simmer 5 minutes. Add cream; return to boiling and cook 1 minute longer, stirring constantly. Remove pan from heat.

- In a blender or food processor, place strained blueberries, raspberries, strawberries, mint, sugar and vinegar. Process until combined. Add cream mixture; process again until well combined.

- Pour soup into a container; cover and refrigerate until thoroughly chilled. Soup can be prepared several days prior to serving.

- To serve, ladle chilled soup into thoroughly chilled bowls. Garnish with mint, lemon and orange zest.

Serves 6

Blueberry Lemon Bread

1 1/2 cups flour

1 teaspoon baking powder

1/4 teaspoon salt

6 tablespoons butter

1 1/2 cups sugar

2 eggs

2 tablespoons lemon zest

1/2 cup milk

1 1/2 cups blueberries

Glaze:

1/3 cup sugar

3 tablespoons fresh lemon juice

- Preheat oven to 325°. Butter and flour 8 1/2 x 4 1/2- inch loaf pan.

- Combine flour, baking powder and salt and set aside. In another bowl, cream butter and 1 1/2 cups sugar until fluffy. Add eggs, beating well. Add lemon zest. Add dry ingredients alternating with milk. Fold in blueberries. Pour into loaf pan and bake until golden brown, approximately 1 1/4 hours.

- For glaze, mix together 1/3 cup sugar and lemon juice in saucepan and bring to a boil. Poke holes in bread with toothpick and pour the glaze over the bread. Cool 30 minutes.

Yields 1 loaf

Zucchini Apple Harvest Bread

1 Macintosh apple

3 eggs

2 cups sugar

2 zucchini, shredded

2 teaspoons vanilla

1 cup vegetable oil

3 cups flour

1 teaspoon salt

1 teaspoon baking powder

$^1/_4$ teaspoon baking soda

1 tablespoon cinnamon

$^1/_2$ to 1 cup chopped walnuts
(optional)

• Preheat oven to 350°. Grease two $8^1/_2$ x $4^1/_2$ x $2^5/_8$-inch loaf pans or 4 mini loaf pans. Peel, core and shred apple.

• Whisk eggs. Add sugar, zucchini, apple, vanilla and oil. Mix well. Sift together dry ingredients and add to zucchini mixture. Fold in chopped walnuts. Pour batter into prepared loaf pans. Bake for 45 to 50 minutes or until knife comes out clean.

Yields 2 loaves or 4 mini loaves

Cranberry Walnut Bread

2 cups flour

1 cup sugar

1 1/2 teaspoons baking powder

1 teaspoon salt

1/2 teaspoon baking soda

1/4 cup shortening

1 egg

3/4 cup orange juice

1/2 cup walnuts

1 cup chopped cranberries

grated rind of 1 orange

• Preheat oven to 350°. Grease and flour 1 loaf pan.

• Sift together all dry ingredients. Cut in shortening. Beat egg well, add orange juice and mix. Pour into dry ingredients. Mix until dampened. Add walnuts, cranberries and orange rind. Spoon into prepared loaf pan. Bake for 1 hour.

Yields 1 loaf

Sun-dried Tomato Bread

*¹/₃ cup oil-packed sun-dried
   tomatoes*

1 bunch scallions

2 ¹/₂ cups flour

2 teaspoons baking powder

1 ¹/₄ teaspoons salt

¹/₂ teaspoon baking soda

5 ounces Provolone cheese, grated

³/₄ teaspoon dried rosemary

³/₄ teaspoon ground pepper

¹/₃ cup pine nuts, lightly toasted

*2 tablespoons vegetable shortening
   at room temperature*

2 tablespoons sugar

2 cloves garlic

2 large eggs

1 ¹/₄ cups buttermilk

• Preheat oven to 350°. Grease one 9x5 pan or three 5x3x2 pans. Drain sun-dried tomatoes, reserving 2 tablespoons of the oil. Thinly slice scallions, including 1 inch of the green part.

• Into a large bowl, sift together the flour, baking powder, salt and baking soda. Add the Provolone cheese, scallions, rosemary, pepper, sun-dried tomatoes and pine nuts. Toss mixture until combined. In a small bowl, whisk together the shortening, reserved oil and sugar until mixture is smooth.

• Cook garlic in boiling water for 15 minutes. Drain, peel and mash with a fork. Combine garlic, eggs and buttermilk. Add to shortening mixture. Blend until well combined. Add the liquid ingredients to the flour mixture and stir until batter is just combined. Pour batter into pan. Bake in the middle of oven for 45 to 50 minutes or until knife comes out clean. Cool bread in pans on wire rack 5 minutes. Turn loaves out onto rack and cool completely. Bread keeps wrapped tightly in foil and refrigerated for up to 4 days.

Yields 1 loaf or 3 mini loaves

Apple Rosemary Tea Bread

¾ cup plus 1 tablespoon milk

½ cup raisins, coarsely chopped

4 tablespoons plus 1 teaspoon
    unsalted butter

2 Granny Smith apples, peeled,
    cored and diced

1 tablespoon plus ½ cup sugar

1 teaspoon chopped fresh rosemary

1 ½ cups flour

2 teaspoons baking powder

¼ teaspoon salt

1 large egg

- Preheat oven to 350°. Butter and flour three 5½ x 2½ x 2-inch loaf pans. Set them aside.

- Heat milk to scalding. Remove from heat and add raisins. Stir in 4 tablespoons of the butter and let cool.

- In a small sauté pan over medium heat, cook apples in remaining 1 teaspoon butter with the 1 tablespoon sugar until apples are glazed and somewhat soft, about 3 minutes. Add rosemary.

- Combine flour, remaining ½ cup sugar, baking powder and salt. Whisk the egg into cooled milk-raisin mixture. Add the diced apples to dry ingredients but do not combine. Pour wet mixture over the dry and mix with a few quick strokes, until dry ingredients are just moistened. Do not over mix.

- Fill prepared pans to about ¾ full. Bake for 30 minutes or until a toothpick inserted into middle comes out clean. Let cool.

- Serve slices with warmed honey (optional).

Yields 3 small loaves

Orange Tea Bread

grated rind of 1 large orange

1 ³/4 cups sugar

4 eggs

1 cup milk

³/4 cup unsalted butter, melted

2 ³/4 cups flour

2 teaspoons baking powder

1 teaspoon salt

Glaze:

juice of 1 orange

¹/4 cup sugar

• Preheat oven to 350°.

• Combine orange rind, sugar, eggs and milk in a large bowl. Beat until well blended. Add melted butter. Sift flour, baking powder and salt together. Add to wet ingredients and blend until smooth. Pour batter into 5 small bread pans 5³/4 x 3¹/4 x 2-inches. Batter should fill ¹/2 of the pan.

• Bake for 30 to 35 minutes or until cake tester comes out clean. Combine juice and sugar to form glaze. Pour over cooling loaves.

Makes 5 small loaves

Recipe Variation

To make Lemon Tea Bread, substitute orange rind and juice with rind and juice of 2 lemons.

Rosemary Scented Rolls

7 ½ tablespoons olive oil

3 or 4 fresh rosemary sprigs

3 cups flour

2 packets active dry yeast

2 tablespoons sugar

½ cup golden raisins

2 tablespoons freshly chopped
  rosemary

1 teaspoon salt

1 ¼ cups warm water

beaten egg, to glaze

• In a small saucepan, combine olive oil and rosemary sprigs and heat slowly until oil begins to ripple. Remove from heat, cover, and let stand 15 minutes. Discard rosemary and set aside.

• In a large bowl, combine flour, yeast, sugar, raisins, rosemary and salt. Make a well in center. Add oil and warm water. Stir to form a soft dough. Turn dough out onto a well-floured surface and knead until smooth and elastic, at least 5 minutes. Place in an oiled bowl, cover with oiled plastic wrap, and leave in a warm place to double in bulk, about 1 hour.

• Divide dough into 12 sections and knead each piece into a ball. Place on two oiled baking sheets and flatten balls to ½-inch thickness. Snip a cross on top of each with scissors, cover loosely with plastic wrap and leave to double in bulk, 15 to 30 minutes.

• Preheat oven to 400°. Uncover rolls and glaze with beaten egg. Bake for 15 to 20 minutes or until rolls are well browned and sound hollow when tapped. Cool on a wire rack.

Yields 12 rolls

Hearthside Bread

2 packages active dry yeast

1/2 cup warm water

2 2/3 cups boiling water

3/4 cup molasses

1 1/2 tablespoons salt

2 tablespoons oil

1 cup quick cooking oats

1 cup bran

2 cups whole wheat

6 cups unbleached white flour

• Proof yeast in warm water. Combine boiling water, molasses, salt, oil, oats and bran. Cool. Add yeast. Stir in whole wheat and 2 cups flour; gradually add flour to make a soft dough. Knead until smooth.

• Place in a greased bowl and cover; let rise in warm place until doubles in size, about 1 hour. Punch down; divide in half. Shape into loaves. Place in greased 9x5 loaf pans. Let rise about 1 hour. Bake at 350° for about 35 to 40 minutes.

Yields 2 loaves

Whole Wheat Soda Bread

1 1/4 cups whole wheat pastry flour

3/4 cup unbleached white flour

1 teaspoon baking soda

1 tablespoon wheat germ

1 tablespoon oat bran

1 teaspoon cream of tartar

1/2 teaspoon sea or Kosher salt

2 tablespoons applesauce

1 teaspoon honey

1 1/2 cups nonfat buttermilk

sesame seeds, for top

• Preheat oven to 400°.

• Mix all the dry ingredients together except sesame seeds. Blend in wet ingredients until well combined.

• Shape dough into a ball and place in a greased 8-inch ceramic soufflé dish or cake pan. Press the dough to fill the shape of the pan and score with a criss cross pattern across the whole top with a sharp knife. The dough should fill up the space of the pan with plenty of space left for the bread to rise properly. Sprinkle the top generously with sesame seeds and bake for 45 minutes.

• Let the bread cool at least 5 to 10 minutes before cutting.

Yields 1 loaf

Herbed Focaccia

pizza dough (see recipe on page 98)
or use 1 pound store bought dough

$^1/_4$ cup extra virgin olive oil

2 tablespoons dried rosemary

$^1/_4$ cup grated Romano cheese

1 teaspoon garlic powder

1 teaspoon onion powder

1 tablespoon dried basil

salt and freshly ground pepper
to taste

2 tablespoons extra virgin olive oil,
for topping

• Preheat oven to 400°. Cut dough in half and lightly knead forming a larger circle.

• Lightly brush 2 large cookie sheets with 1 tablespoon of the oil. Place each piece of dough onto cookie sheets. Brush each piece with remaining oil, covering all of dough. Sprinkle each piece with herbs and cheese. Bake for 15 minutes or until golden brown. Remove immediately and brush 1 tablespoon of oil on each piece for a golden crust. Cut into pieces and serve hot.

Serves 4 to 6

English Muffin Bread

6 cups flour

2 packages yeast

1 tablespoon sugar

2 teaspoons salt

$^1/_4$ teaspoon baking soda

2 cups milk

$^1/_2$ cup water

cornmeal

• Combine 3 cups of the flour, yeast, sugar, salt and soda. In a separate pan, heat the milk and water until very warm. Add to the dry mixture and beat well. Stir in enough of the remaining 3 cups of flour to make a stiff batter. Spoon into two 8$^1/_2$ inch x 4$^1/_2$-inch loaf pans that have been greased and sprinkled with cornmeal. Sprinkle more cornmeal on the top of the dough. Cover and let rise in a warm place for 45 minutes.

• Bake in a 400° oven for 25 minutes. Remove from pans immediately and cool. Slice, toast and serve.

Yields 2 loaves

Effortless French Bread

1 ½ packages yeast

2 teaspoons sugar

½ cup warm water,

3 ¼ cups unbleached flour

2 teaspoons salt

1 cup warm water

- Preheat oven to 450°.

- Add yeast and 1 teaspoon of sugar to the warm water. Let this mixture proof for about 5 minutes or until it has doubled in size and is foamy.

- In a food processor, using the metal blade with motor running, add flour, salt, remaining 1 teaspoon of sugar and the yeast mixture. Blend these ingredients and slowly add up to 1 cup of warm water. If the dough is too wet, add more flour. If it is too dry, add more water. The dough should form a smooth ball if it is the right consistency.

- Knead the dough on a floured doughboard or countertop for a couple of minutes.

- When it is the right texture, cut the dough in half and shape it into loaves by rolling the dough and pulling it lengthwise. Place them side by side in a greased baguette pan.

- Cover the loaves and let them rise in a warm place for 45 minutes to 1 hour. Place a shallow pan of water in the bottom of the oven and bake loaves for 15 minutes or until the bread has a hollow sound when you hit it with a knife.

Yields 2 loaves

Downeast Dinner Rolls

1 package yeast

¹/₄ cup sugar

¹/₂ cup warm water

¹/₂ cup warm milk

¹/₂ cup oil

1 teaspoon salt

3 cups flour

2 eggs, beaten

4 tablespoons butter, melted

• In a large bowl, dissolve yeast and sugar in warm water and let stand 3 to 5 minutes. To bowl, add water mixture, milk, oil and salt. Stir to evenly mix. Add flour in batches and continue mixing until well blended and a ball has formed.

• Lightly grease a large bowl and add dough. Cover bowl and let dough rise until doubled in size. Punch dough down and turn onto a lightly floured board. Roll out dough and cut or shape into approximately 1¹/₂ dozen rounds. In 2 to 3 greased round pans, place rolls touching each other. Cover and allow to rise 1¹/₂ hours.

• Preheat oven to 400°. Brush egg on top of rolls. Bake for 20 to 25 minutes. While rolls are warm, brush with melted butter.

Yields 1 ¹/₂ dozen

Crispy Crust Pizza Dough

1 package active dried yeast

¹/4 cup warm water

2 teaspoons salt

2 tablespoons honey

2 tablespoons olive oil

³/4 cup cold water

3 cups flour

Preparing Pizza Crust by Hand

On a lightly floured work surface, place the flour and make a small well in the center. Add the salt and honey liquid and the yeast into the well. Slowly work the flour into the wet ingredients from the center outward. Continue this process until a dough ball forms. On a floured work surface, knead the dough until smooth. Place dough in a lightly oiled bowl and cover for 30 minutes.

• In a small cup, dissolve the yeast in ¹/4 cup warm water and proof for 10 minutes.

• In a small bowl, mix the salt, honey, olive oil and the cold water.

• In a food processor, add the flour and with motor running, slowly pour the salt and honey liquid into the flour and then pour the yeast mixture. Process until the dough forms into a large ball. On a floured work surface, knead the dough until smooth. Place dough in lightly oiled bowl and cover for 30 minutes.

• Divide the dough into four equal pieces and shape into a smooth small ball. Put dough onto a plate and cover with a damp towel and refrigerate, freeze or use immediately.

• To form dough into 7-inch diameter, flatten ball of dough into a circle and working with floured fingers (or a rolling pin), gently stretch the edges, working clockwise to form a 7-inch circle.

• Once pizza is topped with your favorite toppings, bake at 450° for 12 to 15 minutes or until crust is golden brown and cheese is bubbly.

Yields four 7-inch individual pizzas

Maine Potato Pizza Dough

2 medium Maine potatoes

1 package active dried yeast

³/4 cup warm water

1 teaspoon sugar

2 ³/4 cups flour

1 teaspoon salt

• Boil the potatoes until tender. Drain, cool and remove skin.

• In a small bowl, proof the yeast with 2 teaspoons of the water and sugar and set aside.

• Sift the flour and salt into a medium bowl. Press potato through a strainer into flour. Stir in yeast mixture and remaining water. Mix into a soft dough and transfer to a lightly floured surface.

• Knead for 10 minutes, until smooth. Place in a lightly oiled bowl for about 45 minutes, until doubled in size.

• Punch down dough and knead briefly. Divide into 2 or 4 pieces. (May be frozen at this point).

• With hands, shape piece into desired size and crust is ready for your favorite toppings!

Yields four 7-inch individual pizzas

Sauces For Pizza

Spicy Marinara Sauce:

1 can whole peeled tomatoes
  (28 to 32 ounces)

¼ cup extra virgin olive oil

4 cloves of garlic, chopped

⅓ cup Burgundy wine

1 teaspoon salt

1 teaspoon freshly ground pepper

½ teaspoon red pepper flakes

1 tablespoon fresh or dried basil,
  chopped

• Cut up tomatoes into small pieces and save juice.

• In a medium saucepan, heat oil and add garlic, sautéing for 1 minute, until lightly golden. Add remaining ingredients including juice from tomatoes. Simmer for 15 to 25 minutes.

Yields enough for four 7-inch individual pizzas.

This sauce is easily doubled and freezes well.

Olive Oil Herb Sauce:

1 cup extra virgin olive oil

1 tablespoon fresh basil, chopped

1 tablespoon fresh oregano, chopped

2 tablespoons freshly grated
  Romano cheese

3 cloves of garlic, chopped

½ teaspoon kosher salt

1 teaspoon freshly ground pepper

• Mix all ingredients in a small bowl. Using a pastry brush, coat each individual pizza with ¼ of the mixture.

Yields enough for four 7-inch individual pizzas.

Basil Pesto Pizza Sauce

*1 cup tightly packed fresh basil
leaves*

*$^1/_2$ to $^3/_4$ cup grated Parmesan
cheese*

$^1/_2$ to $^3/_4$ cup olive oil

$^1/_3$ cup pine nuts

$^1/_3$ cup parsley

3 to 5 cloves garlic

salt and pepper to taste

• Place all of the ingredients in a blender or food processor and process until smooth.

Helpful Hints For Pizza Making

- Always start with a very hot oven - at least 450°.

- Use fresh ingredients whenever possible.

- Fresh herbs have much more flavor than dried.

- You will save time, money and waste if you use the supermarket salad bar to purchase toppings (i.e., spinach, vegetables and cheeses).

- A pizza stone and wooden paddle make a crispy crust pizza and unbeatable flavor (do not forget to coat the paddle with cornmeal for easy pizza removal).

- Cut or slice your vegetables thin and they won't have to be precooked.

Create Your Own Winning Combinations
Food trends have come and gone but pizza has remained a favorite for everyone. Favorite toppings are turning to the more sophisticated and unusual while making a pizza has become a social event - pizza making parties are popping up everywhere, with bowls of various toppings just waiting to be made into a one-of-a-kind masterpiece.
Fresh herbs:
   Basil, Dill, Oregano, Marjoram, Parsley, Thyme, Rosemary, Chives
From the summer harvest:
   Tomatoes, Zucchini, Eggplant, Onions, Spinach, Summer, Squash, Asparagus
Cheeses:
   Fresh Mozzarella, Fontina, Feta, Ricotta, Goat Cheese, Gorgonzola, and of course, freshly grated Parmesan and Pecorino Romano
Meats and Seafood:
   Prosciutto, Grilled Chicken, Duck, Pepperoni, Shrimp, Clams, Anchovy, Turkey, Sausage, Tuna, Crabmeat, Smoked Salmon
Miscellaneous:
   Capers, Kalmata Olives, Sundried Tomatoes, Roasted Peppers, Pine Nuts, Wild Mushrooms, Roasted Garlic, Artichoke Hearts, Carmelized Onions, Sliced Red Onions

Salads

MAINE
Ingredients
Potatoes

*T*ravel to the northern reaches of Maine and you'll find yourself in what looks like western European countryside. Long stretches of land lay before you covered with pleasantly groomed fields. If you visit in July, the fields come alive with delicate white potato blossoms.

Nearly eighty thousand acres in Aroostook County are devoted to potatoes. This is no accident. "The County" has just the right climate and conditions for cultivating this popular Maine crop.

The Scotch-Irish introduced potatoes to Maine. Although highly prized by these immigrants, they were held in low regard by their English neighbors. At first the English did not understand how to cultivate them. They tried several ways of cooking and eating the greens, not realizing the value of the root. It was not until the following spring, while plowing the fields, that they accidentally dug up the tuber and learned that *this* was the potato! The new lands cleared and burned were rich with sandy loam and produced abundant crops. In time the English learned to cook and cultivate them.

The "County's" potato crop benefited from the "Aroostook War." During this border dispute with Great Britain, the northern portion of Maine almost became a part of Canada. Settlement was interrupted and much of the valuable lumber was cut and hauled. This resulted in miles of barren land, ideal for potato crops. Today in Northern Maine, businesses and schools close down during harvest time, so that men, women, and children can harvest the crop.

Blissful Herb Vinaigrette Potato Salad

1 ¹/2 pounds small red new potatoes

²/3 cup olive oil

4 tablespoons white wine vinegar

2 tablespoons Dijon mustard

2 tablespoons lemon juice

2 cloves garlic, minced

1 tablespoon basil

1 tablespoon tarragon

1 tablespoon dried chives

¹/2 tablespoon oregano

2 tablespoons chopped shallots

2 tablespoons chopped fresh dill

3 sprigs fresh dill, for garnish

salt and pepper to taste

• Boil potatoes with skins on. Quarter the cooled boiled potatoes, keeping skins on.

• In a large bowl, whisk together remaining ingredients. Toss gently with potatoes. Refrigerate at least 1 hour. Garnish with dill sprigs.

Serves 4 to 6

Herbs

Use fresh herbs whenever possible, but when only dried herbes are available, use less, approximately 1 teaspoon to every tablespoon of fresh. Rub the herbs in your palm to release the flavor and oils.

Roasted Red Pepper Potato Salad

3 pounds red-skinned or white
   potatoes

two 12-ounce jars roasted peppers,
   reserve juice

6 ounces soft goat cheese

¹/₃ cup olive oil

1 teaspoon salt

1 teaspoon freshly ground pepper

¹/₃ cup chopped sun-dried tomatoes,
   packed in oil, drained

¹/₂ cup thinly sliced scallions

¹/₃ cup chopped fresh basil

• Steam the potatoes in a large pot over
  medium-high heat until tender, approximately
  20 to 25 minutes. Drain and cool.

• Cut the peppers into strips and toss with the
  goat cheese, olive oil, reserved pepper juice,
  salt and pepper.

• Quarter the potatoes and gently fold with the
  pepper mixture, tomatoes, scallions and basil.

• Serve at room temperature.

Serves 6 to 8

Horseradish & Yogurt Potato Salad

¹/₄ cup plain yogurt

2 tablespoons grated horseradish

1 tablespoon red wine vinegar

¹/₃ cup extra virgin olive oil

*coarse salt and freshly ground
    pepper to taste*

6 scallions, chopped

2 pounds red potatoes

1 bunch watercress, leaves only

• Combine the yogurt, horseradish, vinegar and oil. Mix thoroughly and season to taste with salt and pepper. Stir in scallions.

• Scrub potatoes. Leave skins on. Boil in water until tender. Drain and cut into thick slices while they are still hot.

• Place the potatoes in a serving bowl and toss with the dressing. Add the watercress leaves just before serving and toss.

Serves 4 to 6

Note: If using bottled horseradish packed in vinegar, check seasoning before you add the red wine vinegar.

Grilled Tuna & Dijon Herb Potato Salad

2 pounds red-skinned potatoes

5 tablespoons cider vinegar

¹/4 cup olive oil

2 tablespoons white wine vinegar

1 large head Romaine lettuce

2 tablespoons drained capers

1 pound tuna steak, grilled
    and sliced

Dressing:

2 tablespoons fresh basil

1 tablespoon fresh parsley

1 ¹/2 tablespoons Dijon mustard

1 tablespoon water

1 tablespoon white wine vinegar

¹/2 teaspoon salt

1 teaspoon pepper

¹/2 cup olive oil

1 tablespoon chilled whipping cream

• Cook potatoes in large pot of boiling water until tender, about 30 minutes. Drain and cool. Cut into 1-inch cubes and transfer to a large bowl. Sprinkle with cider vinegar. (Can be made 4 hours ahead. Let stand at room temperature).

• Whisk oil and white wine vinegar in another large bowl. Add lettuce and toss to coat.

• To prepare dressing, chop basil and parsley in food processor. Add and blend next 5 ingredients in processor. With machine running, add oil in slow, steady stream. Add cream; blend mixture until thick and creamy. (Can be prepared 1 day ahead. Cover and refrigerate. Bring to room temperature before using).

• Add capers to potatoes. Mix enough dressing into potatoes to coat. Spoon salad and tuna slices on top of Romaine leaves and serve.

Serves 6 to 8

This is also great without the tuna.

Savory Rice Salad

1 cup rice

1 chicken bouillon cube

4 scallions, finely chopped

3/4 cup finely chopped peppers
   (any combination of red,
   yellow or green)

12 pimiento stuffed olives, sliced

12 ripe black olives, sliced

two 6-ounce jars marinated
   artichoke hearts, quartered
   (reserve liquid from 1 jar)

1/4 cup mayonnaise

2 teaspoons curry powder
   or to taste

• Cook rice according to package directions
  with bouillon cube added to water. Cool.

• In medium bowl, gently mix rice with
  remaining ingredients including reserved
  liquid from the artichoke hearts.

• Refrigerate at least one hour.

Serves 4 to 6

Summer Seafood Salad

2 cups cooked rice

1/2 pound cooked lobster meat

1/2 pound cooked shrimp

6 ounces crabmeat

1/2 cup sliced celery

1 scallion, sliced

Dressing:

1/2 cup lemon juice

2 tablespoons dried dill or
    4 to 5 tablespoons fresh dill

2 cloves of garlic, minced

4 ounces Feta cheese, crumbled

• In a large bowl, combine rice, lobster, shrimp, crabmeat, celery and scallions.

• In a small bowl, combine lemon juice, dill weed and garlic. Toss with rice mixture and top with cheese. Refrigerate.

Serves 6-8

Suggestion

To enhance the flavor of the rice — after peeling the shrimp, boil the shells in water for 5-10 minutes. Discard the shells and then use this water to cook the rice.

Shrimp Remoulade

1 egg

1 cup olive oil

2 tablespoons lemon juice

salt and white pepper to taste

1 tablespoon chopped gherkin pickles

1 tablespoon drained capers

2 teaspoons Dijon mustard

1 tablespoon fresh tarragon

1 tablespoon fresh flat leaf parsley

2 pounds medium shrimp peeled
    and deveined

red leaf lettuce

• To make mayonnaise, blend together in blender or food processor, egg, $1/4$ cup of the olive oil, lemon juice, salt and pepper. While machine is running, add remaining oil in a steady stream until thickened.

• Mix in pickles, capers, mustard, tarragon and parsley. More herbs, capers or pickles can be added to taste. Makes about $1^1/3$ cups.

• Cook shrimp by blanching in large pot boiling water for 2 to 3 minutes. Drain and run cold water over shrimp. When cool, mix remoulade sauce with shrimp. Chill for several hours.

• Serve on bed of red leaf lettuce.

Serves 4 to 6

Chilled Lobster Salad
with Tomato Lime Vinaigrette

1 ¹/2 cups seeded, chopped tomato

¹/3 cup peeled, seeded and diced
   cucumber

¹/3 cup finely chopped scallions

2 tablespoons finely chopped
   fresh basil

¹/4 teaspoon salt

¹/8 teaspoon pepper

¹/2 yellow pepper, chopped

4 cups tightly packed torn
   mixed greens

³/4 pound cooked lobster meat,
   cut into bite sized pieces

Vinaigrette:

¹/2 cup peeled, seeded, chopped,
   tomato

2 tablespoons fresh lime juice

1 tablespoon balsamic vinegar

1 tablespoon olive oil

1 clove garlic

¹/2 teaspoon sugar

• Mix together first eight ingredients. Set
  lobster aside.

• To make vinaigrette, position knife blade in
  food processor bowl; add vinaigrette ingredients and process until smooth.

• Pour vinaigrette over salad. Toss and divide
  evenly among 4 serving plates; top each with
  lobster.

Serves 4

Cut an "x" on the bottom of tomato, being careful to cut through
skin only. Drop in boiling water for 20 seconds. The skin will be
very loose and easy to peel.

Lobster Salad with Saffron Mayonnaise

4 lobster tails, steamed and chilled

¹/4 cup chopped celery

¹/4 cup chopped scallions

1 large egg

2 tablespoons lemon juice

1 ¹/2 tablespoons Dijon mustard

1 ¹/2 cups olive oil

zest of 1 lemon

¹/2 teaspoon saffron, soaked in 1
    tablespoon of hot water*

¹/2 teaspoon thyme

salt and pepper to taste

*available in specialty shops as well as some
 super markets

- Remove lobster meat from shell, reserving tail shells (for serving).

- Combine lobster, celery and scallions. Set aside.

- In a food processor, pulse the egg, lemon juice, mustard, 1 tablespoon of olive oil, lemon zest, saffron (including the steeping liquid) and thyme for about 60 seconds. While machine is running add remaining oil in a steady stream until thickened. Add salt and pepper to taste.

- Mix mayonnaise with lobster, celery and scallions. Chill. Spoon into reserved lobster tails.

Serves 4

Cool Shrimp & Scallops

2 cups white wine

1 cup water

¹/2 pound thin asparagus

1 pound sea scallops

1 pound medium shrimp, peeled
and deveined

2 ripe tomatoes, chopped

¹/4 cup chopped fresh basil

³/4 cup extra virgin olive oil

¹/2 cup red wine vinegar

¹/2 teaspoon salt

freshly ground pepper to taste

fresh parsley and lettuce for garnish

4 large lettuce leaves

• In large sauté pan or skillet, bring wine and water to a boil. Cut asparagus into 1-inch pieces. Add asparagus to pan and quickly poach for 5 minutes. Remove asparagus and set aside.

• Add scallops to liquid and poach for 10 minutes, then add shrimp and continue poaching for 5 more minutes.

• In bowl, combine tomatoes, basil, oil, vinegar, salt and pepper, tossing all together. Drain seafood and toss with tomato mixture and asparagus.

• Refrigerate for at least 1 hour. Best when made one day ahead. Garnish with parsley and serve on lettuce leaves.

Serves 4

Marinated Steak Salad

Marinade:

1/2 cup red wine

1/4 cup olive oil

1/4 cup loosely packed fresh cilantro, in large pieces

salt and pepper to taste

4 cloves garlic, coarsely chopped

2 tablespoons soy sauce

1 1/2 to 2 pounds London Broil

Salad:

1 pound red potatoes

1 medium purple onion, sliced

1 small red pepper, sliced

1 small yellow pepper, sliced

1/2 pound snow peas

1 cup loosely packed fresh cilantro

1 small head of red leaf lettuce

2 to 3 thinly sliced scallions, for garnish

Dressing:

1 cup extra virgin olive oil

1/3 cup red wine vinegar

6 to 8 cloves garlic, crushed

salt and pepper to taste

• Mix marinade ingredients and pour over steak. Let marinate for 3 to 4 hours or overnight in refrigerator.

• After steak has marinated, drain marinade. Broil or grill the steak 4 inches from heat for 12 to 15 minutes, until medium-rare, turning meat once. Cut into 1 1/2-inch long strips.

• Boil potatoes until soft but not mushy. Cut into quarters. Combine all vegetables, potatoes and steak. Mix in cilantro.

• Combine dressing ingredients and add to vegetables and steak. Serve on fresh red lettuce leaves. Garnish with thinly sliced scallions.

Serves 6

Tarragon Hazelnut Chicken Salad

2 pounds cooked chicken breast

¹/2 cup hazelnuts

1 small red onion, coarsely chopped

4 stalks celery, diced

6 tablespoons chopped fresh tarragon

4 tablespoons finely chopped
  fresh parsley

¹/2 cup low-fat yogurt

¹/4 cup mayonnaise

salt and pepper to taste

- Cut chicken into bite-size pieces.

- Roast, skin and coarsely chop hazelnuts.

- Toss all the ingredients except the yogurt, mayonnaise and salt and pepper in a large bowl.

- Mix the yogurt and mayonnaise and add until the proper coating is achieved. Add salt and pepper.

Serves 6

Fort Williams Chicken Salad

9-ounce package French cut
   green beans or 9 ounces snowpeas

3 cups shredded cooked boneless
   chicken breast (about 1 1/2
   pounds)

3 cups cooked spiral shaped pasta

1 cup fresh blueberries

3/4 cup thinly sliced celery

1/4 cup thinly sliced scallions

2 tablespoons finely chopped
   fresh oregano

1/2 cup plus 2 tablespoons plain
   low-fat yogurt

1/4 cup plus 1 tablespoon
   low-fat mayonnaise

3 tablespoons blueberry vinegar*

1/2 teaspoon salt

1/2 teaspoon coarsely ground pepper

* available in specialty shops

• Thaw and chop green beans and place
between paper towels and squeeze until
barely moist. Combine beans and next 6
ingredients in a large bowl.

• Combine yogurt, mayonnaise, blueberry
vinegar, salt and pepper in a bowl and stir
well. Pour over chicken mixture and toss
gently. Cover and chill for 2 hours. Serve
over lettuce, if desired.

Serves 6

Apple Pecan Chicken Salad

2 small cloves garlic, minced

1 tablespoon Dijon mustard

1 tablespoon white wine vinegar
or rice vinegar

2 tablespoons minced savory

1/4 teaspoon salt

1/4 teaspoon freshly ground pepper

1/4 cup plus 2 tablespoons olive oil

1 small red onion, thinly sliced

2 large tart green apples,
such as Granny Smith

1 medium sweet red pepper, julienned

3/4 pound cooked chicken,
cut into 1-inch pieces

1 cup toasted pecans

- In a small bowl, combine garlic, mustard, vinegar, savory, salt, black pepper and olive oil.

- Put the onion slices in a small bowl. Cover with cold water and soak for 5 to 10 minutes; drain well.

- Peel and core the apples; cut into 1/2-inch pieces. In a large bowl, combine the onion, apple, red pepper and chicken. Pour the vinaigrette over the salad and toss well. Spoon the salad onto a serving platter. Crumble the pecans and sprinkle on top.

Serves 3 to 4

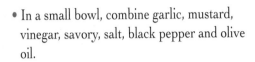

Apple Walnut Vinaigrette Salad

1 to 2 large heads green leaf
   lettuce or combination of greens
   such as Bibb or Boston

1 Granny Smith apple, peeled, cored
   and cubed

2 ounces Monterey Jack cheese,
   cut in small cubes

1/4 cup chopped walnuts

1/4 cup white or yellow raisins

1/4 to 1/2 cup Vinaigrette Dressing
   (recipe follows)

salt and pepper to taste

• Tear lettuce into bite-size pieces.

• In a large salad bowl toss the lettuce, apples,
  cheese, walnuts and raisins.

• In a small bowl whisk together the
  vinaigrette ingredients.

• Pour dressing over salad and gently toss. Add
  salt and pepper to taste.

Serves 4-6

Vinaigrette Dressing:

1/2 cup olive oil

1 tablespoon lemon juice

2 tablespoons vinegar

1 tablespoon Dijon mustard

1 clove garlic, minced

1/2 teaspoon each of basil, tarragon
   and oregano

Strawberry Romaine Salad

1 cup extra-virgin olive oil

³/4 cup sugar

¹/2 cup red wine vinegar

2 cloves garlic, minced

¹/2 teaspoon salt

¹/2 teaspoon paprika

¹/4 teaspoon ground white pepper

1 head romaine lettuce

1 head Boston lettuce

1 pint strawberries, sliced

1 cup shredded Monterey Jack cheese

¹/2 cup walnuts, toasted

• Combine first seven ingredients in large jar. Cover tightly, and shake vigorously.

• Tear lettuce into bite-sized pieces and combine with strawberries, cheese and walnuts in a large salad bowl. Pour dressing over salad and toss.

• Dressing may be refrigerated for up to 1 week.

Serves 12

Tossed Spinach & Pears

10 ounces spinach, washed and dried

2 medium pears, peeled and cut in wedges

¹/4 cup golden raisins

¹/4 cup blanched slivered almonds

Dressing:

¹/2 cup olive oil

2 tablespoons cider vinegar

1 tablespoon grated Parmesan cheese

1 teaspoon salt

¹/2 teaspoon Worcestershire sauce

¹/4 small onion

¹/4 teaspoon each sugar, dry mustard, basil, oregano and pepper

• In a large salad bowl, gently toss spinach, pears, raisins and almonds.

• To prepare dressing, mix all ingredients in a blender.

• Pour dressing over salad mixture and serve immediately.

Serves 6

Pear & Stilton Cheese Salad

Dressing:

1 teaspoon salt

1/2 teaspoon fresh ground pepper

1/4 teaspoon sugar

1/2 teaspoon dry mustard

juice of 1/2 lemon

1 clove garlic, minced

5 tablespoons tarragon wine vinegar*

1/2 cup extra virgin olive oil

1 egg

1/4 cup light cream

Salad:

1 head of Boston lettuce

4 ripe pears (2 Bartlett and 2 red), sliced

juice of 1/2 lemon

1/2 cup Stilton cheese,* crumbled

1/2 cup walnuts

*Available in specialty shops.

• In a jar, mix the dressing ingredients, shaking well.

• Arrange the salad greens on a plate. Slice pears and brush with lemon juice. Layer the pears on top of greens and then top with cheese and walnuts. Pour the dressing over all and serve.

Serves 4 to 6

Baby Greens & Wild Flowers

1 bunch watercress leaves only

1 small head Bibb lettuce

1 small head red leaf lettuce

1 small head radicchio

1 head Belgian endive

1 bunch arugula

1 bunch chicory

1 bunch baby beet greens

1 tablespoon chopped fresh basil

*pansies, nasturtiums or any edible
    flowers, for garnish*

Dressing:

¹/₄ cup champagne vinegar

2 shallots, chopped

2 cloves garlic, minced

²/₃ cup extra virgin olive oil

¹/₂ cup chopped fresh basil

*salt and fresh ground white pepper
    to taste*

• In a small bowl, whisk together the dressing ingredients. Refrigerate until needed.

• Gently toss greens. Arrange on plates and drizzle with dressing. Garnish with flowers.

Serves 8 to 10

Sweet Pepper, Tomato & Green Bean Salad

Dressing:

2 tablespoons balsamic vinegar

1 tablespoon Dijon mustard

1 tablespoon fresh lemon juice

1 clove garlic, minced

dash of Worcestershire sauce

¼ cup extra virgin olive oil

salt and pepper to taste

Salad:

1 pound thin green beans,
   stems trimmed

1 large yellow pepper, cut in
   thin strips

2 cups cherry tomatoes, halved

1 small red onion, coarsely chopped

¼ cup chopped fresh basil

• To prepare dressing, whisk together balsamic vinegar, mustard, lemon juice, garlic and Worcestershire sauce. Gradually whisk in oil. Season with salt and pepper. (This can be made 1 day ahead. Bring to room temperature and rewhisk before using).

• Cook green beans in a large pot of boiling salted water until crisp-tender, about 5 minutes. Transfer beans to a bowl of ice water. Cool and drain. Combine green beans, peppers, tomatoes, onion and basil in a large bowl. Add dressing. Toss to coat. Season with salt and pepper.

Serves 6

Tri-Pepper Slaw

3 tablespoons Dijon mustard

1 tablespoon sugar

1 ¹/₂ teaspoons dry mustard

1 teaspoon coarse (kosher) salt
   or to taste

¹/₂ teaspoon cayenne pepper

¹/₄ teaspoon freshly ground
   white pepper

¹/₄ teaspoon freshly ground
   black pepper

1 ²/₃ cups mayonnaise

2 ¹/₂ pounds green cabbage,
   quartered, cored and shredded

5 medium carrots, shredded

• In a medium bowl, whisk the mustard, sugar, dry mustard, coarse salt, cayenne, white and black peppers. Whisk in the mayonnaise. (The dressing can be refrigerated, covered, for up to 2 days).

• One to two hours before serving, toss the cabbage and carrots together in a large salad bowl. Add the dressing and mix thoroughly. Cover and refrigerate the slaw until ready to serve, stirring once or twice. When ready to serve, season to taste and toss once again.

Serves 8 to 12

Zesty Zucchini Salad

1/4 cup pine nuts

1 pound zucchini

1 pound summer squash

6 tablespoons olive oil

1 teaspoon salt

1 teaspoon freshly ground pepper

1 large shallot, minced

2 tablespoons fresh lemon juice

1 teaspoon dry mustard

2 bunches of arugula, trimmed

1 medium head radicchio

1 medium head Boston lettuce

2 tomatoes, chopped

• Preheat oven to 350°. Spread pine nuts on a small baking sheet. Toast for about 5 minutes, until golden. Remove pine nuts from oven and increase temperature to 450°.

• Cut the zucchini and squash into 2-inch x 1/2-inch sticks. In a large bowl, toss the zucchini and squash with 2 tablespoons of the oil and 1/2 teaspoon each of salt and pepper. Set the zucchini and squash, skin side down, on a nonstick baking sheet. Roast for about 15 minutes, until lightly browned. Let cool slightly, then transfer to a large bowl. (Zucchini and squash may also be grilled, if desired).

• In a small bowl, whisk the minced shallot with the lemon juice, mustard and remaining salt and pepper. Whisk in the remaining 4 tablespoons olive oil. Pour half of the dressing over the zucchini and toss.

• Tear the greens into bite size pieces. In a large shallow bowl, toss the greens with the remaining dressing. Make a well in the center and add the zucchini and squash strips. Sprinkle with the toasted pine nuts and tomatoes and serve.

Serves 6 to 8

One lemon yields four tablespoons of lemon juice. Squeeze lemon through a strainer of cheesecloth to obtain clear lemon juice.

Broccoli Sunflower Salad

2 bunches fresh broccoli

1 cup raisins

1 small red onion, diced

4-ounces roasted sunflower seeds

2 cups shredded Cheddar cheese

1 pound cooked bacon, crumbled

Dressing:

1 ¹/₂ cups mayonnaise

¹/₄ cup lemon juice

¹/₄ cup sugar

• Cut the broccoli into small flowerets.

• Plump raisins by soaking in hot water for 20 minutes.

• One hour before serving, toss onion, sunflower seeds, cheese and bacon.

• Stir together dressing ingredients, pour over salad and toss.

Serves 10

Healthy Alternative

For a healthier salad, try light mayonnaise, turkey bacon, low-fat cheddar cheese and fewer sunflower seeds. You'll never know the difference!

Warm Brussels Sprouts Salad

Vinaigrette:

¹/2 cup extra virgin olive oil

1 tablespoon white wine vinegar

1 tablespoon lemon juice

¹/2 tablespoon Dijon mustard

1 clove garlic, crushed

*salt and freshly ground pepper
to taste*

Salad:

*24 to 30 brussels sprouts, trimmed
and cleaned*

1 head radicchio

1 tablespoon olive oil

*¹/2 cup chopped walnuts,
lightly toasted*

4 ounces goat cheese

- Combine all vinaigrette ingredients in a bowl large enough to hold the brussels sprouts. Mix well.

- Steam brussels sprouts until tender but still crisp. Sprouts should be bright green. While still hot, add to vinaigrette and set aside to marinate.

- Separate, clean and dry radicchio leaves. Heat olive oil in sauté pan and braise radicchio until tender.

- With a slotted spoon, transfer sprouts to a large bowl. Toss with radicchio and walnuts until well coated with dressing. Add more vinaigrette if necessary.

- Arrange on salad plates. Top with crumbled cheese. Serve warm.

Serves 4

Fiddlehead Ferns with Wild Blueberry Vinaigrette

¹/₃ cup blueberry vinegar*

1 scant tablespoon Dijon mustard

¹/₂ cup extra virgin olive oil

*salt and freshly ground pepper
    to taste*

³/₄ pound fresh fiddlehead ferns*

1 small head red leaf lettuce

1 head radicchio

1 small head bibb lettuce

1 cup fresh blueberries

*Available in specialty shops. Fresh
fiddleheads are available in May and
early June in most produce sections of
supermarkets in Maine.

• Whisk vinegar and mustard together in a
small bowl. Add oil, salt and pepper and
whisk.

• Wash fiddleheads. Drop into boiling water
for 1 minute. Rinse under cold water.

• Wash lettuce and break into large pieces.

• In a salad bowl, combine the lettuce with the
ferns. Toss with the vinaigrette and mix in
fresh blueberries.

Serves 8 to 10

Olive Oil

Olive oil is an all-natural oil
that contains no cholesterol,
chemicals or artificial
additives. It is high in
monounsaturated fat which
helps to maintain healthy
cholesterol levels. It makes
good foods tastier and better
for you!

Black Bean Cumin Salad

two 16-ounce cans black beans,
  rinsed and drained

3 cups cooked corn kernels

1/3 cup chopped scallions

1/3 cup chopped fresh parsley

2 large tomatoes, chopped

1/3 cup olive oil

1/3 cup lemon juice

2 teaspoons ground cumin

1/2 teaspoon black pepper

salt to taste

fresh cilantro for garnish

• In a large bowl, combine all ingredients.
  Refrigerate overnight. Garnish with fresh
  cilantro.

Serves 12

Chickawaki Chick Pea Tabouleh

^{1}/2 cup bulgar wheat

1 ^{1}/2 cups hot water

juice of ^{1}/2 a lemon

^{1}/3 cup chopped parsley

1 cup chopped tomatoes, seeded

1 clove garlic, minced

^{1}/4 cup chopped scallions,
   including 1 inch of green

^{1}/4 cup chopped onion

15-ounce can chick peas

2 tablespoons red wine vinegar

^{1}/4 cup olive oil

^{1}/2 teaspoon salt

• Soak bulgar wheat in hot water and lemon juice until plumped, approximately 1 hour.

• Meanwhile, combine parsley, tomatoes, garlic, scallions and onion. Add chick peas.

• Whisk together red wine vinegar, olive oil and salt to make dressing. Add dressing to vegetable mixture. Toss with bulgar wheat and tomato mixture. Chill.

Serves 4-6

Fresh Mozzarella & Tomato Salad

4 ripe tomatoes

¹/4 cup extra virgin olive oil

1 cup chopped, loosely packed
   fresh basil leaves

freshly ground pepper

1 pound fresh mozzarella*

*Available in specialty shops.

• Slice tomatoes. Place on large platter.
  Drizzle oil over tomatoes. Top with basil and
  pepper. Let stand at room temperature for 1
  to 2 hours.

• Slice mozzarella and top tomato slices with
  mozzarella. Serve immediately.

Serves 8

Olive Oil
Which one to buy?

Extra-Virgin or Virgin are the
strongest of all the olive oils and
should be saved for salad
dressings and hearty dishes that
can stand up to its strong flavor.
It is not recommended for
heated cooking. Look for a
dark green color for the best
flavor.

Pure Olive Oil is the most
popular and the best for heated
cooking. It has a milder flavor
than Extra Virgin Oil. To ensure
a high quality oil, look for an
imported variety that is cold-
pressed, preferably from the first
pressing. All olive oils should
be stored in a cool, dark place
and used within 6-8 months of
opening.

Parmesan Orzo Pasta Salad

1 ¹/₂ cups orzo pasta
(rice shaped pasta)

³/₄ cup olive oil

9-ounce package frozen
artichoke hearts

¹/₂ cup chicken broth

1 large egg yolk

2 tablespoons white wine vinegar

1 teaspoon Dijon mustard

2 tablespoons lemon juice

salt and pepper to taste

¹/₂ pound proscuitto, chopped

2 tablespoons fresh minced basil

1 cup grated Parmesan cheese

¹/₄ cup minced fresh flat leaf parsley

4 scallions, minced

• Cook orzo according to package directions. Rinse in cold water, drain and coat with ¹/₄ cup of the oil.

• In a small saucepan, cook artichokes in chicken broth until thawed. Cut into bite-size pieces.

• Blend egg yolk, vinegar, mustard, lemon juice, salt and pepper in food processor. Slowly drip in remaining ¹/₂ cup oil, until mayonnaise is formed.

• Add proscuitto, basil, Parmesan, parsley and scallions to mayonnaise and mix by hand. Add all ingredients to orzo and gently mix. Serve immediately or refrigerate.

Serves 4

Bountiful Bow Tie Chicken

1 pound bow tie pasta

two 6 1/2 ounce jars marinated artichoke hearts

2 cloves garlic, minced

1/4 cup lemon juice

2 tablespoons balsamic vinegar

1 tablespoon Dijon mustard

1 teaspoon chopped fresh thyme

3/4 cup extra virgin olive oil

freshly ground pepper to taste

1/2 pound asparagus

4 boneless chicken breast halves, poached

1 yellow or orange pepper, chopped

1/2 pound cherry tomatoes, quartered

1/2 cup chopped oil-cured olives

2 shallots, chopped

• Cook pasta according to package directions, drain well and cool.

• Drain artichoke hearts and reserve marinade. In a bowl, whisk together the marinade, garlic, lemon juice, vinegar, mustard, thyme, oil and pepper.

• Steam asparagus until just tender, drain and chop into bite-size pieces. Cut chicken into bite-size strips.

• In a separate bowl, toss the artichokes, asparagus, pepper, tomatoes, olives and shallots with the cooked chicken and pasta. Toss with the dressing, cover and refrigerate at least one hour.

Serves 8 to 10

Tomato Basil Tortellini Salad

1 pound cheese tortellini

2 cups corn kernels

1 1/2 pounds fresh tomatoes

1/4 cup chopped fresh basil

2 tablespoons chopped fresh parsley

3 tablespoons olive oil

1 tablespoon red wine vinegar

1 clove garlic, crushed

1/2 teaspoon salt

1/2 teaspoon pepper

*2 tablespoons freshly grated
   Parmesan cheese*

• Cook tortellini, drain, set aside. If using fresh corn, cook corn and remove from ear. Seed and dice the tomatoes.

• In large bowl combine corn, tomatoes, basil and parsley. In small bowl whisk oil, vinegar, garlic, salt and pepper; stir into tomato mixture. Add tortellini; toss gently, sprinkle with grated Parmesan.

Serves 6 to 8

Spinach Dressed Chicken & Pasta

4 cups cooked chicken

1 pound penne pasta

1 cup chopped sun-dried tomatoes

$^1/_4$ cup chopped pine nuts

5 to 6 large leaves red leaf lettuce
   for garnish

Dressing:

$^1/_2$ pound fresh spinach

$^1/_4$ cup chopped fresh parsley

1 scallion

1 clove garlic

2 tablespoons olive oil

salt and pepper to taste

1 teaspoon dried dill weed

2 tablespoons balsamic vinegar

1 cup buttermilk

- Cut the chicken into bite size pieces. Cook the pasta according to package directions, drain and rinse. Soften the sun-dried tomatoes by soaking in hot water and squeeze dry.

- To prepare dressing, steam spinach and squeeze dry. In a blender or food processor with knife blade inserted, process the spinach with remaining dressing ingredients until creamy. Gently toss dressing with chicken, pasta, pine nuts and tomatoes. Refrigerate at least 1 hour and serve on large platter on bed of lettuce.

Serves 4

How to use sun-dried tomatoes

Whether using store bought or prepared-at-home sun-dried tomatoes, the preparation is the same. (Unless your using oil-packed sun-dried tomatoes, then this process is not necessary.) They must be softened in very hot water for at least 10 minutes, then drained and squeezed dry to remove all the water. Save this flavorful water for making stocks or boiling pasta. If storing for later use, place in an airtight container and refrigerate.

Confetti Pasta Salad
with Creamy Balsamic Dressing

1 cup sun-dried tomatoes

1 pound tri-color rotini pasta

2 scallions, chopped

¹/₄ cup pine nuts

1 ¹/₂ cups fresh or frozen peas

2 ripe tomatoes, chopped

³/₄ cup crumbled feta cheese

¹/₄ cup grated Romano or
   Parmesan cheese

2 cloves garlic, minced

1 small red onion, chopped

salt and pepper to taste

Dressing:

1 cup extra virgin olive oil

²/₃ cup balsamic vinegar or
   red wine vinegar

2 tablespoons Dijon mustard

2 tablespoons dried basil

4 cloves garlic, minced

1 teaspoon salt

1 teaspoon pepper

²/₃ cup low-calorie mayonnaise

• Soften sun-dried tomatoes by soaking in hot water and squeeze dry; chop. Cook pasta according to directions, rinse under cold water and drain. Toss pasta with all ingredients except dressing.

• Whisk oil and vinegar together. Add remaining ingredients and whisk until thoroughly blended.

• Toss pasta mixture with half of dressing.

• Refrigerate at least 2 hours. After salad has been refrigerated, the dressing is absorbed by the pasta and the remaining dressing can be added as desired to retain the creamy consistency.

Serves 8 to 10

Mayonnaise & More

Fresh Mayonnaise

3 egg yolks

4 teaspoons lemon juice

1 teaspoon white wine vinegar

1 tablespoon Dijon mustard

2 1/4 cups sunflower oil

1 scant teaspoon salt
  and freshly ground pepper

- Put egg yolks, lemon juice, vinegar and mustard in a food processor and process until light and thoroughly combined.

- While machine is running, add the oil in a steady stream until thickened.

- Add salt and pepper to taste.

Herb Mayonnaise

1 cup fresh mayonnaise

1 cup chopped fresh dill, basil
  cilantro or tarragon

1 tablespoon lemon juice

- Whisk dill, basil or cilantro and lemon juice into 1 cup of mayonnaise.

- Serve with steamed vegetables, seasoned grilled meats or chicken.

Egg White Mayonnaise

2 large egg whites

2 teaspoons Dijon mustard

1 teaspoon red wine vinegar

salt and freshly ground pepper

1 cup safflower oil

1/2 cup extra virgin olive oil

1/4 cup water

- Process the egg whites, mustard, vinegar, salt, pepper and 3 tablespoons of safflower oil in a food processor for 1 minute.

- With the machine running, add the remaining oil in a steady steam until thickened. After incorporating the oil, with processor still running, slowly pour in the water.

- Cover tightly and refrigerate up to 2 weeks.

Yields 1 1/2 cups

Dilled Cucumber Salad Dressing

1 cup peeled, seeded and diced
   cucumber

1 bunch scallions, sliced,
   green part only

$^{1}/_{4}$ cup safflower oil

$^{1}/_{4}$ cup sour cream or yogurt

1 tablespoon lemon juice

$^{1}/_{4}$ cup fresh dill weed

$^{1}/_{2}$ teaspoon salt

$^{1}/_{8}$ teaspoon ground pepper

2 cloves garlic, minced

- Combine all ingredients in a food processor
  or blender.

- Blend until smooth. Refrigerate for up to one
  week.

Yields approximately 1 $^{1}/_{2}$ cups

> For a cucumber garnish —
> before slicing, flute the
> cucumber by running the
> tines of a fork lengthwise
> down the cucumbers.

Feta Cheese Dressing

4 ounces feta cheese, crumbled

$^{1}/_{3}$ cup mayonnaise

$^{1}/_{3}$ cup sour cream

juice of 1 lemon

1 large clove garlic, minced

freshly ground pepper, to taste

- In a medium bowl, combine all ingredients
  and mix well.

- Refrigerate for up to one week.

Yields approximately 1 cup

Balsamic Mustard Vinaigrette

¹/2 cup extra virgin olive oil

¹/3 cup balsamic vinegar

2 tablespoons Dijon mustard

salt and pepper to taste

¹/2 teaspoon sugar (optional)

• Whisk olive oil and vinegar. Add mustard, salt and pepper and mix thoroughly. Add sugar if desired. (Ingredient amounts can be altered to taste).

Yields 1 ¹/2 cups

Green Onion Salad Dressing

4 scallions

2 tablespoons oil

¹/4 cup light mayonnaise

1 tablespoon white wine vinegar

1 tablespoon Dijon mustard

¹/4 teaspoon fresh ground pepper

1 clove garlic, minced

8-ounces plain low-fat yogurt

• Combine all ingredients in a blender or food processor. Blend until smooth. Cover and refrigerate for up to one week.

Yields 1 ¹/2 cups.

Blackberry Vinegar

3 cups fresh blackberries

2 cups rice vinegar

2 cups sugar

- In a food processor, using knife blade, process berries until smooth. In a medium bowl, combine berries with vinegar and let stand at room temperature for 24 hours.

- Strain mixture into a large saucepan. Stir in sugar and bring to boil. Reduce heat to medium and cook 5 minutes. Remove from heat and let cool.

- Pour into airtight containers. Keeps for 3 months.

Yields 4 cups.

Blackberry Vinaigrette

1 teaspoon cornstarch

1/4 cup water

1/4 cup Blackberry Vinegar

1/4 teaspoon salt

2 tablespoons lemon juice

1 clove garlic, minced

dash of pepper

- Place cornstarch in a small saucepan and slowly add water, whisking until well blended over medium heat. Stir in vinegar, salt, lemon juice, garlic and pepper. Bring to a boil. Reduce heat to medium and cook 2 minutes. Cool, cover and chill. Keep refrigerated.

Yields 3/4 cup.

Vegetables, Pasta & Rice

MAINE
Ingredients

Sweet Corn

*M*aine has had a long love affair with sweet corn. For the Indians and early settlers, corn was essential for surviving the harsh winter months. It was one of the few crops that would not rot in storage. Local Indians taught the first settlers to plant corn and to fertilize it by burying one or two fish in each seed hill.

The Indians had several creative ways of preparing corn. Hominy or crushed corn, was used as a staple in other foods or eaten a la carte. Samp was whole corn hulled in scalding water with lye leached from maple heaps. Nokehike, a popular Indian snack, was corn picked, pounded and mixed with maple sugar. Suckatash consisted of corn in milk, boiled together with shelled beans. Upaquontop was a broth made of boiled bass heads thickened with hominy.

Sweet corn became an industry in Maine in the 1800's, when it was the state's most profitable crop. In fact, the sweet corn canning industry originated in Maine.

Fresh grilled, boiled or steamed sweet corn complements any summer meal. No lobster bake would be complete without a few delicious ears!

Sweet Corn & Cheddar Cheese Soufflé

4 tablespoons butter

1 cup fresh or frozen corn kernels

3 tablespoons flour

1 cup milk

4 egg yolks

1/2 teaspoon dry mustard

1/2 teaspoon salt

1/4 teaspoon freshly ground pepper

1 bunch of fresh chives, chopped

3/4 cup grated sharp Cheddar cheese

5 egg whites

pinch of salt

• Preheat oven to 400°. Butter 8-cup soufflé dish.

• Melt 1 tablespoon of the butter in heavy medium skillet over medium heat. Add corn and sauté until tender, about 3 minutes. Remove from heat. Melt remaining butter in heavy medium saucepan over medium heat. Add flour and stir 3 minutes. Gradually whisk in milk. Boil until very thick, stirring constantly, about 1 minute. Remove from heat. Whisk in yolks 1 at a time. Whisk in mustard, salt and pepper. (Can be made 2 hours ahead. Dot top with butter and let stand at room temperature. Before continuing, rewarm over low heat until just lukewarm, stirring constantly). Add corn, chives and cheese.

• Using clean dry beaters, beat egg whites and pinch of salt until stiff but not dry. Stir 1/4 of whites into yolk mixture to lighten. Gently fold in remaining whites. Spoon into prepared dish. Place in oven. Reduce temperature to 375° and bake until puffed and golden on top and soufflé still moves slightly when top is gently touched, about 30 minutes. Serve hot.

Serves 4

Hearty Harvest Ratatouille

¹/₄ cup olive oil

4 cloves garlic, minced

1 bay leaf

1 medium onion, chopped

salt to taste

1 small eggplant, cubed

3 tablespoons dry red wine

¹/₂ cup tomato juice

1 teaspoon basil

1 teaspoon marjoram

¹/₂ teaspoon oregano

dash of ground rosemary

2 small or 1 medium zucchini, cubed

2 medium peppers, cubed

1 teaspoon salt

pepper to taste

2 medium tomatoes, cut in chunks

2 tablespoons tomato paste

freshly chopped parsley

• Heat olive oil in large, heavy cooking pot. Add the garlic, bay leaf and onion; salt lightly. Sauté over medium heat until onion starts to become transparent. Add eggplant, wine and tomato juice. Add herbs. Stir to mix well then cover and simmer 10 to 15 minutes over low heat.

• When eggplant is tender enough to be easily pricked by a fork, add zucchini and peppers. Cover and simmer 10 minutes. Add the 1 teaspoon salt, pepper, tomatoes and tomato paste. Mix well. Continue to stew until all vegetables are tender. Just before serving, mix in the fresh parsley.

Serves 4 as entree or 8 as a side dish

Serving suggestion: Serve on a bed of brown rice, accompanied by French bread. Top with grated cheese.

Spinach & Cheese Soufflé

grated Parmesan cheese for dish

parchment paper

string

3 tablespoons softened unsalted
   butter plus more for dish

2 shallots, minced

4 tablespoons flour

1 cup milk

pinch of nutmeg

salt and freshly ground pepper

pinch of cayenne pepper

1 cup grated Gruyere cheese

4 egg yolks

$^{1}/_{2}$ pound fresh spinach

6 large egg whites

pinch of cream of tartar

• Heat oven to 400°. Butter soufflé dish, dust with Parmesan and tap out excess. From baking parchment, cut a collar to extend 3 inches above the rim of dish. Tie collar around dish with kitchen string, then, using a pastry brush, butter the inside. Chill.

• In a medium saucepan over medium-low heat, sauté shallots in butter until soft. Add flour and cook 2 to 3 minutes. Add milk, nutmeg, salt, pepper and cayenne. Stir until smooth. Bring to a boil; lower heat and simmer 5 minutes, stirring constantly. Add Gruyere and stir until melted. Adjust seasonings if necessary — the base should be over-seasoned because the egg whites will dilute the flavor. Stir in yolks, one at a time. Transfer mixture to a large bowl and cover with plastic wrap, pressing it onto the surface. Keep warm.

• Cook spinach until wilted. Drain thoroughly. Stir spinach into cheese mixture. In a large bowl, beat whites and cream of tartar until stiff. Stir $^{1}/_{4}$ of whites into cheese-spinach mixture to lighten. Gently and quickly fold in remaining whites. Spoon into prepared dish. Bake for 15 minutes at 400°, then reduce heat to 375° and bake 15 minutes longer. Remove collar and serve immediately.

Yields one 1-quart soufflé

Summer Squash Tart

2/3 cup freshly grated Parmesan
    cheese

1/4 cup mixed, chopped fresh herbs
    such as savory, thyme, parsley,
    basil and oregano

2 tablespoons unsalted butter, melted

2 tablespoons canola oil

12 sheets phyllo dough, defrosted

6 teaspoons wheat germ

1/2 sweet red onion, chopped fine

1 medium zucchini, thinly sliced

1 medium summer squash,
    thinly sliced

2 medium tomatoes, thinly sliced

- Preheat oven to 400°. Place cheese and herbs in a small bowl and set aside.

- Combine melted butter and oil and, with a pastry brush, lightly grease a baking sheet. Place 2 sheets of phyllo, one on top of the other, on the baking sheet. Brush lightly with the oil and butter mixture. Sprinkle with 2 tablespoons of the herb-cheese mixture and 1 teaspoon of wheat germ. Repeat 5 more times, until all the sheets have been used, ending with a layer of phyllo. Brush this top sheet with the oil and butter.

- Leaving a 1½-inch border free, sprinkle the onion on the top sheet. Place the zucchini and squash, in alternating rows, overlapping as necessary. Top with sliced tomato. Sprinkle with remaining cheese, herbs and wheat germ. Drizzle with any remaining oil and butter.

- Bake 15 to 20 minutes or until phyllo is lightly browned and the cheese has melted. Remove pan to cooling rack and serve immediately.

Serves 3 or 4 as a light lunch or side dish

Vegetable Bake with Goat Cheese

1 medium onion

2 medium red and yellow peppers

4 tablespoons olive oil

¹/₃ cup finely chopped garlic

¹/₂ peeled eggplant, thinly sliced

salt and pepper to taste

6 tomatoes, thinly sliced

2 large zucchini, thinly sliced

3 tablespoons chopped fresh herbs (such as thyme, oregano and parsley)

8 ounces soft mild goat cheese

Savor the flavors of fresh herbs and vegetables and serve as a light luncheon or brunch dish.

• Preheat oven to 350°. Cut onion into ¹/₂-inch slices. Cut peppers into ¹/₂-inch strips.

• Heat 2 tablespoons of the olive oil in heavy large skillet over medium heat. Add onion and pepper strips and sauté until tender, about 5 minutes. Add half of garlic and sauté 1 minute. Spread mixture evenly on bottom of 9x13x2-inch glass baking dish.

• Arrange eggplant slices evenly over onion and pepper mixture. Season with salt and pepper. Top with alternate rows of tomato and zucchini, overlapping slightly. Sprinkle with herbs and remaining garlic. Drizzle with remaining 2 tablespoons olive oil. Season with salt and pepper.

• Bake until vegetables are very tender and beginning to brown on top, basting occasionally with pan juices, about 50 minutes. Crumble goat cheese and sprinkle on top. Bake until cheese melts, about 5 more minutes.

Serves 6

Old Port Baked Beans

2 cups Maine pea beans

¹/₄ pound salt pork

1 medium onion

1 teaspoon salt

¹/₂ cup dark molasses

¹/₂ teaspoon dry mustard

1 tablespoon sugar

• Wash beans and discard imperfect ones. Cover with cold water and soak overnight. Drain, place in large heavy saucepan and cover with fresh water. Cook very slowly over medium heat until skins burst when you take a few on the tip of a spoon and blow on them. Drain, reserving cooking water.

• Rinse salt pork to remove excess salt. Scald salt pork. Cut off ¹/₄-inch slice and put in 2-quart bean pot with the onion. Cut through remaining pork every half inch, making cuts 1-inch deep. Put beans in pot and bury pork in the beans leaving rind exposed.

• Bring reserved water to boiling point and add 1 cup of it to salt, molasses, mustard and sugar. Mix together. Pour mixture over beans and add enough water (preferably the reserved cooking water) to cover beans.

• Cover bean pot. Bake 6 to 8 hours at 300°. Add water as needed to keep beans moist. Uncover the last hour of baking so pork rind will be brown and crisp.

Serves 6 to 8

Baked Onions Amandine

2 dozen small white onions

¹/₄ pound butter

¹/₂ cup sliced almonds

¹/₄ cup dark brown sugar

1 clove garlic, minced

¹/₂ teaspoon salt

¹/₄ teaspoon freshly ground pepper

¹/₄ cup white wine

• Preheat oven to 350°. Peel onions by cooking in boiling water for a minute or so until the skin slips off easily. Set aside.

• In a heavy skillet, melt butter and stir in almonds and sugar. Add garlic, stir for a minute and add salt, pepper and wine. Add onions to butter mixture and stir until onions are well coated. Pour mixture into a glass baking dish and bake for 1 hour.

Serves 6

Perfect Peas

2 cups fresh or frozen peas

4 small white onions, peeled and sliced

8 Boston lettuce leaves, shredded

salt and freshly ground pepper to taste

pinch of sugar

2 tablespoons butter

¹/₄ cup water

1 teaspoon flour or cornstarch

• Combine peas, onions, lettuce, salt, pepper, sugar and 1 tablespoon of the butter in a bowl. Mix well and add the water. Place in a sauce-pan. Cover and bring to a boil. Simmer until tender.

• Meanwhile, cream the remaining 1 tablespoon butter and the flour. Add to the saucepan, stirring with a wooden spatula. Blend well. When liquid has thickened and returned to a boil, remove from heat and serve immediately.

Serves 4

Grilled Sweet Corn

8 fresh ears sweet corn-on-the-cob

butter

salt and freshly ground pepper

• Carefully pull the husks back over the corn without breaking off. Remove silk and discard. Replace husks. Soak corn in cold water for 25 to 30 minutes.

• Prepare grill. Remove corn from water and drain. Pull husks back and rub corn with butter. Replace husks. Place corn on grill and cook for 12 to 15 minutes, turning corn every 5 minutes.

• When finished cooking, remove husks and discard. Serve corn with butter, salt and pepper.

Serves 4

Sesame Grilled Eggplant

1 pound unpeeled eggplant

¹/2 teaspoon salt

1 tablespoon sesame seeds

¹/4 teaspoon crushed red pepper

3 tablespoons rice vinegar

2 tablespoons dark sesame oil

1 ¹/2 teaspoons lemon juice

2 cloves garlic, crushed

vegetable oil cooking spray

• Cut eggplant diagonally in 1-inch slices. Place slices on several layers of paper towels; sprinkle salt over cut sides of eggplant. Let stand 15 minutes; blot dry with paper towels.

• Combine sesame seeds and next five ingredients; stir well. Brush over both sides of eggplant slices; let stand 10 minutes. Coat grill rack with cooking spray and place on grill over medium-hot coals.

• Place eggplant on rack and cook 5 minutes on each side, basting with remaining sesame seed mixture.

Serves 6

The Eggplant

The eggplant is actually a berry and a member of the nightshade family. Other members of this family include tomatoes, potatoes and petunias. Some varieties may be orange, green or even striped and shaped like round balls.

Brussels Sprouts with Lime

1 pound brussels sprouts

4 tablespoons unsalted butter

1 medium onion, thinly sliced

*1 tablespoon chopped fresh fennel
or dill weed*

*1 tablespoon juniper berries, crushed
or 2 to 3 tablespoons gin*

juice of 1 lime

*salt and freshly ground pepper
to taste*

1 tablespoon chopped fresh tarragon

2 tablespoons chopped parsley

• Clean and trim the brussels sprouts. Drop
into boiling salted water. Bring to boil then
adjust heat to a simmer. Cook until tender,
about 10 to 15 minutes. Drain and rinse with
cold water.

• Melt 2 tablespoons of butter in a large skillet
over medium-high heat. Add onions and
sauté until golden, about 4 to 5 minutes. Add
brussels sprouts, fennel or dill weed, juniper
berries or gin and lime juice. Cover and
simmer until vegetables are tender, about 5 to
7 minutes. Season with salt and pepper to
taste.

• Toss in 1 to 2 tablespoons butter, broken into
pea-size pieces, along with tarragon and
parsley. Mix everything to coat and serve.

Serves 4 to 6

Lemon Parmesan Fiddleheads

1 pound fiddleheads*

¹/₄ of a lemon, juiced

¹/₄ cup grated Parmesan cheese

3 tablespoons butter, melted

• Brush off the fiddleheads and wash. Steam or cook them in boiling water for 7 to 10 minutes or until they are tender. Drain.

• Put the fiddleheads in a bowl. Sprinkle with freshly squeezed lemon juice. Add the cheese and butter and toss.

Serves 4

* Available in specialty shops. Fresh fiddleheads are available in May and early June in most produce sections of supermarkets in Maine.

Fresh Fiddleheads

The fresh fiddlehead season is very short, therefore buying in bulk and freezing allows you"fresh" fiddleheads for months after the harvest. Blanch the fresh, cleaned fiddleheads in a large pot of boiling water for two minutes. Remove and place in cold water. When cool, drain well, and place into freezer bags. Remove as much air as possible and freeze immediately. They keep for months!

Vegetable Sauté

1 pound fresh broccoli flowerets
  or 1 pound green beans

2 tablespoons olive oil

2 cloves garlic, minced

10 medium mushrooms, sliced

1/4 cup bread crumbs

salt and pepper to taste

• Steam vegetable until tender-crisp, about 3 to 5 minutes.

• While vegetable is steaming, heat oil in a large non-stick skillet. Add garlic and mushrooms and sauté for 2 to 3 minutes. Add steamed vegetable to skillet and toss. Pour bread crumbs on top and toss to coat vegetable. Drizzle with additional oil if needed. Salt and pepper to taste.

Serves 2 to 4

Creamy Dilled Spinach

2 tablespoons olive oil

1 small yellow onion, minced

8-ounces fresh mushrooms, sliced

10-ounces fresh spinach, washed

3 tablespoons fresh dill, chopped

1/3 cup sour cream

salt and pepper to taste

• Heat olive oil over medium-high heat and sauté minced onion until translucent. Add sliced mushrooms and sauté until partially cooked. Add spinach and cover. Cook until spinach is wilted. Toss with dill, sour cream, and salt and pepper to taste. Serve immediately.

Serves 4 to 6

Zucchini Pancakes

2 medium zucchini

$^1/_2$ cup brown rice flour

$^1/_4$ cup nonfat milk

2 egg whites

$^1/_4$ cup onion

2 tablespoons oat bran

$^1/_4$ cup Parmesan or Romano cheese

2 tablespoons baking powder

$^1/_4$ teaspoon nutmeg

salt and pepper to taste

nonfat sour cream for garnish

diced tomato for garnish

• Wash and grate the zucchini. In a medium size bowl, mix the zucchini with the next 7 ingredients. Add nutmeg and salt and pepper to taste and stir well.

• Cook on a hot nonstick griddle or crepe pan sprayed with cooking spray or butter. Drop heaping tablespoons onto pan/griddle. Cook until lightly browned on both sides, about 2 minutes per side. Serve with nonfat sour cream and diced tomato.

Serves 2 to 4

Broccoli Melange

4 slices bacon

2 cloves garlic, slivered

1/2 cup olive oil

1 bunch (1 1/2 pounds) broccoli

1/2 cup water

1/2 teaspoon salt

1/2 teaspoon crushed red pepper
    flakes

2 medium tomatoes, diced

1/3 cup sliced almonds

- Cut bacon into 1/2-inch pieces and place in a large skillet and cook over medium heat until bacon is golden brown, stirring frequently. Using a slotted spoon, transfer cooked bacon to paper towels to drain. Set aside.

- Pour off bacon fat from skillet. Add olive oil and garlic to skillet and sauté until garlic is golden brown, stirring constantly.

- Cut broccoli in flowerets and add broccoli with water, salt and red pepper flakes to skillet.

- Cover the skillet and cook broccoli mixture for 5 minutes. Remove cover from skillet and cook 2 minutes longer or until broccoli is tender. Add tomatoes, reserved cooked bacon and sliced almonds to the skillet.

- Toss broccoli mixture gently to combine. The tomatoes should become warm but should not cook completely or release their liquid. Transfer to a serving bowl and serve immediately.

Serves 6

Asparagus with Orange Butter

20 stalks of asparagus

3 tablespoons butter

¹/₃ cup pecans, chopped

1 teaspoon orange zest

- Trim stalks of asparagus and blanch in a skillet filled with 1 inch of boiling water for 2 to 3 minutes.

- Melt butter over medium heat in small saucepan. Add pecans and cook until nuts are toasted, about 4 minutes.

- Stir in orange peel and cook 1 more minute, stirring occasionally. Pour over asparagus and enjoy.

Serves 4

Tied Asparugus Bundles

Garnish with leek "ribbons". Blanch leek leaves in boiling water until tender and bright green — about two minutes. Remove, drain well and cool. Cut leaves into 1/2-inch wide strips. Use strips to tie individual serving bunches of asparagus.

Honey Spiced Turnips & Carrots

¹/₂ pound carrots

³/₄ pound turnips

¹/₂ cup orange juice

¹/₄ teaspoon ground ginger

1 teaspoon honey

• Peel and grate carrots and turnips.

• In a large skillet, over medium heat, add all ingredients and toss well to coat. Cover and cook, stirring occasionally, until vegetables are just tender, about 15 minutes. Serve immediately.

Serves 4

Penobscot Pickles

3 medium cucumbers

1 tablespoon salt

1 tablespoon dill

2 cloves garlic, minced

8 peppercorns

1 teaspoon mustard seed

1 cup white vinegar

2 cups cold water

• Cut up cucumbers into desired size pieces and place in bowl. Add salt and dill and mix thoroughly. Let stand ¹/₂ hour.

• Place garlic in a 1.5 liter jar. Add pepper-corns, mustard seed, vinegar, water and cucumbers. Stir and cover.

• Store at least overnight before eating. This will last 2 weeks in the refrigerator.

Zucchini & Carrots Parmesan

¹/₂ cup chicken broth

1 pound zucchini, shredded

2 carrots, shredded

*1 tablespoon freshly grated
Parmesan cheese*

- In a medium skillet, boil the chicken stock over medium-high heat until reduced by half, about 2 minutes. Add the carrots and cook for 5 to 7 minutes. Add zucchini and season with salt and pepper.

- Cook, stirring frequently, until the vegetables are just tender, about 4 minutes. Transfer to a serving dish and sprinkle the Parmesan cheese on top.

Serves 4

Honey Glazed Carrots

1 pound baby carrots

2 tablespoons honey

¹/₄ cup orange juice

1 tablespoon butter

¹/₈ teaspoon nutmeg

2 tablespoons parsley

- Cook carrots in boiling water until tender and drain.

- In a medium saucepan, combine cooked carrots, honey, orange juice, butter and nutmeg. Cook on medium heat until it boils. Reduce heat to medium-low and continue cooking for 5 minutes.

- Toss with parsley and serve.

Serves 4

Baked Herbed Tomatoes

2 medium tomatoes, halved
   horizontally

$1/2$ cup seasoned bread crumbs

$1/4$ cup onion, finely chopped

2 cloves garlic, minced

$1/2$ cup fresh basil leaves,
   finely chopped

$1/4$ teaspoon dried thyme

$1/4$ cup grated Parmesan
   cheese

$1/3$ cup dry white wine

3 tablespoons extra virgin olive oil

salt and pepper to taste

- Preheat oven to 450°.

- Remove seeds and pulp from tomatoes and discard. In a bowl, mix the remaining ingredients. Spoon mixture evenly into tomatoes.

- Place tomatoes cut sides up in a shallow baking pan.

- Bake for 15 minutes.

Serves 4

Baked Leeks & Garden Fresh Tomatoes

4 leeks

4 tablespoons butter

4 ripe tomatoes

salt and pepper to taste

2 to 3 tablespoons chopped fresh basil

1 1/2 teaspoons cornstarch

1/2 cup heavy cream

• Preheat oven to 375°.

• Trim off green part of leeks. Wash white part thoroughly and cut into 1 inch pieces. Melt butter in a shallow baking dish, add leeks and bake for 10 minutes.

• Cut tomatoes in half horizontally, sprinkle with salt, pepper and basil. Put tomatoes cut side down on the leeks and reduce oven temperature to 350°. Bake 5 minutes, then turn tomatoes over and bake 5 minutes longer. Remove from oven.

• Mix cornstarch with cream and whisk until smooth. Remove tomatoes to a hot platter and stir the cream mixture into the leeks, cooking on medium heat until the sauce thickens slightly.

• Use a spatula to spread the resulting leek sauce over the tomatoes.

Serves 4

Cherry Tomato Basil Compote

1 ¹/₂ tablespoons olive oil

3 cloves garlic, thinly sliced

1 pint red cherry tomatoes

1 pint yellow cherry tomatoes

salt and ground pepper to taste

10 large basil leaves

• Heat oil in a large skillet over medium-low heat. Add garlic and cook until soft and golden, about 3 minutes. Add tomatoes. Season well with salt and pepper and cook, stirring often, until tomatoes are just warm and ready to burst, about 3 to 5 minutes. Add basil and cook until just wilted, about 1 minute.

• Serve as a side dish or spoon over grilled meat.

Serves 4 to 6

Green Beans & Tomato Sauté

1 pound fresh green beans

1 large onion, chopped

3 tablespoons olive oil

2 large tomatoes, quartered

salt and pepper to taste

¹/₄ teaspoon cinnamon

• Sauté green beans and onion in olive oil until beans begin to soften. Add tomatoes. Sauté tomatoes until juices begin to appear (about 3 minutes). Add salt, pepper and cinnamon. Cover and cook 20 minutes until green beans are tender.

Serves 4

Cheesy Shredded Potatoes

9 medium red potatoes, peeled and grated

$^{1}/_{2}$ pound sharp Cheddar cheese, grated

1 teaspoon dry mustard

1 $^{1}/_{2}$ teaspoons salt

dash pepper

pinch of nutmeg

1 cup heavy cream

1 cup milk

paprika

• Preheat oven to 325°.

• Boil grated potatoes in large pot until nearly done. Remove potatoes, drain well and let cool. Place the potatoes in large casserole, being careful not to press the potatoes down firmly into dish.

• In 1-quart saucepan combine cheese, mustard, salt, pepper, nutmeg, cream and milk, stirring over low heat until cheese melts. Pour over potatoes. Do not stir. Sprinkle with paprika. Bake uncovered 45 to 60 minutes.

Serves 8

Lovely Light Sweet Potatoes

2 large sweet potatoes

$^{1}/_{2}$ cup fresh orange juice

$^{1}/_{4}$ teaspoon nutmeg

$^{1}/_{4}$ teaspoon ginger

• Peel potatoes and cut into large pieces. In a saucepan, boil potatoes until tender. Drain and place in a serving bowl.

• Mash potatoes then add orange juice, nutmeg and ginger. Mix well and serve.

Serves 2

Two Potato Spinach Bake

4 large baking potatoes

4 sweet potatoes

3 tablespoons butter

1 small onion, minced

3 tablespoons flour

2 teaspoons salt

pinch of pepper

2 1/2 cups milk

two 10-ounce packages frozen chopped spinach

• In 8-quart pot over high heat, put unpeeled washed potatoes (both types) in enough water to cover. Bring to a boil then reduce heat to low, cover and simmer 20 to 30 minutes until potatoes are fork tender but not soft. Drain and cool potatoes until easy to handle.

• Meanwhile, preheat oven to 375°. In 2-quart saucepan over medium heat, melt butter. Add onion and sauté until tender. Stir in flour, salt and pepper until blended. Gradually whisk in milk and cook until sauce thickens.

• Thaw spinach and squeeze dry. Peel baking and sweet potatoes and cut into 1/4 inch slices.

• In greased 2-quart casserole, arrange 1/2 of potato slices, top with all of the spinach and pour 1/2 of the sauce on top. Repeat with remaining potatoes and sauce. Cover and bake for 30 minutes. Uncover and bake 15 minutes longer, until hot and bubbly. Serve immediately.

Serves 8

Potato Gratin with Boursin

2 cups whipping cream

5 ounces Boursin cheese

3 pounds red potatoes, unpeeled,
   thinly sliced

salt and pepper to taste

1 ½ tablespoons chopped fresh
   parsley

- Preheat oven to 400°. Butter a 9x13 pan. Stir together whipping cream and cheese in a large saucepan over medium heat until cheese melts and mixture is smooth. Remove from heat.

- Layer half of the potatoes in the buttered pan. Season with salt and pepper. Pour half of the cheese mixture over the potatoes. Arrange the remaining potatoes, salt and pepper, and pour the remaining cheese mixture on top. Bake approximately 1 hour. Add parsley and serve.

Serves 8

Potato Tomato Gratin

4 large tomatoes

2 ½ pounds potatoes, peeled and sliced

salt and pepper to taste

3 large onions, thinly sliced

4 large cloves garlic, finely chopped

1 tablespoon chopped fresh thyme

1 cup dry white wine

¼ cup olive oil

- Boil a pot of water. Blanch tomatoes for 10 seconds. Drain, peel, core and slice tomatoes.

- Preheat oven to 400°. Arrange half of potatoes in shallow baking dish. Season with salt and pepper. Top with half of onions, half of tomatoes, half of garlic and half of thyme. Repeat layering. Pour wine and oil over gratin.

- Bake approximately 1 hour 30 minutes.

Serves 8

Oven Roasted Country Potatoes

*8 medium sized new potatoes,
   unpeeled*

¹/4 cup extra virgin olive oil

*salt and freshly ground pepper
   to taste*

*2 tablespoons chopped fresh
   rosemary*

- Cut potatoes into cubes (approximately 8 to 10 pieces per potato), and place in large bowl.

- Pour the olive oil over the potatoes. Sprinkle with salt, pepper and rosemary. Toss to evenly coat.

- Spread potatoes evenly on a cookie sheet with raised edges.

- Bake at 350° for 1 to 1¹/2 hours or until golden and crisp (evenly roasted), turning with spatula 2 or 3 times during the cooking. More oil may be added while roasting, if necessary.

Serves 4

Recipe Variation

Suggested optional
ingredients:
Caraway seeds
1 small chopped onion
chopped shallot
2 chopped cloves garlic,
6 ounces bacon (uncooked
and finely chopped)

Roasted Garlic Mashed Potatoes with Caramelized Onions

Caramelized onions:

2 tablespoons butter

1 large Vidalia or Spanish onion, peeled and sliced thin

2 tablespoons sugar

Potatoes:

1 head roasted garlic (see below)

3 large russet potatoes

6 red potatoes

2 tablespoons butter

³/4 cup milk

salt and pepper to taste

- To carmelize onions, melt butter in saucepan. Add onions. Cook until translucent, about 15 minutes. Add sugar and brown onions. Cook another 5 to 10 minutes. Set aside to cool.

- Leaving the skins on, quarter the potatoes. Boil in large pan until tender. Drain. Transfer to large mixing bowl. Mash potatoes with masher or fork until large lumps disappear. Add butter and milk. Using electric mixer, mix until all ingredients are blended. Fold in onions and garlic. Salt and pepper to taste. Serve.

Serve 6 to 8

Roasting Garlic

8-10 heads of garlic
olive oil
2 teaspoons oregano
2 teaspoons thyme
pepper

- Trim tops of garlic heads.
- Place in ovenproof dish tightly arranged.
- Drizzle olive oil over top or brush with pastry brush.
- Add oregano, thyme and pepper to taste
- Bake at 325° for 40 minutes. Reduce heat to 250°. Bake 1 hour.

Angelic Shrimp & Lobster

3 tablespoons butter

3 cloves garlic, chopped

2 shallots, finely chopped

1 cup white wine

1 cup chicken broth

freshly ground pepper to taste

dash red pepper flakes

1 pound medium to large shrimp,
    peeled and deveined

1 pound cooked lobster meat, chopped

1 cup light cream
    (milk may be substituted)

1 pound angel hair pasta

1/4 cup fresh parsley, chopped

• In large skillet, over medium heat, melt butter and sauté garlic and shallots for 2 minutes. Add wine, chicken broth and peppers, bringing to a boil on medium high heat until the liquid starts to reduce. Add shrimp and cook approximately 5 minutes, until opaque. Add lobster just to heat through. Reduce heat to simmer, add cream and turn heat off after 1 to 2 minutes.

• Meanwhile, cook angel hair pasta according to package directions.

• Remove seafood from sauce and set aside. Toss pasta with sauce. Place seafood on top of pasta, sprinkle with parsley and serve immediately.

Serves 4-6

Top It Off!

Enjoy a refreshing glass of
Pinot Blanc or Piont Grigio
with this "heavenly" pasta.

Scallops with Spicy Tomatoes & Fettuccine

1 ½ pounds sea scallops

2 tablespoons olive oil

2 scallions, finely chopped

2 tablespoons minced garlic

2 cups chopped fresh tomatoes

³/4 cup red wine

3 tablespoons red wine vinegar

4 tablespoons chopped flat-leaf
parsley

1 tablespoon chopped fresh basil
leaves or 1 teaspoon dried

1 teaspoon salt

1 teaspoon freshly ground pepper

³/4 pound fettuccine

¹/4 cup freshly grated Parmesan
cheese

4 sprigs fresh parsley for garnish

• Rinse scallops and set aside.

• In a large sauté pan heat oil and add scallions, garlic, tomatoes, wine, vinegar, parsley,
basil, salt and pepper. Cook on medium high
for approximately 5 minutes until vigorously
boiling. Reduce heat to medium low and
cook for 15 minutes.

• Cook pasta according to package directions.
While pasta is cooking add scallops to
tomatoes and cook for 5 to 7 minutes until
scallops are done.

• Add drained pasta to tomato sauce, toss.
Sprinkle each serving with grated cheese and
garnish with parsley.

Serves 4

Littlenecks & Linguine

3 tablespoons extra-virgin olive oil

4 cloves garlic, finely chopped

1/3 cup chopped onion

36 littleneck clams, scrubbed

1 cup chopped fresh plum tomatoes

1/2 cup dry white wine

1 pound linguine

pinch of dried hot red pepper flakes

1 tablespoon chopped flat leaf parsley

1 tablespoon shredded fresh
    basil leaves

• Heat the oil in a heavy saucepan. Add the garlic and onion and sauté over low heat until tender. Add the clams.

• Stir in the tomatoes and wine. Cover the pan and cook over medium-low heat until the clams have opened. Discard any unopened clams.

• While the clams are cooking, bring a large pot of salted water to a boil for the linguine. Cook the linguine until al dente. Drain and divide onto four warm plates.

• Season the clams with hot pepper. Spoon the clams in their shells along with the sauce in the pan over each serving of linguine. Sprinkle with parsley and basil.

Serves 4

The Secret to Clean Clams

To remove the excess sand from clams and mussels, put them into a large pot of water with about a cupful of cornmeal and refrigerate. As they digest some of the cornmeal, they exhale it along with some of the inside sand. If they float in this water, they should be discarded, as they are dead and should not be cooked. Drain and rinse thoroughly before cooking.

Spinach Linguine with Crab, Tomatoes & Capers

2 cloves garlic, minced

3 scallions, minced

2 tablespoons olive oil

2 tomatoes, peeled, seeded and chopped

*4 tablespoons chopped fresh basil
leaves or to taste*

*1 teaspoon dried hot red pepper
flakes or to taste*

salt and pepper to taste

*1 tablespoon capers, rinsed and
drained*

¼ pound crabmeat

2 tablespoons unsalted butter

2 tablespoons dry vermouth

½ pound spinach linguine

- In a skillet, sauté the garlic and the scallions in the oil over medium-low heat, stirring, until the garlic is pale golden. Add the tomatoes, basil and red pepper flakes and cook the mixture, stirring occasionally, for 20 minutes. Season the sauce with salt and pepper and stir in the capers.

- In a small skillet, heat the crab meat in the butter over medium heat, stirring, for 5 minutes. Stir in the vermouth and cook the mixture for 1 to 2 minutes or until most of the liquid is evaporated. Add the crabmeat to the sauce and keep the sauce warm, covered.

- In a pot of boiling salted water, cook the pasta until it is al dente, drain it, and toss it with the sauce.

Serves 2

Capers

What exactly is a caper? A caper is a small flower bud from the nasturtium or caper bush. It is dried and pickled and added to sauces or used as garnish. Capers keep for months stored in their liquid and refrigerated. They should be rinsed before use.

Seaside Shrimp with Feta & Linguine

2 tablespoons olive oil

2 scallions, chopped

16-ounce can whole tomatoes, chopped

¹/4 pound feta cheese, crumbled

2 tablespoons chopped fresh dill weed plus 2 sprigs for garnish

1 teaspoon salt

1 teaspoon pepper

1 cup dry vermouth

8 ounces linguine

³/4 pound medium shrimp, peeled and deveined

• In a large skillet, heat oil and sauté scallions until tender. Add tomatoes, feta, dill, salt, pepper and vermouth. Bring to a boil, reduce heat and simmer for 20 minutes.

• Cook pasta according to package directions. While cooking, add shrimp to tomato sauce and simmer for 10 minutes.

• Drain pasta, toss with sauce and serve immediately.

• Garnish with dill.

Serves 2

The Great Impasta

While there are no "rules of pasta", when menu planning keep a few things in mind. Cut pasta, such as rigatoni, penne, shells or spiral pasta are best suited for the robust and chunky sauces traditionally made of meats or vegetables so that the sauce is caught in the tube or wraps around the spiral. Long pasta such as spaghetti, fettuccine and linguine are best when topped with olive oil, cream, tomatoes or seafood based sauces.

Creamy Tomato Lobster Linguine

6 tablespoons olive oil

¹/4 cup chopped onion

¹/4 cup chopped shallots

32 ounce can whole tomatoes, drained and chopped

1 ¹/2 teaspoons chopped fresh tarragon

salt and pepper to taste

1 cup heavy cream

1 pound fresh linguine

1 ¹/2 pounds cooked lobster meat

pinch of cayenne pepper

- Heat 2 tablespoons of the olive oil in a saucepan. Add onion and shallots, cover and cook until soft — do not brown. Add tomatoes, tarragon, salt and pepper. Bring mixture to a boil, reduce to simmer and cook covered for 30 minutes. Stir often.

- Remove from heat; cool for 10 minutes before pouring into food processor. Use metal blade to smooth out mixture. Add remaining oil. The above procedure may be prepared in advance.

- Return sauce to pan and add cream. Simmer 15 minutes, whisking often.

- Cook linguine according to package directions. Add lobster meat and cayenne pepper to sauce and adjust seasoning if necessary. Heat lobster through. Serve lobster sauce over linguini.

Serves 4 to 6

Pasta
Fresh or Dried

When buying pasta there are a few considerations to be made. Fresh pasta must be refrigerated and used or frozen within a short time. It also cooks very quickly and must be watched over. The price of fresh pasta is usually considerably higher, per pound than that of dried pasta. Dried pasta has a long shelf life and should be cooked according to package directions, although we recommend cooking "al dente", which loosely translates to "to the bite" or "to the tooth"

Tangy Tomato Lobster Sauce

¹/₂ cup thinly sliced shallots

2 tablespoons unsalted butter

2 tablespoons olive oil

1 ¹/₂ pounds very ripe tomatoes, chopped

¹/₂ cup red wine

¹/₄ teaspoon dried tarragon, crumbled

¹/₂ to 1 teaspoon hot red pepper flakes

salt and pepper to taste

8 ounces linguine or fettuccine

³/₄ pound cooked lobster meat

¹/₄ cup minced fresh parsley

• In a large deep skillet, cook the shallots in butter and oil over medium heat, stirring occasionally, until softened. Add the tomatoes, wine, tarragon, red pepper flakes and salt and pepper to taste. Bring the mixture to a boil, stirring, and boil for 10 minutes or until it is thickened.

• Cook pasta according to package directions. Add the lobster to the skillet and simmer for 2 minutes. Toss with pasta, transfer to a platter and sprinkle with parsley.

Serves 2

Red Wine Clam Sauce

¹/4 pound bacon, chopped

¹/2 cup fresh flat leaf parsley, chopped

3 tablespoons fresh oregano

red pepper flakes to taste

2 cloves garlic, chopped

salt and pepper to taste

³/4 cup red wine

1 pound fresh chopped clams, drained or 10-ounce can whole baby clams, drained

28-ounce can whole tomatoes with juice

1 pound linguine, cooked al dente

¹/4 cup freshly grated Romano cheese

fresh parsley, for garnish

• In a large sauté pan, on medium heat, cook bacon, parsley, oregano, red pepper, garlic and salt and pepper. Stir frequently, for 5 minutes, until bacon is slightly crisp.

• Add wine and continue cooking for 5 to 7 minutes. Lower heat to medium-low. Add clams and tomatoes and cook for 15 minutes.

• Cook linguine according to package directions.

• Toss sauce with linguine. Sprinkle with cheese and garnish with parsley.

Serves 4

Chilled Seafood Terrine

6 lasagna noodles (try spinach for
   a colorful variation)

$1/2$ pound fresh spinach

6 ounces crabmeat

$1/4$ pound cooked shrimp, chopped

3 tablespoons low calorie mayonnaise

1 teaspoon dried dill weed

1 cup low-fat ricotta cheese

1 clove garlic, finely chopped

$1/2$ teaspoon salt

$1/2$ teaspoon freshly ground pepper

$1/4$ cup grated Romano cheese

1 teaspoon olive oil

fresh parsley for garnish

• Cook lasagna noodles according to directions (do not overcook), drain, separate and set aside.

• Cook spinach until wilted. Drain and squeeze dry. Mix together the crabmeat, shrimp, mayonnaise and $1/2$ teaspoon of the dill.

• In separate bowl mix together the ricotta cheese, spinach, garlic, salt, pepper, Romano cheese and remaining dill.

• Brush the entire inside of a loaf pan with the oil. Lay 1 lasagna noodle in bottom of loaf pan and trim off excess. Using seafood mixture first, spread noodle with spoonfuls of seafood and then top the seafood with the cheese mixture. Top with another lasagna noodle and repeat procedure making layers and trimming off excess noodle as necessary. The top of terrine will be a plain noodle.

• Tightly wrap in aluminum foil and refrigerate for at least 2 hours or overnight.

• On a platter, tip loaf pan upside down and slice to serve. Garnish with parsley.

Serves 4

Saucy Sausage Fettuccine

1 small onion, chopped

2 cloves garlic, chopped

2 tablespoons oil

1 pound sweet Italian sausage

1 tablespoon Italian seasoning

1 teaspoon onion powder

1 teaspoon freshly ground pepper

1 teaspoon salt

³/4 cup red wine

28-ounce can Italian tomatoes

1 cup light cream or half and half

¹/4 cup butter

1 pound fettuccine

*¹/2 cup grated Romano or
   Parmesan cheese*

parsley, for garnish

• In a large skillet, on medium heat sauté onion and garlic in oil until transparent. Remove sausage from casing, crumble, and cook until brown, about 10 minutes. Add all spices, wine and tomatoes (cut up tomatoes when adding to skillet), cover and simmer on medium-low for 20 to 30 minutes. (You may refrigerate or freeze at this point, but do not freeze after cream has been added).

• Turn heat to low and add cream and butter after sauce has stopped bubbling.

• Cook fettuccine according to package directions. Drain fettuccine and place in large serving bowl. Add sauce, toss, and mix with grated cheese. Garnish with fresh parsley.

Serves 4 to 6

Lemon Garlic Chicken Pasta

¹/₄ cup flour

*2 tablespoons freshly grated
 Parmesan cheese*

¹/₄ teaspoon garlic powder

1 pound boneless chicken breasts

2 tablespoons unsalted butter

juice of ¹/₂ lemon

¹/₄ cup dry white wine

*1 cup hot water with ¹/₂ cube
 chicken bouillon*

12 ounces angel hair pasta

freshly grated Parmesan cheese

parsley or lemon slices for garnish

• Combine flour, Parmesan cheese and garlic powder. Cut chicken breasts into bite-size pieces. Dredge pieces in flour mixture.

• Melt butter in large frying pan over medium-low heat. Add chicken and cook over medium heat until pieces are browned. Add lemon juice, wine and bouillon to chicken. Cook over medium to medium-high heat until sauce thickens, stirring occasionally. Reduce heat to warm.

• Cook pasta according to package directions and drain. Serve chicken over pasta with freshly grated Parmesan cheese. Garnish with parsley or lemon slices.

Serves 4

Rustic Bolognese Sauce

2 tablespoons olive oil

1 small onion, chopped

3 cloves garlic, chopped

3 carrots, chopped

2 celery stalks, chopped

^{1}/$_2$ pound ground chicken or turkey

^{1}/$_2$ pound ground pork

28-ounce can whole tomatoes

^{1}/$_2$ cup white wine

^{1}/$_2$ teaspoon fennel (optional)

^{1}/$_2$ teaspoon crushed red pepper

1 teaspoon dried basil

1 teaspoon dried thyme

2 tablespoons tomato paste

1 pound fettuccine

grated Parmesan cheese for garnish

• In large pot, heat oil and add onion, garlic, carrot and celery. Sauté for 5 to 7 minutes. Remove vegetables and set aside.

• Add meat to pot and crumble. Cook until brown, about 5 minutes. Add remaining ingredients, breaking up tomatoes, and simmer for at least 45 minutes.

• Cook pasta according to package directions and drain.

• Toss pasta with some of the sauce. Serve with extra sauce and Parmesan cheese.

Serves 4 to 6

Campfire Pasta

2 yellow squash, cut into chunks

2 zucchini, cut into chunks

1 red onion, quartered

1 small eggplant, unpeeled and
    cut into chunks

1 sweet red pepper, quartered

1/3 cup butter

2 to 3 teaspoons dried Italian
    seasoning

1/2 teaspoon pepper

2 teaspoons chicken-flavored
    bouillon granules

2 quarts water

8 ounces linguine, uncooked

1/4 cup grated Parmesan cheese

- Place yellow squash, zucchini, onion, eggplant and red pepper on lightly greased 24 x 18 inch piece of heavy aluminum foil; dot with butter and sprinkle with Italian seasoning and pepper. Fold foil and seal securely. Cook on a grill rack over hot coals 20 to 30 minutes or until vegetables are tender. Remove from heat and keep sealed.

- Combine bouillon granules and water in a pot. Bring to a boil; add linguine and cook until tender. Drain. Top pasta with vegetables and sprinkle with cheese.

Serves 4

Mediterranean Pasta

3 medium tomatoes, diced

1/2 cup chopped imported green
    olives

2 tablespoons capers

1 tablespoon fresh lemon juice

3 cloves garlic, finely chopped

1/3 cup chopped flat leaf parsley

1 tablespoon finely chopped
    fresh mint

1/2 cup extra virgin olive oil

freshly ground pepper to taste

3/4 pound angel hair pasta

1/4 cup grated Romano cheese
    for garnish

• Combine all ingredients except the pasta and
cheese and pepper in a large bowl. Mix
completely. Set aside. Can be made ahead
but bring to room temperature before
serving.

• Cook pasta according to package directions.
Toss the tomato mixture with the steaming
pasta. Serve immediately with fresh pepper
to taste and grated cheese sprinkled on top.

Serves 4

Pasta with Pizzaz

5 tablespoons butter

1 clove garlic, minced

²/3 cup vodka

¹/2 to 1 teaspoon crushed hot red
   pepper flakes

¹/2 teaspoon fennel, optional

1 ¹/2 cups crushed Italian tomatoes

³/4 cup heavy cream

1 pound rotelle pasta (or any
   tubular pasta)

³/4 cup freshly grated Parmesan
   cheese

• Melt butter in a large skillet or saucepan over medium heat. Add garlic, vodka and hot pepper flakes and fennel (if desired). Simmer for 2 minutes.

• Stir in tomatoes and cream. Simmer covered 5 more minutes.

• Cook pasta according to package directions for al dente. Drain well and pour into skillet with red pepper sauce. Stir. Keep warm.

• When ready to serve, sprinkle in Parmesan cheese and toss.

Serves 6

Fennel

The fennel seed is native to the Mediterranean and comes from India. The Puritans called it "meeting seed" and nibbled it during church services. Its slight licorice flavor adds a special touch to tomato sauces, sausage, lamb and hearty breads.

Four Pepper Pesto Pasta

1 large green pepper

1 large red pepper

1 large orange pepper

1 large yellow pepper

2 tablespoons olive oil

$^{1}/_{2}$ onion, chopped

2 cloves garlic, minced

28-ounce can whole tomatoes, chopped

9 ounces spinach fettuccine

$^{1}/_{2}$ cup basil pesto (see recipe on page 101)

freshly grated Parmesan cheese

• Coarsely chop peppers. Heat oil in heavy large skillet over medium heat. Add peppers, onion and garlic and sauté until soft, about 6 minutes. Stir in tomatoes and simmer pepper sauce 7 minutes.

• Meanwhile, cook fettuccine according to package directions. Drain and toss with pesto. Divide evenly among 4 plates. Spoon bell pepper sauce on top. Sprinkle with Parmesan cheese and serve.

Serves 4

Cheese, Glorious Cheese!

We recommend using freshly grated cheese for the best flavor. A piece of hard cheese, such as Parmesan, Romano, or Asiago, will keep for months in the refrigerator. Four ounces of hard cheese will yield approximately one cup of grated cheese. The hard cheeses are also lower in fat than soft cheeses.

Penne with Artichoke Sauce

1 small onion, chopped

3 cloves garlic, finely chopped

3 tablespoons olive oil

1/8 pound thinly sliced prosciutto, chopped

1 cup sliced mushrooms

two 14-ounce cans artichoke hearts, drained and chopped

28-ounce can whole tomatoes, chopped

16-ounce can whole tomatoes, chopped

1 cup dry white wine

1 teaspoon salt

1 teaspoon pepper

1 pound penne pasta

1 cup light cream or milk

1 1/2 cups freshly grated Romano or Parmesan cheese

1 teaspoon grated nutmeg

• In large high sided skillet, sauté onion and garlic in olive oil for 2 to 3 minutes on medium heat. Add prosciutto and mushrooms, quickly tossing until mushrooms are almost limp. Add artichokes, tomatoes, wine, salt and pepper. Cook on medium allowing it to come to a boil. Reduce heat to low and cover. Continue cooking for at least 10 to 15 minutes.

• While sauce is cooking, cook pasta according to package directions. Add cream to sauce and stir. Return cover and let sit until pasta is done.

• Place pasta in large pasta bowl, add sauce, 1 cup of the cheese and nutmeg. Toss. (Extra 1/2 cup cheese can be sprinkled on individually as desired).

Serves 4 to 6

Roasted Red Pepper Ravioli

two 12-ounce jars roasted red peppers

2 small onions, chopped

4 cloves garlic, minced

pinch of red pepper flakes

pinch of salt

freshly ground pepper to taste

1 cup chicken stock

2 teaspoons fresh thyme, chopped

1 teaspoon white wine vinegar or sherry vinegar

1 pound cheese ravioli

¹/₂ bunch fresh flat parsley, chopped

• Drain roasted red peppers, reserve juice. In a large skillet, heat the juice for 1 minute on medium heat. Add onions and garlic and continue to sauté for 2 to 3 minutes. Add roasted peppers, pepper flakes, salt and ground pepper. Add chicken stock and bring to a boil.

• Transfer the sauce to a blender or food processor and purée until smooth and creamy. The sauce may have to be puréed in batches. Return sauce to skillet. Add thyme and vinegar and keep warm.

• Meanwhile, cook ravioli according to package directions. On a large platter, distribute ³/₄ of the sauce evenly and carefully place ravioli on top of sauce. Drizzle some of the remaining sauce over top and garnish with parsley. Serve immediately.

Serves 4

Wild Mushroom Risotto

1 tablespoon olive oil

4 cups chicken broth, approximately

¹/2 pound wild mushrooms

¹/2 cup chopped onion

1 cup Arborio rice

¹/2 cup dry white wine

*¹/2 to 1 cup finely grated Romano
    cheese*

salt and pepper to taste

• Heat oil in a large frying pan or heavy pot. Heat broth in a separate pot. Wash, trim and coarsely chop mushrooms.

• Sauté onion in the oil until golden. Add rice to the onion and stir until well coated. Add the wine and stir; let the wine cook away — about 2 minutes.

• Add about a cup of simmering chicken broth to the rice and cook over high heat, stirring often, until broth has been absorbed. Repeat this process, adding mushrooms as well as broth. While stirring, continue adding broth as it is absorbed into the rice. You may need more or less than four cups to achieve a creamy consistency while the center of the rice is still firm.

• When rice is done and there is still enough broth left in the rice to make it slightly runny, stir in the cheese. Season with salt and pepper and serve.

Serves 2

Summer Bounty Risotto

2 chicken bouillon cubes

3 1/2 cups water

2 teaspoons olive oil

1/2 cup chopped scallions

2 cups diced zucchini

1/2 cup chopped carrot

1 1/2 cups chopped tomato, peeled
 and seeded

1/2 teaspoon basil

1/4 teaspoon marjoram

1 cup Arborio rice

2 tablespoons grated Parmesan
 cheese

• Simmer bouillon cubes and water in saucepan. (Do not boil.) Keep warm.

• Heat oil in large saucepan over medium-high
heat. Add scallions and cook 1 minute. Add
zucchini and carrot. Reduce heat and cook,
uncovered, for 5 minutes, stirring constantly.

• Add tomato, basil and marjoram; cook 10
minutes, stirring frequently. Add rice and 1/2
cup warm bouillon; cook 5 minutes or until
liquid is absorbed.

• Add remaining bouillon 1/2 cup at a time,
cooking 5 minutes between each addition and
stirring constantly. (Mixture will be creamy).
Stir in cheese.

Serves 4 to 6

Pine Nut & Parsley Couscous

1 ¹/2 tablespoons unsalted butter

1 ¹/2 cups water

1 cup couscous

¹/3 cup pine nuts, toasted lightly

¹/4 cup minced fresh parsley leaves

¹/3 cup thinly sliced scallion

1 tablespoon white wine vinegar

• In a saucepan, combine the butter and water. Bring to a boil and stir in the couscous. Remove from heat. Let the couscous stand, covered, for 5 minutes. Fluff it with a fork and stir in the pine nuts, the parsley, the scallion and the vinegar.

Serves 4

Parmesan Baked Rice

3 tablespoons butter

²/3 cup long grain rice

13 ³/4-ounce can chicken broth

¹/4 cup grated Parmesan cheese

2 tablespoons chopped parsley

salt and pepper to taste

• Preheat oven to 350°.

• Melt butter in medium skillet. Add rice. Stir until rice is coated and golden brown. Remove from heat.

• Stir in remaining ingredients. Bake in 1-quart casserole, covered, for 50 minutes. Stir after 30 minutes.

Serves 4

Casco Bay Rice

1 cup long grain rice, uncooked

6 ounce jar marinated artichoke
   hearts

1 medium red onion, minced

3 tablespoons sherry

1 cup dry white wine

8 ounces medium shrimp, peeled
   and deveined

1 teaspoon dried basil

1 teaspoon salt

freshly ground pepper, to taste

6 ounces crabmeat

1 medium very ripe tomato, diced

• Cook rice according to package directions to make 3 cooked cups. Drain artichoke hearts and reserve marinade. Chop artichokes and set aside.

• In a large skillet, heat reserved marinade for 20 seconds and add onion. Over medium heat, cook onion until dark golden brown, about 3 to 5 minutes. Add sherry and wine and bring to a boil. Add shrimp, basil, salt and pepper and cook for 5 minutes. Add crabmeat, tomatoes and cooked rice, tossing to mix evenly. Serve hot.

Serves 6 to 8

Plum Tomato & Scallion Rice

2 teaspoons olive oil

1/3 cup long grain rice

1 1/2 cups low-salt chicken broth

pinch of saffron

1 large plum tomato, seeded, cubed

2 scallions, sliced

salt and pepper to taste

• Heat olive oil in heavy small saucepan over medium-high heat. Add rice and stir until rice is coated with oil and slightly translucent, about 2 minutes. Add chicken broth and saffron and bring to simmer.

• Reduce heat to low, cover saucepan and cook until broth is absorbed and rice is tender, about 20 minutes. Stir in tomato and scallions. Season with salt and pepper and serve.

Serves 2

Scallions

Scallions, or green onions are baby onions with a mild flavor. Both the bulbs and the green tops contain the flavor; they are very perishable, however, and should be used within a day or two of purchase.

Creamy Onion Orzo

1 tablespoon minced onion

1 tablespoon olive oil

1 tablespoon grated Parmesan cheese

2 tablespoons cream cheese

2 tablespoons skim milk

1/8 teaspoon salt

1/4 teaspoon pepper

1 tablespoon fresh chives

2/3 cup orzo (rice shaped pasta)

1 scallion, finely chopped

• Sauté onion in the olive oil for 2-3 minutes. In a medium bowl, combine Parmesan cheese, cream cheese, milk, salt, pepper, chives and sautéed onion with an electric mixer. Beat until smooth.

• Cook orzo according to package directions. During last few minutes of cooking, add scallions. Drain. Add cheese mixture to orzo and stir well. Serve immediately.

Serves 2

Apricot & Pecan Chicken
201
Baked Country Chicken
200
Braised Chicken with New Potatoes
& Pearl Onions
202
Chicken Oscar
203
Chicken with a Twist
204
Chicken with Heart
205
Cornish Game Hens Oregano
193
Golden Grilled Chicken
208
Harmony Chicken
199

Holiday Roasted Turkey
with Vegetable Gravy
191
Lemon Lime Pesto Chicken
197
Mountainside Mustard Chicken
207
Mushroom Tarragon Chicken
198
Raspberry Grilled Chicken
206
Roasted Herb Chicken & Cranberry Chutney
194
Sassy Salsa Chicken & Sassy Salsa
209
Turkey Dijon
192
Wild Rice Baked Chicken
196

Backyard Venison Burgers
233
Baked Ham with Bourbon Glaze
233
Beef Tenderloin Stuffed with Lobster
214
Braised Beef Short Ribs
212
Butterflied Leg of Lamb
& Spiced Rhubarb Gel
229
Dijon Cider Pork Chops
221
Dilled Veal Vermouth
228
Elegant Beef Wellington
210
Fall Harvest Veal Cutlets
225
Fruit Filled Roasted Pork
222
Hazelnut Crusted Rack of Lamb
232
Kennebunk Kabobs
217

Lamb & Pear Stir Fry
231
Maple Mustard Pork Tenderloin
220
Mustard Grilled Lamb Chops
230
Pork Chops with Apricot Glaze
219
Pork Tenderloin with Currant Sauce
218
Rosemary Grilled Veal Chops
228
Sautéed Veal with Sage & Marsala
227
Sirloin with Green Peppercorn
& Mustard Sauce
216
Thyme for Tenderloin
215
Veal Marengo
226
Veal with Lobster Cream Sauce
224
Vegetable Filled Flank Steak
213

Wild Rice Stuffed Pork
223

Meat & Poultry

MAINE
Ingredients
Wild Turkey

*T*he wild turkey has a long history on the Maine coast. The Indians not only ate turkey, but used its feathers, quills and spurs for clothing and hunting. Turkey feathers were also used to decorate religious implements and headdresses.

The Indians found thirty pound turkeys commonplace until 1700 when Maine's new settlers transformed the landscape with hunting and farming. This trend spread throughout the country and this strong and wary bird's populace dwindled to a mere forty thousand by 1940.

Wild turkeys were reintroduced to Maine in 1977, and the population soon flourished. Limited hunting seasons were introduced in 1987 and up to five hundred hunting permits issued. Today, this wily bird poses a challenge to turkey hunters and rewards the determined with a flavorful treat! If you are fortunate enough to find a wild turkey, prepare it in much the same way you would a domestic turkey.

Holiday Roasted Turkey
with Vegetable Gravy

3 tablespoons chopped fresh
   rosemary

3 tablespoons chopped fresh thyme

3 tablespoons chopped fresh tarragon

1 tablespoon freshly ground pepper

2 teaspoons salt

12 to 14 pound turkey

2 tablespoons vegetable oil

fresh herb sprigs

6 tablespoons butter, melted

6 to 8 small boiling onions

4 carrots, peeled and cut into
   4" strips

4 stalks celery, cut into 4" strips

2 parsnips, peeled and cut into
   4" strips

2 to 3 tablespoons flour

• Heat oven to 425°.

• Mix first five ingredients in a small bowl. Wash turkey and pat dry. If not stuffing bird, place herb sprigs in main cavity and tie legs together to hold shape of turkey. Brush turkey with oil. Rub herb mix all over turkey. Place on rack in roasting pan and drizzle with butter. Arrange vegetables in pan around the turkey.

• Roast turkey for 30 minutes. Remove turkey from oven and loosely cover turkey with aluminum tent. Reduce heat to 350°, return turkey to oven and continue roasting, basting with pan juices every half hour. When a meat thermometer inserted into the thickest part of the thigh reads 180° and juices run clear, turkey is fully cooked. (The total cooking time should be about 3 1/2 hours.) Remove from oven, let cool slightly and transfer to a platter.

• Remove vegetables from pan with slotted spoon. Transfer to a food processor and process until smooth. Place pan with turkey juices over low heat. Add flour and 3 to 4 tablespoons of vegetable mixture to pan. Whisk until thickened. Serve remaining vegetable mixture as a side dish.

Serves 6

Turkey Dijon

1 pound turkey cutlets, thinly sliced

1/4 cup flour

1/4 teaspoon salt

1/4 teaspoon pepper

1 tablespoon butter

1 cup sliced mushrooms

1 cup light cream

1 tablespoon Dijon mustard

2 teaspoons lemon juice

1 teaspoon lemon zest

fresh parsley, for garnish

• Dredge turkey in flour seasoned with salt and pepper. Heat butter in nonstick pan over medium heat. Add turkey and cook approximately 3 minutes per side. Remove turkey to plate and keep warm.

• Add mushrooms and sauté 2 minutes. Pour cream into pan and mix with pan scrapings over medium heat until boiling. Add mustard, lemon juice and lemon zest and cook until thickened, approximately 2 minutes.

• Spoon sauce over turkey and garnish each serving with parsley.

Serves 2 to 4

Cornish Game Hens Oregano

4 Cornish game hens

vegetable oil

salt, pepper, oregano and celery salt
   for seasoning

Stuffing:

4 tablespoons butter

$^1/_2$ cup finely chopped onion

$^1/_2$ cup finely chopped celery

4 cups white bread, cut into
   $^1/_2$-inch cubes

1 teaspoon oregano

$^1/_2$ teaspoon celery salt

dash of pepper

1 tablespoon water

• Wash hens and pat dry. Rub skins with oil. Season inside and out with salt, celery salt, pepper and oregano. Set aside.

• Make stuffing by heating butter in saucepan until bubbly. Add onion and celery. Cook 1 minute. Stir in bread cubes, oregano, celery salt, pepper and water. Loosely stuff each hen with $^1/_4$ of the stuffing. Place hens in a roasting pan.

• Preheat oven to 450°. Roast hens for 20 minutes. Reduce heat to 350°. Roast 30 to 40 minutes longer or until juices run clear when thigh joint is pricked. Remove to a platter or individual plates and serve.

Serves 4

Roasted Herb Chicken with Cranberry Chutney

¹/₂ teaspoon vegetable oil

1 roasting chicken (2¹/₂ pounds)

1 teaspoon salt

1 teaspoon freshly ground pepper

10 fresh tarragon leaves or
  1 teaspoon dried tarragon

1 large lemon, halved

2 shallots, peeled

2 tablespoons Madeira

2 tablespoons dry white wine

• Preheat oven to 350°. Line a shallow roasting pan with heavy-duty aluminum foil. Lightly spread the oil over the foil to cover an area the size of the chicken.

• Reserve neck and giblets. Rub the chicken inside and out with the salt and pepper. Gently tuck the tarragon leaves under the skin of the breast and near the thigh-drumstick joint. Place the lemon in the cavity of the chicken. Place the chicken, breast-side down, on the roasting pan. Nestle the neck, giblets and shallots around the chicken. Roast for 15 minutes.

• Turn the bird breast-side up. Roast for 20 minutes longer, until the skin is brown and crisp and the juices run clear when the leg is pierced with a fork. Transfer the chicken to a carving board, tilting it slightly so the juices from the cavity run into the pan. Cover loosely with foil to keep warm.

• Pour the pan juices into a small saucepan. Skim the fat off the surface. Add the neck, giblets and shallots to the saucepan and place over moderate heat. Add the Madeira and white wine and boil until the liquid is reduced by half, skimming off any fat that rises to the surface, about 3 minutes. Discard the neck, giblets and shallots.

• Carve the chicken into 4 equal portions.
Remove the skin. Pour any juices collected
on the carving board into the gravy. For a
lemony sauce, if desired, squeeze the lemon
into the gravy. Spoon about 2 tablespoons of
the gravy over each serving.

• Serve with *Cranberry Chutney.*

Serves 4

Cranberry Chutney:

2 ¹/₂ cups fresh cranberries

1 cup brown sugar

¹/₂ cup cider vinegar

6 tablespoons candied ginger

¹/₂ cup sliced onions

2 cups white raisins

1 teaspoon chili powder

¹/₂ teaspoon salt

2 cups apple cider

1 lemon, thinly sliced

• In a large saucepan, combine all the ingredients. Bring to a boil, reduce heat and simmer
for 35 to 45 minutes. Stir occasionally to
prevent from sticking to the pan. Can be
served warm or chilled. Can be made a few
days in advance. Also freezes easily.

Yields 2 cups

Wild Rice Baked Chicken

6 boneless chicken breast halves

3 cups chicken broth

1 cup uncooked wild rice

3 tablespoons butter

3 tablespoons flour

1 cup heavy cream

2 tablespoons Madeira

1 cup canned sliced water
    chestnuts, drained

1/2 cup freshly grated Parmesan
    cheese

• Preheat oven to 325°.

• Poach chicken breasts in broth for 15
minutes. Remove and cool, reserving stock.
Cut chicken into large pieces.

• Rinse the wild rice and cook as directed.
Melt butter until foamy. Add flour: cook and
stir for 3 minutes. Gradually add 2 cups
reserved chicken broth. Cook and stir until
thickened. Cool to room temperature and
blend in cream and Madeira. Combine
cooked rice and water chestnuts.

• In a buttered casserole, layer chicken breasts
and rice mixture, making 2 layers. Pour
sauce over and sprinkle with cheese. Bake,
uncovered, for 15 minutes. Cover and bake
for 15 minutes more.

Serves 6

Lemon Lime Pesto Chicken

6 boneless chicken breast halves

2 tablespoons olive oil

2 tablespoons chopped parsley

5 teaspoons lime juice

2 tablespoons lemon juice

*3 generous teaspoons Basil Pesto
(see recipe on page 101)*

1 large clove garlic, minced

salt and pepper

• Whisk together all ingredients except chicken. Pour over chicken and marinate 4-6 hours.

• Place in a baking dish and bake at 350° for 45 minutes.

Serves 4 to 6

Use remaining pesto to toss with 12 ounces of cooked pasta for a complete meal.

Top It Off!

To complement the chicken, serve with a bottle of Beaujolais or Sauvignon Blanc.

Mushroom Tarragon Chicken

1 1/2 cups sliced mushrooms

2 cloves garlic, minced

2 tablespoons butter

1 cup water

4 teaspoons cornstarch

2 teaspoons instant chicken bouillon
or 2 chicken bouillon cubes

2 teaspoons cider vinegar

1/2 teaspoon dried tarragon

4 boneless chicken breast halves

paprika

• Preheat oven to 350°.

• In a small frying pan, sauté mushrooms and
garlic in butter. Stir in water, cornstarch,
bouillon, vinegar and tarragon. Cook
mixture, stirring occasionally until thickened.

• Place chicken in an ovenproof baking dish,
sprinkle with paprika, then spoon tarragon
sauce over chicken.

• Bake for 50 to 60 minutes or until done.

Serves 4

Harmony Chicken

12 boneless chicken breast halves

12 slices prosciutto

12 slices Gruyere cheese

¹/₄ cup flour

2 eggs, lightly beaten

1 cup bread crumbs

4 tablespoons freshly grated
    Parmesan cheese

¹/₄ teaspoon garlic powder

¹/₄ teaspoon dried tarragon

4 tablespoons butter

1 cup chicken stock

1 cup dry sherry

1 tablespoon cornstarch

1 tablespoon cold water

• Preheat oven to 350°.

• Place chicken between sheets of waxed paper
and pound lightly to flatten. Place on each
flattened breast a slice of prosciutto and a
slice of Gruyere cheese. Roll up lengthwise
and close with toothpicks. Dip chicken rolls
in flour, shaking off excess and then dip in
beaten egg. Roll in bread crumbs seasoned
with Parmesan cheese, garlic powder and
tarragon.

• In a large skillet melt butter, and brown all
sides of chicken rolls. Transfer to a baking
dish. Mix chicken stock and sherry and pour
over chicken. Bake, uncovered, for 30 to 40
minutes. Remove chicken rolls and keep
warm.

• Drain juices into a saucepan and bring to a
boil. Dissolve cornstarch in water and blend
into saucepan, stirring constantly until
thickened. Spoon over chicken and serve.

Serves 10 to 12

Baked Country Chicken

4 boneless chicken breast halves

6 tablespoons butter

4 tablespoons flour

1 cup light cream

1 cup chicken stock

salt and freshly ground pepper
   to taste

1/2 cup freshly grated
   Parmesan cheese

1/2 teaspoon rosemary

1/2 teaspoon dried basil

1/4 pound mushrooms, sliced

1/2 cup chopped toasted almonds

1 to 2 avocados, for garnish

- Preheat oven to 350°. In skillet, poach the chicken breasts until tender. Set aside.

- Melt 4 tablespoons of the butter in skillet. Stir in flour and cook for 3 minutes. Slowly add the cream and chicken stock, stirring until smooth and thickened. Season with the salt, pepper, Parmesan cheese and herbs. Set aside.

- Sauté mushrooms in remaining 2 tablespoons butter. Place the chicken in a 2-quart casserole and top with mushrooms. Sprinkle with salt and pepper. Pour sauce over and bake, uncovered, for 25 minutes. Remove from oven. Sprinkle with almonds. Return to oven for 10 minutes.

- Peel and slice avocados lengthwise. Place over casserole before serving.

Serves 6 to 8

Apricot & Pecan Chicken

³/4 pound dried apricots

²/3 cup sherry or white wine

1 ¹/2 cups chicken stock

3 teaspoons vegetable oil

2 tablespoons butter

4 boneless chicken breasts

¹/2 teaspoon salt

¹/4 teaspoon pepper

1 tablespoon shallots, finely chopped

1 tablespoon tomato paste

2 tablespoons grainy mustard

¹/2 cup toasted pecans, chopped

1 scallion, thinly sliced

• Marinate apricots in wine and ¹/2 cup stock overnight or bring stock and wine to boil, turn off heat and steep apricots ¹/2 hour, until soft.

• Heat oil and butter in heavy skillet. Sauté chicken on both sides until lightly golden. Sprinkle with salt and pepper. Drain stock and wine from apricots. Pour over chicken. Add remaining stock, reduce heat to low and cook until chicken feels firm to touch, about 5 to 8 minutes. Transfer chicken to plate. Cover to keep warm.

• Add apricots and shallots to skillet; simmer 2 minutes. Whisk in tomato paste and mustard; simmer 3 minutes; stir. Return chicken to skillet for a minute or two to heat.

• Arrange chicken and apricots on warm plate. Spoon sauce over chicken and sprinkle with pecans and scallions.

Serves 4

Braised Chicken with New Potatoes
& Pearl Onions

4 boneless chicken breast halves

2 teaspoons olive oil

2 tablespoons poultry spice mixture
(recipe follows)

2 cups chicken broth

$^1/_2$ cup pearl onions

2 cups new potatoes, quartered

1 cup baby carrots

4 cloves garlic, minced

1 $^1/_2$ teaspoons butter

2 teaspoons flour

Poultry Spice Mixture

1 teaspoon each:

mustard seed, dried minced garlic,

dried minced onion, dried basil,

dried ground sage, dried marjoram,

dried oregano, ground red pepper,

dried rosemary

1 tablespoon each:

paprika and thyme

• Rub 1 teaspoon of olive oil over chicken breasts then pat on poultry spice mix.

• Heat 1 teaspoon oil in a 2-quart sauté pan on medium-high heat. Sear chicken to brown all sides. Add broth, onions, potatoes, carrots and garlic. Bring to a boil then reduce to a simmer. Cover and cook for 20 minutes or until potatoes are done.

• Remove vegetables and chicken. Increase heat to high and bring stock to a full boil. Reduce by one half. Make a paste of butter and flour then whisk into stock until thickened. Return vegetables and chicken, reheat and serve.

Serves 4

• Combine all herbs and spices and store in an airtight container.

Yields about 4 tablespoons

Chicken Oscar

4 boneless chicken breast halves

1/2 cup flour

salt and freshly ground pepper

4 tablespoons butter

1 cup crabmeat

12 cooked asparagus

Hollandaise sauce
(see recipe on page 15)

• Place chicken between 2 pieces of waxed paper on a cutting board and pound very thin. Combine the flour, salt and pepper in a shallow bowl.

• Heat the butter in a heavy skillet. Dip the chicken pieces lightly in the seasoned flour and shake off excess. When the butter stops foaming, add the chicken and cook 3 to 4 minutes per side, until golden. Remove to a heated serving platter as the remaining pieces are cooked.

• Cover each slice of chicken with crabmeat and top with 3 asparagus. Drizzle hollandaise sauce over asparagus and serve.

Serves 4

Chicken with a Twist

8 boneless chicken breast halves

2 eggs

2 tablespoons milk

3 1/2 cups breadcrumbs

1/2 cup butter

salt and freshly ground pepper

juice of 1 lemon

1 1/2 cups chicken broth

minced fresh parsley

1 thinly sliced lemon

• Pound the chicken breasts between 2 pieces of waxed paper.

• Combine eggs with milk in a shallow bowl and beat well. Put breadcrumbs in a shallow bowl. Dip chicken into egg mixture, then in crumbs, pressing them firmly to make them adhere.

• Heat butter in a large skillet and, when hot and bubbling, add chicken in batches.

• Brown quickly on both sides, sprinkling with salt and pepper as they cook. Each side will take no more than 2 or 3 minutes, just until the coating is lightly browned. Add more butter between batches if needed. When all are done, reduce heat.

• Squeeze the juice of 1 lemon into the pan drippings. Stir in chicken broth, scraping to loosen browned bits from the bottom. Simmer for 15 minutes.

• Pour sauce over cutlets and garnish with chopped parsley and slices of lemon.

Serves 6 to 8

Chicken with Heart

4 boneless chicken breast halves

2 tablespoons flour

1/4 teaspoon freshly ground pepper

1 tablespoon olive oil

1/2 cup thinly sliced red onion

1/4 cup Madeira wine

14 1/2 ounce can artichoke hearts

1 1/2 teaspoons minced fresh lemon
   thyme or 1/2 teaspoon dried
   lemon thyme

1/8 teaspoon salt, optional

• Slice chicken into 2-inch strips.

• In a shallow bowl, combine flour and pepper. Lightly dredge chicken pieces in seasoned flour and shake off excess. (Dredge just before sautéing or flour coating will become gummy).

• In a large skillet, heat oil over medium high heat. Add chicken and sauté, turning once, until lightly golden on both sides, about 2 minute on each side. Transfer chicken to plate.

• Reduce heat to medium, add onion and cook, stirring constantly and scraping any bits that cling to bottom of pan. Add wine, turn heat to high and cook, stirring constantly until wine has reduced to half, about 1 minute. Stir in artichoke hearts, reduce heat to medium and cook, partially covered, stirring frequently for about 3 minutes. Stir in lemon thyme.

• Return chicken to pan. Continue cooking over low heat, partially covered, for an additional 2 minutes. Season with salt. Serve immediately.

Serves 4

Raspberry Grilled Chicken

¹/4 cup white wine

¹/4 cup fresh lemon juice

*2 tablespoons peeled, grated
gingerroot*

2 cloves garlic, minced

4 boneless chicken breast halves

1 ¹/2 cups chicken broth

³/4 cup sliced onion

¹/4 cup dry red wine

1 clove garlic, thinly sliced

1 bay leaf

vegetable cooking spray

1 cup fresh raspberries, divided

1 tablespoon water

1 teaspoon cornstarch

2 tablespoons chopped fresh parsley

2 teaspoons sugar

¹/4 teaspoon salt

fresh rosemary sprigs, optional

• Combine white wine, lemon juice, gingerroot
and garlic in a large bowl. Add chicken breasts;
cover and marinate in refrigerator 2-3 hours.

• In a medium saucepan over medium-high heat,
combine broth, onion, red wine, garlic and bay
leaf; bring to a boil. Cover, reduce heat and
simmer 45 minutes. Strain broth mixture
through a sieve into a bowl, reserving 1¹/2
cups; discard solids. Set aside broth mixture.

• Remove breasts from marinade, reserving
marinade. Coat grill rack with cooking spray;
place breast halves on rack over medium heat.
Cook 5-7 minutes on each side or until juices
run clear, basting occasionally with reserved
marinade. Set aside and keep warm.

• Combine reserved broth mixture and ¹/2 cup of
the raspberries in a saucepan; boil until
reduced to 1 cup, about 5 minutes. Strain and
discard seeds; return purée to pan. Combine
water and cornstarch; stir well and add to
puree. Bring to a boil and cook 1 minute,
stirring constantly. Remove from heat; stir in
parsley, sugar and salt. Spoon 3 tablespoons
puree onto individual serving plates; arrange
breast half on each plate and top with 2
tablespoons raspberries. Garnish with fresh
rosemary if desired.

Serves 4

Mountainside Mustard Chicken

2 boneless chicken breast halves

$^1/_2$ cup unsalted butter, melted

2 tablespoons oil

5 tablespoons Dijon mustard

2 tablespoons minced shallots

2 tablespoons fresh thyme

1 teaspoon fresh ground pepper

$^1/_2$ teaspoon ground red pepper

1 cup bread crumbs

- Place chicken on broiling pan and broil about 3 minutes on each side. Remove from oven.

- In saucepan, melt butter and oil. In a small bowl, combine mustard, shallots, thyme, black pepper and red pepper. Stir $^3/_4$ of butter mixture into mustard mixture and blend well.

- Brush chicken on both sides with generous amount of mustard mixture. Roll chicken in bread crumbs and glaze with remaining butter mixture.

- Broil chicken 6 to 8 minutes, turning 2 or 3 times.

Serves 4

Shallots

Shallots, like onions, are members of the lily family. They have a mild onion flavor with just a hint of garlic. Use in place of onions when a milder flavor is desired.

Golden Grilled Chicken

¹/₂ cup lemon juice

*1 tablespoon finely chopped
    lemon zest*

¹/₄ cup Dijon mustard

*¹/₄ cup finely chopped fresh herbs
    (using equal amounts of
    rosemary, thyme, basil, oregano,
    parsley)*

³/₄ teaspoon salt

¹/₄ teaspoon freshly ground pepper

4 boneless chicken breast halves

*Parsley sprigs, lemon slices,
    fresh herb leaves, for garnish*

• Combine first 6 ingredients in small bowl for marinade. Mix well. In large shallow non-aluminum dish, arrange chicken breasts and pour marinade over them. Marinate for 2 to 4 hours in refrigerator.

• Prepare grill. Remove chicken from marinade and grill 3 inches from flame for 7 to 10 minutes on each side.

• Place on individual plates or on a platter surrounded by parsley sprigs, lemon slices and fresh herb leaves.

Serves 4

Sassy Salsa Chicken

²/₃ cup Sassy Salsa (recipe follows)

¹/₃ cup Dijon mustard

1 tablespoon lemon juice

4 boneless chicken breast halves

3 tablespoons unsalted butter, softened

Sassy Salsa

4 large tomatoes

2 to 6 tablespoons fresh jalapeno chiles (or canned)

4 tablespoons finely chopped cilantro

1 small red onion, finely chopped (¹/₂ cup)

3 medium cloves garlic, minced

1 teaspoon red wine vinegar or lemon juice

1 teaspoon salt

• To prepare salsa, peel, seed and finely chop tomatoes. Seed and finely chop chiles. Combine all ingredients and mix well. Cover and refrigerate. Keeps up to 3 days.

• Combine salsa, mustard and lemon juice together in medium bowl. Reserve 1 tablespoon of mixture.

• In large shallow non-aluminun baking dish, arrange chicken breasts and pour marinade over. Marinate for 1 to 4 hours in refrigerator.

• To make mustard butter, combine butter and reserved marinade mixture and whip until smooth. Place on a waxed paper sheet and roll up in form of a log. Refrigerate until ready to use.

• Preheat broiler or grill if necessary. Place chicken breasts on pan and broil 7 to 10 minutes on each side. When turning, spoon additional marinade over top and broil until very brown and bubbly. (May be cooked on barbeque grill.)

• Place chicken on individual serving dishes.

• Slice mustard butter in equal pieces and arrange slices on chicken pieces. Serve immediately.

Serves 4

Elegant Beef Wellington

4 to 4 ¹/₂ pound beef tenderloin

salt and pepper to taste

Duxelles (recipe follows)

butter pastry (recipe follows)

1 egg

- Preheat oven to 425°.

- Place beef on rack in shallow baking pan. Sprinkle with salt and pepper. Bake for 15 minutes for rare. Let stand until cool. Trim off all fat.

- Prepare pastry.

- Prepare duxelles.

- Roll pastry in rectangle large enough to wrap around beef, about 3 inches longer than roast and 12 to 13 inches wide. Press cool duxelles into pastry, leaving an inch uncovered on all edges. Place beef on pastry. Moisten pastry edges; enclose beef, pressing edges firmly together. Trim off excess pastry from ends so single layer covers ends of roast. Place roll, seam side down, on shallow baking pan. Cut decorations from pastry trimmings; place on top. Brush pastry with egg beaten with 1 tablespoon of water.

- Reduce heat to 400° and continue baking for 30 to 35 minutes until browned. Let stand for 15 to 20 minutes before slicing.

Recipe Variation

For a slightly different presentation, prepare individual Beef Wellingtons. Follow the directions as above with these changes:
- Use 4 single beef tenderloin steaks.
- Bake at 425° for 10 to 15 minutes.
- Cut 2 single pastry sheets in half.
- Place ¹/₄ of the duxelles in the center of each pastry strip and place a steak on top.
- Roll pastry around the steak.
- Place seam side down in a baking dish.
- Bake at 400° for 30 to 35 minutes until pastry is lightly browned.

Pastry:

*(May substitute with 1 package
puff pastry sheets)*

3 ³/4 cups sifted flour

1 teaspoon salt

1 cup cold butter

2 tablespoons shortening

³/4 cup (approximately) ice water

• To prepare pastry, combine flour and salt.
Cut in butter and shortening until particles
are fine. Add water, by the tablespoon, until
a stiff dough forms. Shape dough into a
square. Cover and chill.

Duxelles:

1 pound mushrooms, finely chopped

¹/4 cup chopped scallions

¹/4 cup butter

¹/2 teaspoon salt

¹/2 teaspoon marjoram

2 teaspoons flour

dash of pepper

¹/4 cup beef broth

2 tablespoons parsley, chopped

• Sauté mushrooms and scallions in butter until
liquid evaporates. Stir in salt, marjoram,
flour, pepper and broth. Cook, stirring
constantly, until mixture comes to a boil and
thickens. Remove from heat; stir in parsley.
Cool.

Serves 4

Braised Beef Short Ribs

11-ounce package mixed dried fruit

2 cups port

3 ¹/2 pounds beef short ribs

¹/2 cup flour

salt and freshly ground pepper

¹/4 cup olive oil

¹/2 cup chopped onion

¹/2 cup chopped carrot

¹/2 cup chopped celery

¹/2 cup blanched sliced almonds

2 cups dry red wine

2 to 3 ³/4 cups beef broth

• In a small bowl, marinate the dried fruit with the port for at least 2 hours.

• Dust the beef with flour. (The simplest way is to pour the flour into a plastic bag and, one by one, place the ribs in the bag, coat with the flour, and shake off the excess). Season lightly with salt and pepper. Preheat the oven to 400°.

• In a large ovenproof roasting pan, heat the olive oil. Brown the beef on all sides. Do not crowd the pan, browning in batches if necessary. Add the vegetables, almonds, dried fruit and marinating liquid. Pour in the red wine and bring to a boil. Reduce heat to medium and reduce the sauce by half. (The length of time required depends upon the size of the pan).

• Pour in enough beef broth to cover the ribs and bring to a boil. Cover the pan, transfer to the oven, and bake until the ribs are tender, 35 to 45 minutes. Remove the ribs and keep warm. Reduce the sauce just until it thickens. Correct seasoning to taste and return the ribs to the pan. Serve immediately.

Serves 4 to 6

Top It Off!

Uncork a bottle of Merlot or Cabernet Sauvignon and savor this wonderful winter dinner.

Vegetable Filled Flank Steak

1 1/4 pounds Flank steak
(have butcher slice in half
lengthwise to make 2 thin steaks)

1/4 cup grated Romano cheese

1 small summer squash,
thinly sliced

1 small onion, thinly sliced and
broken into rings

10 medium size mushrooms,
thinly sliced

10 sun-dried tomatoes, soaked in
hot water and squeezed dry

6 slices Muenster cheese

4 large spinach leaves
(stems removed)

2 cups Spicy Marinara Sauce
(see recipe on page 27)

Marinade:

1/2 cup corn or vegetable oil

1/4 cup red wine vinegar

1/2 cup dry red wine

2 cloves garlic, minced

salt and pepper to taste

• Place 1 steak between 2 large sheets of
waxed paper. With a meat mallet, pound
steak. Repeat with remaining steak.

• Divide Romano cheese and vegetables in
half. Sprinkle Romano cheese on steak then
spread squash, onion, mushrooms, tomatoes
and Muenster on top. Top with 2 spinach
leaves.

• Roll up steak and secure with toothpicks,
tucking in ends. Repeat with remaining
steak.

• In a large plastic container, mix marinade
ingredients. Place each steak in marinade
and refrigerate for at least 4 hours.

• Preheat oven to 375°. Remove steak from
marinade and place in large baking dish.
Pour remaining marinade and spicy marinara
sauce over steak and bake for 40 minutes.

• Remove toothpicks and carefully slice (with a
serrated knife) each steak, carefully keeping
round shape. Place steak spirals on oval
platter. Serve immediately. Serve extra
sauce tossed with pasta for a complete meal.

Serves 4

Beef Tenderloin Stuffed with Lobster

3 to 4 pound whole beef tenderloin,
   trimmed

2 cooked lobster tails

1 tablespoon butter, melted

1 1/2 teaspoons lemon juice

6 slices bacon, partially cooked

1 cup butter

1/2 cup sliced scallions

2 cloves garlic, minced

1 cup dry white wine

2 teaspoons fresh tarragon

- Cut tenderloin lengthwise to within 1/2 inch of bottom to butterfly.

- Remove lobster from shells. Cut the lobster tails in half lengthwise. Place lobster, end to end, inside tenderloin.

- Combine the 1 tablespoon butter and lemon juice. Drizzle on lobster. Close tenderloin around lobster; tie tenderloin together securely with string at intervals of 1 inch.

- Place the tenderloin on a rack in shallow roasting pan. Roast in 425° oven for 45 to 50 minutes for rare doneness.

- Lay bacon slices on top; roast 5 minutes longer.

- In saucepan, melt 1 cup butter and sauté scallions and garlic over low heat until tender. Add wine and tarragon and heat through, stirring frequently. Slice tenderloin and arrange on a platter. Pour sauce over tenderloin.

Serves 8

Thyme for Tenderloin

1 ³/4 pounds fresh shiitake
    mushrooms, stems trimmed

two 3.2 ounce packages fresh enoki
    mushrooms, cleaned

¹/2 cup olive oil

2 tablespoons chopped fresh thyme
    or 2 teaspoons dried

salt and fresh ground pepper to taste

6 tablespoons butter

six 8-ounce tenderloin steaks
    1 ¹/4-inch thick

1 ¹/2 cups beef broth

1 cup dry red wine

• Preheat broiler. Toss mushrooms, oil and thyme in bowl. Season with salt and pepper. Arrange mushroom mixture in single layer on baking sheets. Broil until golden and tender, about 3 minutes. Reduce temperature to 250° to keep mushrooms warm.

• Melt butter in large heavy skillet over medium-high heat. Season steaks with salt and pepper. Add steaks to skillet and cook to desired doneness. Transfer steaks to plate.

• Add broth and wine to skillet. Boil until reduced to sauce consistency. Scrape up pan juices and browned bits.

• Divide steaks onto plates. Spoon sauce and mushrooms over steaks.

Serves 6

Sirloin with Green Peppercorn & Mustard Sauce

1 1/2 tablespoons drained green
   peppercorns in brine, rinsed

1 1/2 tablespoons Dijon mustard

1 tablespoon unsalted butter,
   room temperature

2 teaspoons flour

1 tablespoon vegetable oil

salt and pepper to taste

16-ounce top sirloin steak
   (1 1/4-inches thick)

1/2 cup beef broth

1/4 cup whipping cream

• Mash peppercorns in small shallow bowl.
Add mustard, butter and flour and blend
well. (Can be prepared 1 day ahead. Cover
and refrigerate).

• Heat oil in heavy large skillet over high heat.
Season steak with salt and pepper and cook
to desired doneness, about 5 minutes per side
for rare. Transfer steak to platter and keep
warm.

• Pour off drippings from skillet. Add broth
and cream to same skillet; boil until sauce
thickens slightly, scraping up browned bits,
about 3 minutes. Add peppercorn mixture;
boil until sauce thickens enough to coat
spoon, whisking constantly, about 1 minute.
Season sauce with salt and pepper.

• Slice steak crosswise. Arrange slices on
plates. Spoon sauce over steak.

Serves 2

Kennebunk Kabobs

For marinade:

¹/₃ cup olive oil

¹/₄ cup balsamic vinegar

2 tablespoons soy sauce

1 teaspoon lemon juice

2 tablespoons Worcestershire sauce

2 cloves garlic, minced

1 tablespoon Dijon mustard

1 teaspoon chopped parsley

salt and pepper to taste

1 to 1 ¹/₂ pounds cubed beef

1 sweet red pepper

1 sweet yellow pepper

1 large Vidalia or Spanish onion

1 pint cherry tomatoes

1 pint mushrooms

• Combine ingredients for marinade. Place beef in a bowl or glass dish and pour marinade over it. Cover and marinate 1 hour at room temperature. Cut peppers and onion into pieces, large enough to place on skewers. Leave tomatoes and mushrooms whole.

• Prepare grill. Alternate beef and vegetables on skewers. Brush with extra marinade. Grill until desired doneness, turning skewers occasionally.

Serves 4

Pork Tenderloin with Currant Sauce

2 whole pork tenderloins

2 tablespoons dry mustard

2 tablespoons dried thyme

1/2 cup sherry

1/2 cup low-sodium soy sauce

3 cloves garlic, minced

2 tablespoons grated fresh ginger

6 ounces currant jelly

1 tablespoon soy sauce

• Rub each pork loin with mustard and thyme and place in a dish for marinating. In small bowl, combine sherry, 1/2 cup soy sauce, garlic and ginger. Pour over tenderloins. Let marinate 3 to 6 hours in refrigerator.

• Grill or broil tenderloins until desired doneness.

• Meanwhile, heat currant jelly until bubbly. Add the remaining soy sauce.

• Slice tenderloins into medallions. Spoon currant sauce over meat and serve.

Serves 4 to 6

Ginger Root

Ginger Root is available year-round in the produce department of your supermarket. Look for roots with unshriveled skins and few knobs. Wrap loosely and refrigerate. The root may also be frozen and peeled and sliced as needed.

Pork Chops with Apricot Glaze

4 tablespoons apricot spread
(all fruit, not jam)

3 teaspoons dry Madeira wine

2 teaspoons Dijon mustard

2 teaspoons honey

1/4 teaspoon pared and minced
ginger root

4 pork loin chops

salt, pepper and garlic powder
to taste

• In small saucepan, combine apricot spread, wine, mustard, honey and ginger. Cook over medium heat, stirring frequently, until mixture is smooth and thickened, 3 to 4 minutes. Remove from heat; cover and keep warm.

• Season pork chops with salt, pepper and garlic powder and arrange on rack in broiling pan. Broil or grill for 6 minutes. Turn chops over and, using a pastry brush, brush each with 1 teaspoon apricot mixture. Broil until chops are thoroughly cooked, about 6 minutes longer. Transfer chops to serving platter and serve with remaining apricot mixture.

Serves 4

Top It Off!

A fruity red wine or White Zinfandel will enhance the flavor of the apricot glaze.

Maple Mustard Pork Tenderloin

1 whole pork tenderloin

*3 teaspoons minced fresh sage or
1 teaspoon dried*

salt and pepper to taste

1 tablespoon butter

1 cup low-salt chicken broth

2 tablespoons pure maple syrup

*2 tablespoons coarse-grained
mustard*

fresh sage for garnish

• Slice tenderloin into $^1/_3$-inch thick slices.
Sprinkle with $1^1/_2$ teaspoons sage, salt and
generous amount of pepper.

• Melt butter in heavy medium skillet over
medium-high heat. Add pork and cook until
golden brown on both sides and cooked
through, about $1^1/_2$ minutes per side. Transfer
pork to plate, leaving drippings in skillet.
Add broth, maple syrup, mustard and
remaining $1^1/_2$ teaspoons sage to skillet. Boil
until syrupy and thick, about 3 minutes
scraping up browned bits. Reduce heat to
low.

• Return pork and any accumulated juices to
skillet and cook until just heated through,
about 1 minute. Serve pork with sauce.
Garnish with fresh sage.

Serves 4

Dijon Cider Pork Chops

1 tablespoon cooking oil

4 center cut pork chops

2 cups fresh apple cider

2 tablespoons Dijon mustard

1 teaspoon crushed rosemary

¹/4 cup chopped pecans

¹/4 cup raisins

• Heat oil in deep-sided skillet. Over high heat, cover and sear pork chops on both sides. Remove chops from skillet.

• Pour cider into medium bowl. Whisk in mustard and rosemary. Pour cider mixture into skillet, add chops and simmer, covered, for about 30 minutes, until meat is tender.

• Remove chops and reduce cider mixture by half over high heat. Add pecans and raisins and place chops back in skillet to warm.

Serves 4

Fruit Filled Roasted Pork

6-ounce package mixed dried fruit

1/2 cup finely chopped onion

1 tablespoon balsamic vinegar

1/4 cup dry bread crumbs

2 tablespoons margarine, melted

salt and pepper to taste

1/4 teaspoon ground cloves

two 2-pound boneless pork loin
   roasts, tied

3 to 4 sprigs fresh thyme,
   for garnish

Pineapple-Ginger Sauce

3/4 cup packed brown sugar

2 tablespoons cornstarch

3/4 cup unsweetened pineapple juice

1/4 cup balsamic vinegar or
   white wine vinegar

1 1/2 teaspoons grated ginger root

1/4 teaspoon salt

• For stuffing, in a mixing bowl, combine fruit, onion and vinegar. Pour boiling water over to cover. Let stand 25 minutes; drain. Add bread crumbs, margarine, salt, pepper and cloves to fruit. Toss gently to mix.

• Preheat oven to 325°. Untie the roasts and trim fat. Butterfly roasts and flatten to open. Pound with a meat mallet to 1/2 to 3/4-inch thickness. Sprinkle with salt and pepper. Spread stuffing onto the roasts. Roll up the meat and stuffing jelly-roll style. Tightly retie the roasts. Place the roasts on a rack in a shallow roasting pan. Insert a meat thermometer. Roast for 1 3/4 hours for medium.

• Cover meat with foil. Let stand for 15 minutes before carving. Serve with *Pineapple-Ginger Sauce* and garnish with thyme if desired.

• For sauce, in a medium saucepan, stir together brown sugar and cornstarch. Stir in pineapple juice, vinegar, ginger and salt. Simmer for 3 to 5 minutes or until thickened.

Serves 6 to 8

Wild Rice Stuffed Pork

6-ounce package long-grain and
    wild rice

2 tablespoons oil

¹/₂ cup chopped fresh mushrooms

1 scallion, chopped

1 sweet red or yellow pepper, chopped

2 cloves garlic, minced

2 tablespoons chopped fresh parsley

¹/₂ teaspoon freshly ground pepper

2-pound lean boneless pork roast

1 cup apricot spread, melted
    and divided

³/₄ cup white wine

- Prepare rice according to package directions, omitting salt and fat. Set aside. Heat oil in a nonstick skillet over medium-high heat until hot. Add mushrooms, scallion, sweet pepper and garlic; sauté 4 to 5 minutes or until vegetables are tender. Stir in rice, parsley and ground pepper.

- Preheat oven to 350°. Untie roast and trim fat. Butterfly roast and flatten to open. Spread ¹/₄ to ¹/₂ of rice mixture over inside of roast. Retie roast. Set remaining rice mixture aside.

- Place roast in a roasting pan and brush roast with half of apricot spread. Pour white wine in pan. Bake for 1 hour, basting frequently with remaining half of spread. During last 15 minutes of baking, spread remaining rice in pan around roast and finish baking.

- Remove string from roast; slice diagonally across grain into 8 slices. Spread rice on a large serving platter and arrange pork slices on top.

Serves 4

Veal with Lobster Cream Sauce

Sauce:

2 to 3 scallions, minced

2 tablespoons butter

2 tablespoons flour

1 cup white wine or clam juice

2 cups light cream

1/2 teaspoon allspice

1/2 teaspoon white pepper

salt to taste

3/4 to 1 pound cooked lobster meat

- Sauté scallions in butter; add flour to make a paste; gradually add wine and cream, stirring constantly. Add allspice, pepper and salt.

- Simmer, stirring constantly, until thick. Add lobster.

- Heat butter and oil in a frying pan. Salt and pepper cutlets, dip in flour and lay them in pan. Cook 5 minutes, turn, sprinkle with lemon juice and cook until browned, approximately 3 to 5 minutes.

- Transfer cutlets to plates, pour lobster sauce over veal and serve.

Serves 4

Veal:

2 tablespoons butter

2 tablespoons oil

salt and pepper to taste

8 veal cutlets, pounded thin

1/4 to 1/2 cup flour

juice of one lemon

Fall Harvest Veal Cutlets

Veal:

8 veal cutlets

3 apples, chopped

2 eggs, beaten

1/2 tablespoon thyme

salt and pepper to taste

3 to 4 sprigs fresh parsley, chopped

1/4 cup walnuts, chopped

Sauce:

2 cups Gruyere cheese, grated

1 cup dry white wine

1 cup light cream

1/4 cup flour

1 tablespoon basil

1 tablespoon chives

pan juices from veal

- Preheat oven to 500°. Between 2 pieces of waxed paper, pound veal cutlets very thin.

- Combine apples, eggs, thyme, salt and pepper. Stuff cutlets with apple mixture and hold together with a toothpick. Bake uncovered for 15 minutes.

- Meanwhile, in a medium saucepan, combine all sauce ingredients and simmer until cheese is melted, adding pan juices from veal. Pour sauce over veal and sprinkle with parsley and walnuts. Reduce oven temperature to 400°. Return cutlets to oven and bake for 10 to 15 minutes longer. Serve.

Serves 4

Veal Marengo

1 ³/4 pounds veal for stew

6 teaspoons olive oil

¹/2 teaspoon salt

1 onion, cut in 8 wedges

16 ounce can whole tomatoes

³/4 cup dry white wine

water

¹/2 teaspoon saffron

3 cloves garlic, minced

1 teaspoon dried thyme, crushed

¹/4 teaspoon coarsely ground pepper

2 cups mushrooms, quartered

1 tablespoon cornstarch

chopped parsley, for garnish

• Cut veal into cubes. Heat 4 teaspoons oil in Dutch oven or large heavy saucepan over medium heat. Brown veal. Remove from pan; sprinkle with salt and reserve.

• Cook onion in remaining oil over medium heat until crisp-tender, about 3 to 4 minutes; remove from pan and reserve. Return veal to pan. Add tomatoes with liquid, breaking up tomatoes with spoon. Add wine, and enough water (about ³/4 cup) to cover ingredients. Steep saffron in 2 tablespoons hot water for 2 minutes. Stir in saffron, garlic, thyme and pepper. Cover and simmer 45 minutes.

• Add mushrooms and reserved onions. Continue cooking 25 minutes or until veal and vegetables are tender.

• Dissolve cornstarch in 1 tablespoon cold water. Stir into veal. Bring to a boil; cook and stir until sauce is thickened and clear. Garnish with parsley.

Serves 6

Sautéed Veal with Sage & Marsala

eight 2-ounce veal cutlets,
  each ¹/₄-inch thick

2 tablespoons olive oil

¹/₂ cup minced red onion

3 well-ripened plum tomatoes
  (8 ounces), blanched, peeled,
  cored and coarsely chopped

¹/₂ cup Marsala wine

2 tablespoons minced fresh sage
  leaves or 2 teaspoons crumbled
  dried sage

¹/₂ teaspoon freshly ground pepper

4 clusters of fresh sage leaves,
  for garnish

- Place veal between 2 sheets of waxed paper and pound lightly.

- In a 12-inch skillet, heat oil over medium heat. Sauté veal, turning once, until very lightly golden, about 1¹/₂ minutes per side. Transfer veal to platter.

- Add onion to skillet, turn heat to low and cook, stirring constantly, until lightly golden, about 2 minutes. Stir in tomatoes, Marsala and sage. Increase heat to high and cook, stirring frequently, until there is very little liquid left in bottom of pan, about 2 minutes.

- Return veal to pan, spoon sauce over meat and season with salt and pepper. Cook for an additional minute. Transfer veal to platter, spoon sauce over top and garnish with sage leaves.

Serves 4

Dilled Veal Vermouth

1 pound veal cutlets

3/4 cup flour

salt and pepper to taste

5 tablespoons butter

2 tablespoons olive oil

3/4 cup dry vermouth

3 tablespoons drained capers

1/2 pound mushrooms, sliced

1/3 cup chopped fresh dill

• Lightly pound veal. In a shallow dish, mix flour, salt and pepper. Coat veal with flour mixture, shaking off excess.

• Melt 2 tablespoons of butter with oil in large non-stick skillet over medium-high heat. Add veal and cook until light brown, about 1 to 2 minutes per side. Transfer to platter.

• Add 3 tablespoons butter to skillet and melt. Add vermouth, capers, and mushrooms; bring to boil. Add dill. Season with salt and pepper and pour over veal.

Serves 4

Rosemary Grilled Veal Chops

4 veal loin chops

2 tablespoons extra-virgin olive oil

leaves from two sprigs fresh
    rosemary

juice of 1 lemon

salt and finely ground pepper
    to taste

• Brush veal chops with olive oil on each side.

• Press rosemary leaves into both sides of each veal chop. Sprinkle lemon juice on each side and refrigerate 1 hour.

• Grill veal for 5 to 7 minutes over medium-high heat on each side. Remove from grill and sprinkle with salt and pepper.

Serves 4

Butterfly Leg of Lamb

1 leg of lamb, butterflied

¹/₃ cup olive oil

1 tablespoon lemon juice

1 tablespoon chopped rosemary

1 tablespoon freshly ground pepper

1 bay leaf

• Place the lamb in a shallow baking dish.
Combine remaining ingredients and rub over
lamb. Let stand for 2 hours in refrigerator.
Turn meat occasionally to marinate evenly.

• Preheat broiler or prepare grill. Place lamb
as far from broiler as possible or on the grill.
Turn the leg several times while cooking.
Cook for 20 minutes for rare or up to 40
minutes for medium-well. Remove from heat.
Cover with foil and let stand 20 minutes.

• May be served with *Spiced Rhubarb Gel*

Serves 8

Spiced Rhubarb Gel

*2 to 2 ¹/₂ pounds rhubarb,
    cut up but not peeled*

¹/₂ cup cider vinegar

¹/₂ cup water

1-inch cinnamon stick

3 to 4 cloves

4 cups sugar

1 packet or ¹/₂ bottle liquid pectin

• Mix together the rhubarb, vinegar, water and
spices. In a saucepan, heat to boiling. Cover
and simmer for 15 minutes. Strain and save
juice only.

• Measure 2 cups of the juice. Return to
saucepan and add sugar. Bring to a hard boil,
stirring constantly. Add the pectin and boil
hard for 1 minute. Remove from heat and
allow to stand 1 minute. Skim off foam.
Pour into sterilized jars and seal.

Yields about 3 ¹/₂ to 4 cups

Mustard Grilled Lamb Chops

9 lamb chops

1 large clove garlic, crushed

2 teaspoons crumbled dried
 rosemary

4 tablespoons Dijon mustard

freshly ground pepper

6 tablespoons freshly squeezed
 lemon juice (about 1 lemon)

4 tablespoons dry sherry

4 tablespoons soy sauce

2 tablespoons olive oil or
 vegetable oil

- Combine all ingredients except the lamb
chops to make marinade. Add chops and
marinate the lamb for 4 to 6 hours. Prepare
grill to cook. Grill lamb chops to desired
doneness.

- Serve with *Mustard Vinaigrette.*

Serves 2-3

Mustard Vinaigrette:

2 tablespoons Dijon mustard

1 to 2 tablespoons finely chopped
 shallots

1 clove garlic, minced

1/4 cup freshly squeezed lemon juice
 (about 2 small lemons)

salt to taste

3/4 cup olive oil or vegetable oil

2 to 3 tablespoons finely chopped
 fresh mint or 1 tablespoon dried
 mint

- Combine mustard, shallots, garlic, lemon
juice and salt in a bowl. Whisk, to blend
well. Whisk in the oil gradually to emulsify.
Stir in the mint.

- Refrigerate or serve with *Mustard Grilled
Lamb Chops.*

Lamb & Pear Stir-fry

1 to 1 ¹/2 pounds boneless lamb

4 tablespoons sesame oil

6 to 8 cloves garlic, minced

¹/2 cup chopped fresh basil

2 teaspoons dried marjoram

¹/2 cup chopped fresh mint

salt and pepper to taste

1 sweet red pepper, thinly sliced

³/4 cup chopped scallions

2 large ripe pears, cut in thin wedges

1 tablespoon soy sauce

• Slice lamb in thin slices, trim fat and set aside.

• Heat oil in a large skillet or wok, add lamb, garlic, basil, marjoram, mint and salt and pepper. Brown lamb on both sides. Add red pepper and scallions. Stir fry for 1 minute. Add pears and soy sauce. Stir fry for 20 seconds. Serve immediately.

Serves 4

Hazelnut Crusted Rack of Lamb

1 cup ground hazelnuts

1 cup fresh white breadcrumbs

3 tablespoons minced fresh rosemary

three 1 1/2 to 1 3/4 pound racks of
    lamb (8 ribs each), fat and any
    membrane trimmed

3 tablespoons honey-Dijon mustard

salt and pepper, to taste

• Preheat oven to 425°.

• Combine hazelnuts, fresh breadcrumbs and
rosemary. Arrange lamb racks meat side up
in single layer on heavy large baking sheet.
Brush each rack with 1 tablespoon honey-
Dijon mustard. Season lamb with salt and
pepper. Press 1/3 of breadcrumb mixture onto
each. (Racks of lamb can be prepared up to
4 hours ahead. Cover tightly and refrigerate).

• Roast until meat thermometer inserted into
thickest part of lamb registers 130° for
medium-rare, about 35 to 45 minutes. Let
lamb racks stand 10 minutes. Cut between
each rib to separate into chops.

Serves 8

Baked Ham with Bourbon Glaze

¹/2 cup packed dark brown sugar

4 tablespoons Dijon mustard

2 tablespoons bourbon

3 tablespoons whole cloves

5 to 7 pound partially cooked ham

• Preheat oven to 350°.

• In a bowl, mix brown sugar and mustard. Gradually add bourbon to mixture. Mix well. This will make a thick glaze to coat ham.

• Score ham and stud with cloves. Spread glaze to coat top and sides. Place in a roasting pan and bake for 20 minutes per pound.

• Let ham cool for 10 minutes. Slice and serve hot or cold.

Serves 6 to 8

Backyard Venison Burgers

2 ¹/2 pounds ground venison

¹/2 cup minced onion

1 clove garlic, minced

4 tablespoons chopped parsley

²/3 cup dry red wine

2 tablespoons soy sauce

salt and pepper to taste

• Mix all ingredients together. Form into thick patties. Cook on grill or broil in oven, approximately 10 minutes on each side. Serve on favorite buns.

Serves 8 to 10

Seafood

MAINE
Ingredients

Lobster

*T*he highly regarded lobster was not always considered a delicacy. Local Indians used lobster as bait for fishing and as fertilizer for crops. Lobster was eaten only if the Indians failed to catch bass.

Lobster was just as unpopular with the early settlers. Servants and slaves alone partook of this crustacean because of its abundance. A colonial "blue" law was finally enacted forbidding masters to serve lobster to servants more than twice a week. It was even noted in accounts of the American Revolution that British prisoners-of-war threatened to revolt if they were continued to be fed lobster.

Before the 1800's, lobster was relatively unharvested. Most lived long lives and reached amazing proportions - some were recorded to have been five and six feet in length. Food connoisseurs recognized lobster as a delicacy by the turn of the nineteenth century. Today, approximately twenty-five million pounds are harvested annually along the coast. The largest lobster caught in the Gulf of Maine weighed 36 pounds!

A visit to Maine would not be complete without a lobster dinner!

Honest to Goodness Steamed Lobster

1 quart water

4 lobsters (1 ³/4 to 2 pounds each)

• Place 1 quart of water and a steamer or cake rack in a giant pot (at least 4 gallon capacity). Set pot over high heat and bring the water to a boil.

• Add live lobsters, head first, to pot, cover and reduce heat to medium-high. As soon as the water returns to a vigorous boil, steam the lobsters for exactly 20 minutes. (Lobster shells will turn from a deep blue-green to a bright red color as they cook.)

• Remove and serve immediately with *Drawn Butter.*

Serves 4

Drawn Butter

¹/₃ cup butter
4 tablespoons flour
2 cups boiling water
¹/₄ teaspoon salt

Melt butter, stir in flour and slowly add water. Cook for 5 minutes, stirring, add salt.

Fresh Grilled Lobster

2 live lobsters
  (1 ¹/₄ to 1 ¹/₂ pounds each)

2 tablespoons olive oil

6 tablespoons butter

¹/₂ tablespoon fresh basil leaves,
  chopped

3 tablespoons lemon juice

2 tablespoons sherry

• In a large pot filled with 2 inches of water, partially cook lobsters for 4 to 5 minutes or until shell turns red. Remove from water and remove claws. Cut lobster in half lengthwise. Remove tail and vein.

• Prepare grill. In small saucepan, heat oil and butter until butter melts. Add basil, lemon juice and sherry. Cook for 3 to 5 minutes.

• Brush underside of lobsters with butter sauce and place on grill with inside facing down. Crack claws and brush with butter sauce. Place on grill. Grill 8 to 12 minutes, turning and basting halfway through cooking time. Serve immediately, spooning sauce over top.

Serves 4

Spice up your grill

Place thyme, dill, oregano and fennel branches dipped in water directly on hot coals when grilling lobster or any seafood and fish for a hint of herb flavor.

Baked Stuffed Lobster

6 tablespoons unsalted butter,
    softened

¹/₃ cup loosely packed fresh
    tarragon leaves

1 tablespoon fresh lemon juice

²/₃ cup bread crumbs,
    lightly toasted

1 large shallot, minced

3 tablespoons pine nuts, toasted

salt and pepper, to taste

3 quarts water

3 tablespoons salt

1 onion, cut into eighths

1 bay leaf

4 live lobsters,
    (1 ¹/₄ to 1 ¹/₂ pounds each)

2 large potatoes, halved crosswise

• In a food processor, blend together the butter, tarragon, lemon juice, bread crumbs, shallot and pine nuts. Season with salt and pepper. (May be made up to 3 days in advance).

• Preheat oven to 450°. In a large pot, combine the water, salt, onion and bay leaf and bring to a boil. Add lobsters and cook for 5 minutes.

• Cut a crosswise slit at each end of the under-side of the tail. Cut 2 lengthwise slits down the underside from one crosswise slit to the other to remove only a center rectangular section of the underside of the tail shell, leaving about ¹/₄-inch of shell on both sides of the tail. (Leaving the edges intact will keep the meat from curling out of the shell).

• Cut the body down the center of the underside with a knife, leaving the back of the shell intact, and press the body open slightly. Spread ¹/₄ of the stuffing in the body and down the tail of lobsters. Arrange the lobster in 2 jelly-roll pans. Place a potato half on the end of lobster tails to weight.

• Bake for 15 minutes or until the stuffing is crisp and golden and the meat is cooked through. Discard the potatoes. Serve immediately.

Serves 4

Chilled Lobster with Hot Red Pepper Sauce

4 live lobsters,
  (1 ½ pounds each)

1 jalapeno pepper

2 sweet red peppers

2 tablespoons coarse mustard

2 tablespoons red wine vinegar

2 cloves garlic, peeled

½ cup olive oil or vegetable oil

12 to 14 fresh basil leaves

salt and pepper to taste

• Pour about 2 inches of water in the bottom of a large steamer. Add salt. Bring to a boil. Place the lobsters on the steamer rack and cover the pot. Cook over high heat for 15 to 18 minutes. Remove lobsters from the steamer, cool, then chill.

• Split the lobsters in half lengthwise and crack the claws. Remove and discard the small sac near the eyes as well as the vein that runs through the middle of the tail.

• Core, seed and chop the jalapeno pepper and red sweet peppers. Combine with remaining ingredients in blender or food processor and blend until smooth. Top the lobster with sauce and serve.

Serves 4

Lobster Pound

Contrary to public belief, a true "lobster pound" is a sizable cove closed off with a barrier that holds the lobsters in captivity but allows for free passage of sea water.

Broiled Lobster Tails with White Wine

4 lobster tails

2 tablespoons finely crushed saltine crackers

2 tablespoons grated Parmesan cheese

2 teaspoons minced fresh parsley

dash paprika

1 tablespoon butter, melted

2 tablespoons dry white wine

3 tablespoons lemon juice

2 cloves garlic, crushed

• Parboil lobster tails in salted water for 2 minutes.

• Make a lengthwise cut through the top of lobster shells, using kitchen shears, and press shells open. Starting at the cut end of the tail, carefully loosen the lobster meat from bottom of the shells, keeping meat attached at end of tail; lift meat through top shell opening, and place on top of shell. Place lobster tails in a shallow roasting pan.

• Combine cracker crumbs, Parmesan cheese, parsley and paprika in a small bowl; stir in melted butter. Set aside.

• Combine wine, lemon juice and garlic; stir well. Brush lobster with half of wine mixture.

• Broil 5 $\frac{1}{2}$ inches from heat for 9 minutes or until lobster flesh turns opaque, basting with remaining wine mixture after 5 minutes. Sprinkle crumb mixture evenly over lobster meat and broil an additional 30 seconds.

Serves 4

Lobster with Champagne Dipping Sauce

1 bottle (750 ml.) dry champagne

1 cup fresh parsley

1 small bunch fresh thyme

1 bay leaf

4 shallots, chopped

3/4 cup unsalted butter

salt and pepper, to taste

4 live lobsters,
    (1 1/2 to 2 pounds each)

- Place the champagne, herbs and shallots in a medium saucepan; cook over medium heat until just 1 cup of liquid remains, about 25 to 30 minutes. Strain liquid to remove herbs.

- Slowly whisk in the butter, one tablespoon at a time, over low heat. When all the butter has been added, add salt and pepper to taste. Keep mixture warm while preparing the lobsters.

- In a large pot, bring enough salted water to cover the lobsters to a boil. Remove the rubber bands that hold the claws shut. Plunge the lobsters in, head first. Bring water to boil again. Cook lobsters for 10 to 12 minutes from the time the water returns to a boil.

- Serve lobsters accompanied with champagne dipping sauce.

Serves 4

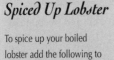

Spiced Up Lobster

To spice up your boiled lobster add the following to the cooking water:
    1/2 tablespoon mustard
        seeds
    1 tablespoon each whole
        black, green and red
        peppercorns
    2 bay leaves.

Two Lights Broiled Lobster

4 live lobsters
  (1 1/2 to 1 3/4 pounds each)
1 lemon, sliced

Herb Sauce

3/4 cup unsalted butter, melted

3 cloves garlic, crushed

2 tablespoons finely chopped fresh
  oregano

2 tablespoons fresh rosemary

salt and freshly ground pepper
  to taste

Basil Oil Sauce

1 cup fresh basil leaves

1 cup olive oil

salt and freshly ground pepper
  to taste

• Bring a large pot of water to boil. Add lobsters, head first, and boil for 2 minutes. Remove parboiled lobsters and place on cutting board, flesh side up. Using a sharp knife, split lobsters in half lengthwise. Place meat side up in roasting pan. Prepare either sauce.

• To prepare *Herb Sauce*, combine butter, garlic, oregano and rosemary in a small bowl . Add salt and pepper to taste. Coat lobsters with sauce.

• To prepare *Basil Oil Sauce*, place basil in food processor and chop well. While machine is running, add oil until smooth. Season with salt and pepper. (Can be made 1 day ahead. Cover and refrigerate). Coat lobsters with sauce.

• Broil lobsters 5 to 6 inches from heat for 10 minutes. Coat again with the herb sauce or basil oil. Finish broiling for 5 more minutes.

•Garnish lobsters with lemon slices. Serve immediately. Serve extra sauce at the table for dipping.

Serves 4

Shrimp & Scallop Cakes

$^1/_2$ cup butter, divided

5 shallots, chopped

1 $^1/_2$ pounds medium shrimp, peeled, deveined, finely chopped

$^1/_2$ pound uncooked sea scallops, finely chopped

1 $^1/_2$ cups bread crumbs

2 eggs, lightly beaten

$^1/_2$ cup minced red bell pepper

2 scallions, finely chopped

salt and pepper to taste

2 tablespoons chopped fresh tarragon or 1 teaspoon dried

• Melt $^1/_4$ cup butter, add shallots and sauté for 2 minutes. Mix in shrimp, scallops, bread crumbs, eggs, red pepper, scallions, salt, pepper and tarragon.

• Form into eight 4-inch rounds.

• In a nonstick skillet, melt 2 tablespoons butter over medium heat. Add cakes in batches and cook on both sides until golden, about 5 minutes per side. Add butter to pan as needed for cooking.

• Serve immediately.

Serves 4

Native Crab Cakes

12 ounces crabmeat

¹/₂ cup bread crumbs

2 large eggs, beaten

2 tablespoons light mayonnaise

2 teaspoons Dijon mustard

2 teaspoons chopped flat leaf parsley

1 teaspoon fresh or dried thyme

¹/₈ teaspoon cayenne pepper

4 scallions, thinly sliced

2 tablespoons unsalted butter

• Combine all ingredients except scallions and butter. Mix well. Add sliced scallions and mix. Form into eight 2-inch crab cakes.

• In a 10-inch skillet, melt butter over medium-high heat. Heat butter until hot but not smoking. Cook the crab cakes for 3 to 4 minutes on each side or until golden.

Serves 4

Gingered Scallops & Vegetables

1 teaspoon minced garlic

2 tablespoons unsalted butter

¹/4 cup thinly sliced scallion

¹/2 teaspoon grated fresh ginger root

¹/2 teaspoon fresh grated lemon rind

1 red bell pepper, thinly sliced

¹/4 pound mushrooms, sliced
   (about 1 cup)

¹/3 cup drained canned water
   chestnuts, thinly sliced

1 tablespoon fresh lemon juice

2 teaspoons sesame oil

³/4 pound sea scallops, rinsed,
   halved horizontally

1 tablespoon minced fresh coriander

salt and pepper to taste

fresh parsley sprigs for garnish

• Preheat oven to 450°.

• In a skillet, sauté the garlic in the butter over medium-low heat, stirring, for 1 minute. Add the scallions, the ginger root and lemon rind and cook the mixture, stirring, for 1 minute. Add pepper, mushrooms and water chestnuts and cook the mixture, stirring, for 2 to 3 minutes. Stir in the lemon juice and salt and pepper.

• Fold 2 pieces of 20 x 12 inch foil in half by bringing the short ends together. Unfold each piece and brush lightly with half of the oil. Arrange half the scallops, seasoned with salt and pepper, just to one side of each fold line and top the scallops with the vegetable mixture. Sprinkle each serving with half of the remaining oil and 1¹/2 teaspoons of the coriander. Fold the foil over the scallop vegetable mixture to enclose it and fold the edges together to form tightly sealed packets.

• Bake the packets on a baking sheet in the middle of the oven for 15 minutes. Transfer the packets to plates and slit them open at the table. Alternatively, open them carefully and transfer the scallop vegetable mixture to plates and pour the juices over them, discarding the foil. Garnish with fresh parsley sprigs.

Serves 2

Sea Scallops with Plum Tomatoes

1 ½ pounds sea scallops

¼ cup milk

salt and freshly ground pepper to taste

5 tablespoons olive oil

2 cups chopped plum tomatoes

2 tablespoons chopped fresh basil leaves

½ cup flour

4 tablespoons butter

1 tablespoon finely chopped garlic

2 tablespoons finely chopped fresh parsley leaves

• Put the scallops in a mixing bowl and add the milk and salt and pepper. Set aside.

• Heat 1 tablespoon of the olive oil in a heavy sauté pan over medium-high heat. Add the tomatoes and salt and pepper. Bring to a boil and cook for 5 minutes or until the moisture has almost evaporated. Add basil.

• Heat 1 tablespoon of the oil in a large nonstick frying pan. Drain the scallops and dredge them in the flour, shake off excess. Add scallops to the pan (do not crowd) and fry over medium-high heat for 3 to 5 minutes per side or until they are golden brown.

• Using a slotted spoon, remove scallops and keep warm. Add more oil to the pan if necessary and another layer of scallops. Repeat until all the scallops are cooked.

• When all the scallops are cooked, pour off the fat from the pan and wipe out. Add butter and cook while swirling until it starts to brown. Stir in garlic quickly. Do not brown garlic.

• Spoon the tomato sauce onto a serving dish. Top with scallops. Pour garlic butter over scallops. Sprinkle with parsley and serve.

Serves 4

Chive & Mustard Shrimp

³/4 pound uncooked shrimp

1 to 2 tablespoons butter

¹/2 tablespoon minced shallots

2 ounces Marsala wine

8 ounces heavy cream

1 tablespoon chopped chives

1 teaspoon Dijon mustard

salt and pepper to taste

- Peel and devein shrimp. Melt butter in sauté pan. Cook shrimp until pink and remove from pan.

- Add shallots and wine to pan and cook until liquid is reduced by half. Add cream, stir well and cook over medium heat until it thickens.

- Add shrimp, chives, mustard, salt and pepper. May be served with pasta or rice.

Serves 2

Fiery Grilled Shrimp

32 large uncooked shrimp

¹/2 cup soy sauce

¹/2 cup olive oil

5 tablespoons Cajun seasoning mix*

¹/4 cup sesame oil

¹/4 cup fresh lemon juice

2 tablespoons minced fresh ginger

2 teaspoons dry mustard

3 teaspoons hot pepper sauce

*available in specialty stores

- Peel and devein shrimp leaving tails intact. In a large bowl, whisk remaining ingredients. Add shrimp to bowl and marinate for 30 minutes.

- Prepare grill. Place shrimp on skewers or on a rack and grill 4 minutes per side, until pink.

Serves 2-4

Citrus Shrimp & Scallop Skewers

1/2 pound sea scallops

12 large shrimp, peeled and deveined

1 teaspoon orange zest

1/2 cup orange juice

2 tablespoons soy sauce

1 teaspoon grated ginger root

1 clove garlic, minced

1/8 to 1/4 teaspoon ground red pepper

12 fresh or frozen pea pods

1 medium orange, cut into 8 wedges

• Halve all large scallops. Place scallops and shrimp in a plastic bag set in a deep bowl.

• For marinade, combine orange zest, orange juice, soy sauce, ginger root, garlic and red pepper. Pour over seafood. Seal bag. Marinate in the refrigerator for 30 minutes. Drain, reserving marinade.

• If using fresh pea pods, cook in boiling water about 2 minutes; drain. If using frozen pea pods, thaw and drain. Wrap one pea pod around each shrimp. Thread pea pod wrapped shrimp onto four 10 to 12-inch skewers alternately with scallops and orange wedges.

• Grill kabobs on an uncovered grill directly over medium-hot coals for 5 minutes. Turn and brush with marinade. Grill 5 to 7 minutes more or until shrimp turn pink and scallops are opaque. Brush occasionally with marinade.

• Alternate cooking method: Place kabobs on the unheated rack of a broiler pan. Broil 4 inches from the heat for 4 minutes. Turn and broil 4 to 6 minutes longer or until shrimp turn pink and scallops are opaque, brushing occasionally with marinade.

Serves 4

Sherry Shrimp Stir-fry

1 tablespoon cornstarch

2 tablespoons soy sauce

¹/₄ cup water

¹/₂ cup sherry

2 teaspoons grated fresh ginger root
  or 1 teaspoon ground ginger

2 tablespoons vegetable or corn oil

1 package frozen pea pods

1 small head fresh broccoli,
  trimmed and chopped

¹/₂ cup sliced scallions

1 small can sliced water chestnuts,
  drained

3 cloves garlic, minced

1 ¹/₄ pounds medium shrimp,
  peeled and deveined

2 cups cooked white rice

• Combine cornstarch, soy sauce, water, sherry and ginger and set aside.

• In a large skillet or wok, heat oil over medium heat. Add next 5 ingredients. Quickly stirring, cook 5 minutes.

• Stir in cornstarch mixture. Add shrimp and continue cooking until sauce thickens and shrimp are pink.

• Serve over hot rice.

Serves 4

Maine Seafood Bake

3 pounds fresh seafood (any combination of scallops, haddock, raw shrimp or cooked lobster meat)

20 butter crackers, crushed

6 tablespoons butter

$^1/_3$ cup sherry

2 tablespoons lemon juice

1 teaspoon salt

1 tablespoon freshly ground pepper

$^1/_2$ teaspoon onion powder

$^1/_2$ teaspoon garlic powder

paprika

2 tablespoons dried parsley

• Preheat oven to 400°

• If using shrimp, peel and devein. Cut larger seafood into bite size pieces. In a 2-quart ovenproof casserole, arrange seafood and sprinkle with cracker crumbs.

• In a small saucepan, melt butter. Add sherry and lemon juice and heat for 2 minutes. Pour butter mixture evenly over seafood. Season with salt, pepper, onion and garlic. Lightly sprinkle with paprika and parsley.

• Bake, uncovered, for 30 minutes.

Serves 6

Seafood Streudel

Streudel:

4 cups fresh spinach

1 clove garlic

8 ounces fresh large scallops

1 egg

1/2 teaspoon salt

1/8 teaspoon hot red pepper

1/2 cup heavy cream

1 teaspoon chopped fresh tarragon

8 sheets phyllo dough

1/2 cup butter, melted

cornmeal

3 ounces cooked shrimp, chopped

Sauce:

1 cup white wine

2 shallots, sliced

10 black peppercorns

1/2 teaspoon tarragon

1/2 cup heavy cream

1/2 cup butter

1/8 teaspoon salt

• Preheat oven to 375°. Remove stems from spinach. Rinse and dry. Chop spinach and set aside.

• Chop garlic in food processor. Add scallops, egg, salt and pepper. Process until smooth. Add cream while motor is running. Stop and add tarragon. Refrigerate.

• Cover phyllo with plastic wrap and a damp towel. Place one sheet on waxed paper. Brush with butter and sprinkle with corn-meal. Repeat with 7 remaining sheets, stacking.

• Evenly spread spinach over phyllo. Spread mousse mixture on spinach. Sprinkle mousse with shrimp. Using waxed paper as a guide, roll up phyllo tightly like a jelly roll. Place on greased baking sheet seam side down. Bake for 20 to 25 minutes until golden.

• Meanwhile, make the wine sauce by gently boiling wine, shallots, peppercorns and tarragon for 10 minutes until reduced. Strain. Gently boil with cream until syrupy. Over low heat, whisk in butter a little at a time. Add salt.

• Slice streudel into 8 slices and top with sauce.

Serves 4

Simply Elegant Seafood Crepes

12 crepes (see recipe on page 57)

1 1/2 pounds cooked seafood
(combination of crabmeat,
scallops and firm white fish)

5 tablespoons butter

5 tablespoons flour

2 1/2 cups milk

1/2 teaspoon salt

1/8 teaspoon white pepper

1 1/2 cups Swiss or Gruyere cheese,
grated

1/2 pound small cooked shrimp,
for topping

1 cup shredded Cheddar cheese

Freezing Crepes

• Seafood Crepes freeze well
and can be reheated frozen at
350° for 35 minutes or until
hot and bubbling.

• To freeze unfilled crepes,
stack between sheets of
waxed paper and wrap tightly
in a plastic bag. Defrost fully
before filling.

• Prepare crepes. Preheat oven to 350°

• Prepare seafood, if not already cooked, by
gently steaming in skillet until just cooked
through. Break or cut into bite-size pieces
and refrigerate.

• For white sauce, melt butter in saucepan over
low heat and mix in flour. Gradually add
milk, stirring constantly. Cook and stir over
medium heat until sauce is thickened. Add
salt and white pepper and remove from heat.

• Reserve one half of sauce. To remaining
sauce, stir in seafood and Swiss cheese. Place
4 tablespoons seafood mixture on each crepe
and roll. Arrange on a buttered 9x13-inch
baking dish, rolled edge down.

• To reserved 1 cup of sauce, add shrimp and
Cheddar cheese and warm until cheese just
melts. Pour over middle of crepes, making a
lengthwise band across crepes.

• Bake for 25 minutes or until hot and bubbling.

Serves 6

Seafood Paella

1 ¹/₂ pounds cooked lobster

12 littleneck clams

12 mussels

1 pound crabmeat

2 tablespoons olive oil

2 cloves garlic, minced

1 onion, finely chopped

¹/₂ teaspoon salt

¹/₂ tablespoon ground pepper

2 tomatoes, chopped

2 cups long-grain rice

4 cups water

1 tablespoon saffron threads

1 sweet red pepper, chopped

1 cup frozen peas

6-ounce jar marinated
    artichoke hearts

12 asparagus tips, steamed

pimiento strips

• Remove meat from lobster; cut into chunks and set aside. Scrub clams and set aside. Scrub and debeard mussels; set aside. Pick over crabmeat and set aside.

• In a heavy deep skillet, heat oil and sauté garlic and onion for 1 minute. Add salt, pepper and tomatoes. Cover and cook 10 minutes. Add rice, water and saffron, stirring to combine. Add pepper and peas. Drain artichokes and add. Cover and cook over low heat for 20 minutes. Add lobster meat, cover, and cook for an additional 10 to 15 minutes.

• Meanwhile, put mussels and clams in a large heavy pot with 1 cup water. Cover and bring to a lively boil and cook until all shells are open. Drain and discard any unopened shells.

• Gently fold crabmeat into rice. Garnish top of rice with clams, mussels, steamed asparagus tips and pimiento strips.

Serves 4-6

Sole & Broccoli Roll-Ups

1 pound fresh sole fillets

1 pound fresh broccoli spears

1 teaspoon salt

1 cup dry white wine

¹/₄ cup water

5 tablespoons butter

2 tablespoons sliced scallions

1 tablespoon lemon juice

1 bay leaf

paprika for garnish

*hollandaise sauce
   (see recipe on page 15)*

chopped parsley for garnish

• Preheat oven to 375°.

• Rinse fish with cold water; pat dry with paper towels. Set aside.

• Steam broccoli for 5 minutes or until crisp-tender; drain. Divide fish and broccoli spears into 4 equal size serving portions. Sprinkle fish with ¹/₂ teaspoon salt.

• To assemble roll-ups, place a small bundle of broccoli spears on each fish portion alternating direction of flowerets within each bundle; roll up. Set aside.

• In large skillet, combine wine, water, butter, scallions, lemon juice and bay leaf; bring to a boil.

• In an oven proof baking dish, place fish bundle, seam side down. Sprinkle with remaining ¹/₂ teaspoon of salt. Pour sauce over fish. Sprinkle with paprika. Bake for 20 minutes or until fish flakes easily.

• Prepare hollandaise and keep warm.

• Remove to a platter. Spoon hollandaise sauce over each bundle and garnish with parsley.

Serves 2 to 3

Beyond the Bay Cod

1 pound cod fillet

1 bay leaf

*salt and freshly ground pepper
   to taste*

1 cup water

2 tablespoons unsalted butter

¼ cup flour

*2 tablespoons grated fresh
   horseradish*

1 cup sour cream

fresh dill sprigs, for garnish

lemon slices, for garnish

- Skin the cod and cut into 4 pieces. Place the fillets in a skillet with the bay leaf. Sprinkle with salt and pepper. Pour in the water and heat until simmering.

- Cook over low heat for 3 to 5 minutes, until fish is just cooked. Carefully transfer fillets to a glass baking dish. Reserve the cooking liquid.

- Preheat oven to 425°. Melt butter in a small saucepan. Add flour slowly. Gradually combine the reserved fish liquid with the butter mixture, stirring constantly. Add the horseradish and bring to a low boil until very thick. Season with salt and pepper. Add the sour cream. Spoon sauce over fish.

- Bake for about 10 minutes, until the sauce is just starting to brown. Garnish with dill and lemon slices. Serve immediately.

Serves 2 to 4

Blackened Bluefish

four 7-ounce bluefish fillets

¹/₂ cup butter, melted

1 tablespoon paprika

¹/₂ teaspoon salt

¹/₂ teaspoon freshly ground pepper

¹/₂ teaspoon freshly ground
   white pepper

1 teaspoon dried minced onion

¹/₂ teaspoon crumbled dried thyme

¹/₄ teaspoon garlic powder

1 lemon, sliced, for garnish

• Prepare grill for cooking.

• Place a large cast iron skillet over high heat and allow to preheat 3 to 4 minutes. (Heat will cause a good deal of smoke, so ensure proper ventilation).

• Brush fillets with half the melted butter. Combine remaining ingredients, and sprinkle both sides of fish with spice mixture.

• Carefully place the bluefish, a piece at a time, in dry hot skillet. Drizzle remaining butter over fish. Sear fish 30 seconds on each side, turning once.

• Place skillet on grill. (You may cook fish indoors up to an hour before grilling.) Grill fish, turning every minute for 3 to 4 minutes, until it is cooked and darkened. Add more butter if necessary.

• Remove bluefish and garnish with lemon slices.

Serves 4

Sea Bass Kabobs

3 small onions

juice of 3 lemons

1/4 cup olive oil

1/8 teaspoon cayenne pepper

2 teaspoons cumin

1 tablespoon tomato paste

1 bay leaf

2 pounds sea bass filet, cubed

6 baby zucchini

2 dozen cherry tomatoes

olive oil

lemon wedges, for garnish

• Puree onions in a food processor. In a small bowl combine onions, lemon juice, olive oil, cayenne pepper, cumin and tomato paste. Mix well. Add bay leaf.

• Place fish in a large bowl and cover with above marinade. Toss to coat completely. Cover and chill for 1 hour.

• Preheat broiler. Cut zucchini into 1-inch slices. On 6 large or 12 small skewers, place fish cubes, zucchini and cherry tomatoes, alternating. Brush with olive oil and place under broiler.

• Cook for 12 to 15 minutes, turning occasionally until fish is opaque and the zucchini is just tender. Serve immediately with lemon wedges.

Serves 6

Top It Off!

A well-chilled glass of Chardonnay will keep you cool while grilling the colorful kabobs.

Grilled Tuna with Vera Cruz Sauce

2 pounds fresh tuna steaks

¹/4 cup vegetable oil

¹/4 cup lime juice

4 tablespoons vegetable oil

2 onions, sliced

3 cloves garlic, minced

4 large tomatoes, peeled and
    quartered

¹/2 cup sliced green olives

salt and freshly ground pepper
    to taste

• Prepare grill. Brush tuna with oil and sprinkle with lime juice. Place on a hot grill. Cook until thickest part of the fish is done.

• Meanwhile, make the sauce. Heat the oil in a saucepan. Saute onions and garlic until tender. Add tomatoes and olives, and continue cooking over medium heat 6 to 8 minutes or until slightly thickened. Season with salt and pepper.

• Remove from heat. Top grilled tuna with sauce and serve immediately.

Serves 4

Grilled Swordfish with Julienne Vegetables

2 swordfish steaks, halved

salt and pepper to taste

1 zucchini

2 carrots

juice of 1 lemon

1/2 cup olive oil

2 tomatoes, peeled, seeded and diced

salt and pepper to taste

3 parsley sprigs, chopped

6 basil leaves, minced

• Season swordfish with salt and pepper. Grill steaks 4 to 5 minutes per side.

• Cut zucchini in half and set aside one half. Slice one half into thin slices, blanch in boiling water, drain and set aside.

• Cut remaining half zucchini and carrots into julienne strips.

• In a small bowl, combine lemon juice, oil, tomatoes, salt, pepper, parsley, zucchini strips, carrots, and basil. Mix well.

• To serve, arrange zucchini slices on plate and place swordfish on top. Spoon vegetable medley on top of swordfish.

Serves 4

Grilling Seafood

Be careful not to overcook fish when grilling. Just a few minutes too long and the seafood will be dry and lose its wonderful flavor. Check the fish, if it doesn't flake when pricked with a fork, it isn't done. Check again in one minute.

Lemon Saffron Swordfish

4 scallions

$^{1}/_{2}$ cup dry white wine

$^{1}/_{4}$ cup fish stock or bottled clam juice

$^{1}/_{4}$ teaspoon saffron threads

four 8-ounce swordfish steaks

4 tablespoons fresh lemon juice

5 teaspoons olive oil

2 cloves garlic, minced

1 small red pepper

1 small yellow pepper

$^{1}/_{4}$ cup chilled unsalted butter, cut into pieces

lemon wedges for garnish

- Chop scallions, separating the white and green parts. Combine white part of scallions, wine, fish stock and saffron threads in heavy small saucepan. Bring to a boil. Boil sauce over medium-high heat until reduced to $^{1}/_{2}$ cup, about 7 minutes. (Sauce can be prepared 1 day ahead. Cover tightly and refrigerate).

- Place fish in single layer in large glass baking dish. Pour lemon juice and 2 teaspoons oil over fish. Sprinkle with garlic. Turn fish to coat. Let stand 15 minutes at room temperature.

- Cut peppers into $^{1}/_{4}$-inch strips. Heat 1 teaspoon oil in heavy nonstick skillet over medium heat. Add peppers and sauté until tender, about 8 minutes. Set aside. Heat remaining 2 teaspoons oil in large skillet over medium-high heat. Add fish, reserving marinade in dish. Cook fish just until cooked through, about 3 minutes per side.

- Rewarm peppers and divide among plates. Top with fish. Add sauce and any remaining marinade to fish cooking skillet and bring to boil. Remove from heat. Add butter and whisk just until melted. Spoon sauce over fish. Sprinkle with reserved scallions. Garnish with lemon wedges.

Serves 4

Lemon Thyme Broiled Trout

¹/4 cup olive oil

juice of 1 lemon

1 teaspoon dried thyme

4 cloves garlic, minced

salt and pepper to taste

4 whole trout (8 ounces each),
  filleted (with heads and tails
  removed)

¹/2 cup dry white wine

- Preheat broiler. In a small bowl, combine olive oil, lemon juice, thyme, garlic, salt and pepper.

- In a large ovenproof skillet, place fish skin side down. Lay fish so it is open and will lie flat in a butterflied position. Drizzle half of the oil mixture over fish. Place under broiler. Cook for about 3 minutes or until fish is opaque but not quite done.

- Remove skillet from oven and place on top of stove over medium heat. Mix wine with remaining oil mixture. When pan is hot, add wine mixture and cook. Continue to pour liquid over fish until fish is tender and just begins to flake, about another 3 minutes.

- Remove trout and serve immediately.

Serves 4

Stuffed Rainbow Trout

$^{1}/_{2}$ cup butter

$^{1}/_{4}$ cup chopped onion

$^{1}/_{4}$ cup chopped celery

$^{1}/_{4}$ cup chopped green pepper

$^{1}/_{2}$ cup sliced mushrooms

8 ounces crabmeat

$^{1}/_{2}$ cup fresh bread crumbs

2 tablespoons chopped parsley

$^{1}/_{4}$ cup slivered almonds

2 rainbow trout ($^{3}/_{4}$ pound each)

4 tablespoons lemon juice

• Preheat oven to 450°. Line a baking pan with foil. Lightly butter foil.

• Heat 4 tablespoons butter in sauce pan. Add onion, celery, pepper and mushrooms and sauté about 4 minutes. Add crab, bread crumbs, parsley and almonds.

• Sprinkle cavity of each fish with half of lemon juice and spoon in stuffing. Secure opening with toothpick. Pour remaining lemon juice over fish. Dot with remaining 4 tablespoons of butter.

• Tent loosely with foil. Cook 10 minutes tented and 5 minutes uncovered.

Serves 2

Tarragon Mustard Marinated Salmon

2 tablespoons Dijon mustard

1 tablespoon olive oil

1 tablespoon brown sugar

3 tablespoons chopped fresh tarragon

salt and freshly ground pepper
  to taste

1 salmon fillet (about 1 ¹/₂ pounds)

1 lime or lemon, quartered

• Combine the mustard, oil, sugar, tarragon, salt and pepper and mix well. Place the fish in a glass dish. Pour the marinade over the fillets. Cover with foil and refrigerate overnight. Can marinate up to two days.

• Preheat broiler. Broil the salmon about 3 to 5 minutes on each side or until it is cooked. Do not overcook or it will be dry. Serve with lemon or lime.

Serves 4

Healthy Halibut in Tarragon

1 pound halibut steaks or fillets

¹/₂ cup plain low-fat yogurt

¹/₂ medium red onion

1 tablespoon fresh tarragon

¹/₂ cup part skim mozzarella
  cheese, grated

• Preheat oven to 400°. Place halibut in baking pan. Combine all other ingredients in food processor and lightly process.

• Spread mixture over halibut. Bake for about 10 minutes per inch thickness of fish. Fish is done when flesh turns just opaque throughout.

Serves 4

Salmon with Cider & Braised Leeks

2 cups bottled clam juice

2 shallots, chopped

1 1/2 teaspoons peppercorns

1 1/2 teaspoons coriander seeds

1 bay leaf

1 cup apple cider

1 cup whipping cream

2 leeks

4 strips bacon cut into
    1/2-inch slices

1/4 cup dry white wine

four 8-ounce salmon fillets,
    skin removed

salt and pepper to taste

1 tablespoon butter

• Boil first 5 ingredients in heavy medium saucepan until reduced by 1/4, about 6 to 8 minutes. Add cider and boil until mixture is reduced by 1/2, about 8 to 10 minutes. Add cream. Boil until mixture is sauce consistency, about 10 minutes. Strain mixture into small saucepan. Set aside.

• Slice leeks into matchstick size strips. Cook leeks and bacon in heavy skillet until golden brown, stirring occasionally. Add wine and boil until almost no liquid remains. Cover and keep warm.

• Preheat broiler. Season salmon with salt and pepper. Broil until fish flakes easily with a fork, about 3 minutes per side.

• Bring sauce to simmer. Whisk in butter until melted. Divide leeks and bacon onto 4 plates. Place salmon on leeks. Spoon sauce over salmon.

Serves 4

Steamed Haddock with Saffron Sauce

3 pounds tomatoes

*¹/4 teaspoon saffron threads**

2 small zucchini, thinly sliced

*salt and freshly ground pepper
to taste*

*2 tablespoons grated
Parmesan cheese*

¹/4 cup fresh lemon juice

2 scallions, coarsely chopped

1 ¹/2 pounds haddock

* Available in specialty shops

- Peel, seed and dice tomatoes. Place tomatoes and saffron into 3-quart heavy bottomed saucepan over medium-high heat. Cook at a simmer until juice evaporates and saffron threads break down, about 20 minutes. Add zucchini. Cook 1 minute. Season to taste with salt and pepper. Remove from heat. Stir in cheese.

- Yields about 4 cups. (Can be made ahead of time and refrigerated). Use ¹/4 to ¹/2 cup of sauce per serving.

- Fill a steamer pan with 2 inches of water. Add lemon juice and scallions and bring to a boil. Reduce heat to simmer. Add haddock to steamer rack and steam until just opaque throughout, about 6 to 8 minutes per inch thickness. Serve immediately topped with sauce.

Serves 4

Saffron

Saffron is the thread-like stigma of a crocus. Grown in Spain, it takes 225,000 hand-picked stigmas to make 1 pound, thus making saffron the most expensive spice in the world. It only takes a few threads to add the orange-red color and distinctive flavor to rice, sauces, soups, and paella.

Baked Haddock with Olives & Tomatoes

2 tablespoons olive oil

¹/4 cup chopped onions

¹/2 cup sliced fresh mushrooms

16-ounce can whole tomatoes,
    drained and chopped
    or 2 cups fresh tomatoes

¹/4 cup white wine

¹/4 cup diced ripe olives

2 tablespoons chopped parsley

1 ¹/2 pounds haddock

• Preheat oven to 350°. Saute onions and mushrooms in olive oil until tender. Add tomatoes and wine. Simmer ten minutes. Stir in ripe olives and parsley.

• Arrange haddock in baking dish. Top with tomato mixture. Bake at 350° for 30 minutes covered.

Serves 4

As an alternative to haddock, choose any mild fresh fish such as cod, snapper, grouper or orange roughy.

Mussel Potato Gratin

4 pounds mussels, scrubbed
   and debearded

3 tablespoons chopped fresh
   flat-leaf parsley

2 cloves garlic, minced

salt and freshly ground pepper,
   to taste

6 tablespoons extra-virgin olive oil

1/4 cup unseasoned dry bread crumbs

1/4 cup freshly grated Romano cheese

5 plum tomatoes, peeled and seeded

1 1/2 pounds new potatoes, boiled

• Steam the mussels in a large covered pot filled with 2 inches of water. As soon as the mussels open, remove from broth and cool. Reserve broth and strain to remove grit. Detach mussels from shells. Clean mussels and put in a bowl. Pour the broth over the mussels.

• Add the parsley, garlic, salt, pepper and 3 tablespoons each of the olive oil, bread crumbs and grated cheese to the mussels. Toss to coat.

• Preheat the oven to 450°. Halve the tomatoes and cut into 1/4-inch strips. Place strips in a colander to drain.

• Peel the potatoes and slice them 1/4 inch thick. Brush a 9x13-inch baking dish or oval gratin dish with 1 tablespoon of the olive oil. Add the potatoes in an even layer. Sprinkle with salt. Spread the mussel mixture evenly over the potatoes. Sprinkle with salt again and arrange the tomato strips decoratively on top. Scatter the remaining 1 tablespoon each of bread crumbs and grated cheese over all and drizzle with remaining 2 tablespoons olive oil.

• Bake the gratin on the top shelf of the oven for 15 to 18 minutes, until a light brown crust begins to form on top. Allow the dish to settle for at least 5 minutes before serving.

Serves 4

Basil Tomato Mussels

4 tablespoons olive oil

³/4 cup finely chopped onion

1 tablespoon finely chopped garlic

4 tablespoons red wine vinegar

3 cups chopped or crushed Italian canned tomatoes

¹/2 teaspoon crumbled dried oregano

¹/4 teaspoon hot red pepper flakes

freshly ground pepper to taste

3 to 4 pounds mussels, scrubbed and debearded

¹/2 cup finely chopped fresh flat leaf parsley leaves

4 tablespoons finely chopped fresh basil leaves or 2 teaspoons dried basil

loaf of French bread

• Heat the oil in a large pot. Add the onion and garlic, and cook until the onion is tender. Add the vinegar, tomatoes, oregano, hot pepper flakes and pepper and bring to a boil. Cover and cook for 5 minutes.

• Add the mussels to the pot along with the parsley and basil. Cover and bring to a boil. Cook for 4 to 5 minutes or until all the mussels have opened. As they cook, shake the pan to distribute them evenly.

• Serve the mussels in hot soup bowls with the liquid poured over them.

• Serve with crusty bread for dipping.

Serves 4

Penobscot Bay Clam Stuffing

8 ounces fresh chopped clams,
   drained

2 teaspoons lemon juice

1 tablespoon butter

1 teaspoon oregano

2 tablespoons fresh parsley,
   finely chopped

dash of Tabasco

white pepper to taste

1 onion, finely chopped

1 green pepper, finely chopped

2 cloves garlic, minced

³/4 cup Italian bread crumbs

grated Parmesan cheese

paprika

• Preheat oven to 350°.

• In a medium saucepan, combine clams, lemon juice, butter, oregano, parsley, Tabasco and white pepper. Simmer for 15 minutes.

• Add onion, pepper and garlic to clam mixture. Remove from heat. Add bread crumbs and mix well. Put stuffing in an ungreased baking dish. Sprinkle with Parmesan cheese and paprika. Bake for 20 minutes.

Yields 4 cups

Stuffing can be made ahead of time and refrigerated or frozen before being baked. If frozen, add 5 to 10 minutes to the baking time.

Elegant Oysters

24 oysters, on the half shell

1 cup Hollandaise sauce (see recipe on page 15)

2 large shallots, finely chopped

¹/₂ cup champagne

fresh dill, for garnish

• Preheat broiler. Loosen oysters in their shells. Arrange oysters on a large ovenproof pan and set aside.

• Prepare the Hollandaise sauce. Add the shallots and champagne. Stir well. Spoon the sauce over each oyster. Place oysters under the broiler for about 2 minutes. Garnish with fresh dill, and serve immediately.

Serves 4 to 6

Steamed Herb Clams

72 littleneck clams

1 ¹/₂ cups white wine

2 onions, chopped

1 teaspoon dried thyme or 1 tablespoon fresh

1 whole bay leaf

2 tablespoons fresh parsley, chopped

freshly ground pepper

loaf of French bread

• Scrub the clams well, and place in a large pot with remaining ingredients (except bread). Place over medium-high heat, and steam until the clams open. Discard any clams that do not open.

• Serve clams in shallow bowls with steaming broth over them and French bread for dipping.

Serves 6

Desserts & Beverages

MAINE
Ingredients

Apples

*M*ore than three hundred varieties of apples, many originating in Maine, were available to the state's early settlers. Apples were grown even before the first colonists began harvesting them. Explorers introduced this sweet and versatile fruit to the Indians, who quickly adapted it to their diets. Young trees, growing in tubs, were transported across the Atlantic with great bother and considerable risk. Seeds were more easily imported and sown by hand. Due to the varying soils and conditions, these seeds produced several indigenous varieties. One of the most rare, was the "The Black Oxford," a nearly black apple. In spite of its strange color, this tasty fruit kept well, often until the following year's harvest.

Throughout the years, many of Maine's apples have been used for making cider. Puritans claimed that the necessary step to making a "perfect" cider was leaving the crushed apples out for at least two days and two nights, thus fermenting the juice into a potent alcohol. This Puritan "spirit" continues to be popular today.

> "In this apple in your fingers
> The splendor of the Maine year lingers,
> This globe arching your hand apart
> Is Maine's cool and beautiful heart."
> —Robert Peter Tristam Coffin
> *Poems For A Son With Wings* (1945)

Apple Cranberry Pear Pie

2 Granny Smith apples or
   other tart apples

2 pears

2 cups cranberries

1 tablespoon cinnamon

¹/₂ teaspoon nutmeg

¹/₄ cup sugar

1 double pie crust
   (see recipe on page 273)

• Preheat oven to 400°. Peel, core and cut apple into cubes. Peel, core and cut pears into slices. In a bowl, combine apples, pears, cranberries, cinnamon, nutmeg and sugar. Toss until coated.

• Place one rolled-out pie pastry into 9-inch pie plate. Turn fruit and spices into plate. Place second pastry on top. Crimp edges of crust. Cut decorative shapes out of extra pastry and place on top of pie. Cut slits in top crust for vents. Sprinkle with sugar.

• Bake for 40 to 45 minutes or until crust is lightly browned.

Serves 8

Sour Cream Apple Pie

Crust:

1 cup flour

3 ounces cream cheese, softened

1/2 cup butter

Filling:

6 large McIntosh apples

1 2/3 cups sour cream

1 cup sugar

1 large egg

1/3 cup flour

2 teaspoons vanilla extract

1/2 teaspoon salt

Topping:

1 cup chopped walnuts

1/2 cup flour

1/2 cup butter

1/3 cup sugar

1/3 cup brown sugar

1 tablespoon cinnamon

pinch of salt

- Preheat oven to 450°.

- Combine crust ingredients. Blend well with pastry cutter. Press into 9-inch pie pan.

- Peel, core and slice apples. Combine sour cream, sugar, egg, flour, vanilla and salt. Mix well. Stir in apples. Pour mixture into pie crust. Bake for 10 minutes. Reduce oven temperature to 350° and bake 35 minutes.

- While pie is baking, combine all topping ingredients. Mix well. Spoon over baked pie. Bake an additional 15 minutes. Serve cold.

Serves 8

Red, White & Blueberry Pie

Double pie crust:

2 1/2 cups flour

1 teaspoon salt

1 teaspoon sugar

*1 cup cold unsalted butter cut into
    small pieces*

1/4 cup ice water

Filling:

1 cup sugar

5 tablespoons flour

1/2 teaspoon cinnamon

2 1/2 cups blueberries

1 1/2 cups raspberries

1 1/3 tablespoons butter

sugar, for garnish

• Put flour, salt and sugar in a food processor.
Add the butter and process about 10 seconds
or until mixture resembles coarse meal.

• Add water a teaspoon at a time until the dough
holds together without being wet or sticky. If
it is crumbly, add more water. Split dough in
half and press into a flat circle. Wrap in
plastic wrap and chill for an hour.

• On a floured surface, roll out the chilled
dough to 1/8-inch thickness. Place one pastry
in the pie plate. Trim the edges. Roll out top
crust, saving extra pieces of dough for
decoration. Preheat oven to 350°.

• For filling, mix together sugar, flour and
cinnamon in a large bowl. Lightly stir in the
berries. Pour mixture into pie plate. Dot with
butter. Cover with top crust. Use cookie
cutter to cut shapes from extra crust. Place on
top and sprinkle with sugar. Make slits in
crust to release steam. Bake 35 to 45 minutes.

Serves 8-10

Bottomless Blueberry Pie

Dough:

1 ¹/₃ cups flour

2 tablespoons sugar

¹/₄ teaspoon salt

¹/₂ cup cold unsalted butter

1 large egg yolk

1 ¹/₂ tablespoons ice water

Filling:

2 tablespoons cornstarch

2 tablespoons rum or water

2 teaspoons lemon juice

¹/₂ cup sugar

¹/₄ teaspoon cinnamon

6 cups blueberries

Egg wash:

1 egg

2 teaspoons water

1 ¹/₂ tablespoons sugar

- To make dough, in a bowl, stir together flour, sugar and salt. Cut butter into flour mixture until the mixture resembles coarse meal. Beat egg yolk lightly with ice water. Add the yolk mixture to flour and butter and toss until the liquid is incorporated. Form the dough into a ball. Dust the dough with flour and chill, wrapped in plastic wrap, for 1 hour.

- To make filling, in a large bowl, stir together the cornstarch, rum, lemon juice, sugar and cinnamon. Add the blueberries and combine the mixture well.

- Preheat the oven to 350°.

- Pour the filling into a 6- to 7-cup gratin dish or other deep baking dish. Roll out the dough slightly larger than the dish on a floured surface and drape it over the filling. Fold the overhang under, pressing the dough to the edge of the dish and crimp the edge decoratively. Make slits and holes in the crust for air vents.

- Beat egg with water and brush the crust with the wash and sprinkle it with the sugar. Bake the pie on a baking sheet in the middle of oven for 1 to 1¹/₄ hours or until the filling is bubbly and the crust is golden. Transfer the pie to a rack and let it cool.

Serves 6

Raspberry Glacé Pie

4 cups fresh raspberries

1 cup sugar

1/2 cup water

2 heaping tablespoons cornstarch

one 9-inch baked pie shell

• Set 3 cups of raspberries aside. Combine remaining cup of berries with sugar, water and cornstarch in a medium-sized pot. Cook over medium heat until mixture thickens.

• Put the remaining 3 cups of raspberries in the pie shell. Add the thickened raspberry mixture and then turn berries over a few times. Chill for 1 hour.

• Serve with whipped cream.

Serves 8

Blueberry Honey Ice Cream

4 cups fresh or thawed frozen
   blueberries

2/3 cup honey

juice of 1 lime

1/2 teaspoon vanilla extract

1/8 teaspoon salt

4 cups heavy cream

• Purée blueberries in a blender. Add honey, lime juice, vanilla and salt; blend.

• Stir mixture into cream. Pour into a 4-quart freezer can of electric or hand-cranked ice cream freezer.

• Freeze according to manufacturer's instructions.

Yields 2 1/2 quarts

Strawberry-Rhubarb Crisp

1 cup packed brown sugar

1 1/2 cups flour

3/4 cup cold unsalted butter,
  cut into pieces

3 tablespoons anise seed,
  coarsely chopped

1 pound rhubarb

1/2 quart strawberries

juice of 1/2 lemon

zest of 1 lemon

1/2 teaspoon vanilla extract

1 cup sugar

• Preheat oven to 400°. Using a food processor with a metal blade, mix brown sugar and flour together. Add butter and anise seed. Mix until large pea-size chunks form and crumbs hold together. Set aside.

• Trim off rough ends of rhubarb and cut into 1-inch lengths. Remove stems on strawberries and cut into quarters. Place rhubarb and strawberries in a bowl. Add lemon juice, zest, vanilla and sugar and toss gently.

• Place rhubarb-strawberry mixture into a 9-inch pie pan. Cover with brown sugar-anise topping. Bake 45 minutes or until fruit juices are bubbling.

Serves 6

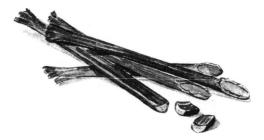

Very Berry Peach Crisp

4 cups fresh sliced peaches

3 cups fresh blueberries
   or thawed frozen

3 teaspoons lemon juice

3 tablespoons sugar

3 tablespoons flour

Topping:

1/2 cup firmly packed brown sugar

1/2 cup quick cooking rolled oats

2 tablespoons flour

2 tablespoons chopped pecans,
   almonds or walnuts

1/2 teaspoon cinnamon

1/8 teaspoon nutmeg

2 tablespoons butter

• Preheat oven to 350°. In an 8-inch square baking dish, toss peaches, blueberries, lemon juice, sugar and flour.

• In a bowl, mix together all topping ingredients except for butter. Cut in butter until crumbly. Sprinkle mixture over fruit.

• Bake for 30 minutes or until bubbly and golden brown. Serve immediately.

Serves 8

Lemon "Tart"!

Tart dough:

1 cup flour

1 ¹/₂ tablespoons sugar

pinch of salt

³/₄ cup chilled unsalted butter, cut up

grated rind of ¹/₂ lemon

Lemon curd filling:

zest of 3 lemons

1 cup sugar

7 large egg yolks

³/₄ cup fresh lemon juice

pinch salt

³/₄ cup unsalted butter, melted

whipped cream

- Preheat oven to 375°.

- To make the dough, combine flour, sugar and salt in a food processor fiited with a steel blade. Add butter and lemon rind and continue to process until dough forms. Press dough into a 9-inch tart pan or springform pan with removable bottom. Bake 15 to 18 minutes or until lightly golden.

- For the filling, combine lemon zest and sugar in the bowl of a food processor fitted with a steel blade. Process until zest is as fine as the sugar. Add egg yolks, lemon juice and salt. With the motor on, add hot butter through feed tube and process until ingredients are combined.

- Transfer mixture to a medium stainless steel sauce pan. Cook filling over medium-low heat until thickened, about 25 minutes. DO NOT BOIL. Filling should be the consistency of jello. Remove from heat and allow filling to cool. Filling will continue to thicken as it cools.

- Pour cooled lemon filling into tart shell. Refrigerate until it is ready to be served. Top each individual piece with a dollop of freshly whipped cream.

Serves 10

Crimson Poached Pears

2 cups dry red wine

juice of 1 lemon

1 strip of lemon peel

1 cup sugar

2 sticks of cinnamon

6 small pears, peeled
(leave stems on)

whipped cream, if desired

• Bring first five ingredients to a boil in a medium saucepan, stirring constantly, for 2 minutes.

• Reduce temperature to simmer, add pears and cook for approximately 20 minutes until pears are slightly soft. Baste pears frequently.

• Remove pears and discard lemon peel and cinnamon sticks. Boil syrup another 1 to 2 minutes until thickened; spoon over pears and serve warm with whipped cream, if desired.

Serves 6

Chocolate Creme Brulée

5 large egg yolks

½ cup sugar

*2 ounces bittersweet or semi-sweet
  chocolate, chopped*

2 cups whipping cream

1 tablespoon vanilla extract

*2 to 4 tablespoons sugar for
  caramelizing*

• Preheat oven to 300°.

• Whisk egg yolks and sugar in a large bowl.
  In a heavy saucepan, bring chocolate and
  cream to a simmer and stir with a wooden
  spoon until chocolate is melted. Whisk hot
  cream into yolks. Whisk in vanilla. Divide
  custard among 4 ramekins or glass custard
  cups.

• Place ramekins in a baking pan. Add enough
  hot water to pan to come halfway up sides of
  ramekins. Bake until custard is set in the
  center, approximately 55 minutes. Remove
  custards from the water and cool. Cover and
  refrigerate for at least 2 hours. (Can be
  refrigerated overnight).

• To serve, preheat broiler. Sprinkle ½ to 1
  tablespoon sugar over each custard. Broil
  until sugar caramelizes, approximately 3
  minutes. Cool 5 minutes and serve.

Serves 4

Chocolate Mousse with Pear Purée

16 ounces bittersweet chocolate

8 ounces semi-sweet chocolate

$^1/_2$ cup espresso

$^1/_2$ cup orange flavor liqueur

4 egg yolks

1 cup heavy cream

$^1/_4$ cup granulated sugar

6 egg whites

dash of salt

Pear Purée

6 tablespoons unsalted butter

6 large ripe pears, peeled and sliced

$^2/_3$ cup sugar

4 tablespoons brandy

• Melt both chocolates in saucepan with espresso and liqueur. Let cool to room temperature. Beat in egg yolks, one at a time.

• In a separate bowl, whip cream until thickened, gradually adding sugar. Beat until stiff. Beat egg whites with salt until stiff. Gently fold into cream. Stir about half of cream mixture into chocolate. After thoroughly mixed, add remaining cream mixture.

• Pour half of mousse into 8 champagne or wine glasses or dessert glass.

• To prepare Pear Purée, melt butter in large saucepan. Add pears and sauté until very soft and mushy, about 20 minutes. Add sugar to pears and simmer about 10 more minutes. Pour into food processor and puree, adding brandy.

• Divide purée among the 8 glasses and top with remaining half of mousse. Chill for at least 2 hours before serving.

Serves: 8

Almond Buttercream Gateau

Macaroon base:

¹/₃ cup sugar

3 ¹/₂ ounces almond paste

1 egg white

Cake layer:

3 cups sifted flour

1 tablespoon baking powder

¹/₂ teaspoon salt

6 egg whites, room temperature

2 cups sugar

*³/₄ cup unsalted butter, room
temperature*

2 teaspoons vanilla extract

1 cup milk

- Preheat oven to 375°. Cover a baking sheet with foil. Butter and flour the foil.

- Process sugar and almond paste until well-blended. Add egg white and process until mixture forms loose ball. Place in center of the prepared baking sheet. Gently spread mixture to resemble an 8-inch round circle.

- Bake 10 minutes or until golden brown. Cool completely before removing foil.

- Grease and flour two 9-inch round cake pans.

- Sift together flour, baking powder and salt. Set aside.

- Beat egg whites until foamy. Gradually add ¹/₂ cup of the sugar, beating until stiff peaks form. Set aside.

- In a mixing bowl, cream the butter and the remaining 1¹/₂ cups of sugar until fluffy. Add vanilla and stir. Add flour mixture, alternating with milk. Fold in egg whites.

- Pour into prepared pans and bake for approximately 35 minutes or until tester comes out clean. Cool slightly and then remove to racks.

Frosting:

1 ¹/₂ cups sugar

¹/₂ cup water

1 tablespoon light corn syrup

2 egg whites

dash of salt

¹/₄ teaspoon cream of tartar

1 teaspoon vanilla

¹/₂ cup butter

toasted almonds, for garnish

• Combine sugar, water and corn syrup in a saucepan over medium heat, stirring until sugar is dissolved. Bring to a boil and cook without stirring until syrup reaches 240° on candy thermometer.

• While syrup is cooking, beat egg whites with dash of salt until foamy. Beat in cream of tartar. Beat until egg whites just hold stiff peaks. Add syrup in a steady stream, beating constantly. Add vanilla and continue to beat on medium speed until completely cool. Beat in butter one tablespoon at a time and beat until smooth and creamy.

• To assemble place macaroon on serving plate. Thinly spread with some frosting. Layer with one cake and frost. Repeat with remaining cake and frost. Garnish with toasted almonds if desired.

Serves 8 to 10

Bourbon Chocolate Torte

2 cups pecans

1/2 pound unsalted butter

8 ounces bittersweet chocolate

1 1/2 cups sugar

1 cup unsweetened cocoa powder

6 eggs

1/3 cup bourbon

parchment paper

Glaze:

4 ounces bittersweet chocolate

1/2 cup unsalted butter

• Preheat oven to 325°. Spread pecans on baking sheet and roast until fragrant, approximately 10 minutes. Set aside. Cut a circle of parchment or waxed paper to fit bottom of 9-inch round cake pan. Butter pan well and line with paper circle.

• Melt butter and chocolate in double boiler. Stir until very smooth. Set aside to cool. Mix sugar, cocoa and eggs until well combined. Add melted chocolate, stirring to combine. Coarsely chop 1 1/2 cups of the pecans and stir in. Stir in bourbon. Pour into pan.

• Place pan inside larger pan. Fill larger pan with hot water to level of 1 inch in outer pan. Bake at 350° for 45 minutes. Cool. Remove from pan, leaving paper. Wrap cake and refrigerate overnight. Remove from refrigerator and place upside down. Peel off paper. Prepare glaze as directed. Drizzle spoonfuls of glaze over edges and sides of cake and spoon remaining glaze over top. Smooth with spatula. Decorate with whole pecan halves.

• For glaze melt chocolate and butter in double boiler over simmering water. Stir until smooth. Cool 5 minutes before glazing.

Serves 8-10

Glazed Truffle Cake

2 ounces unsweetened chocolate

1 cup sugar

1/4 cup butter

2 eggs, separated

1 teaspoon vanilla

1 1/2 cups sifted flour

1/2 teaspoon baking powder

1/2 teaspoon baking soda

1/2 teaspoon salt

3/4 cup milk

Truffle filling:

3/4 cup chocolate chips

1 cup heavy cream

Chocolate Glaze:

1 ounce unsweetened chocolate

2 tablespoons butter

1 1/2 cups sifted confectioners' sugar

1 teaspoon vanilla extract

2 to 3 tablespoon boiling water

sliced almonds, toasted, for garnish

• Preheat oven to 350°. Lightly butter two 8-inch round cake pans and line bottom with waxed paper.

• Melt chocolate and set aside to cool. Cream sugar and butter. Add egg yolks and vanilla. Beat until fluffy. Stir in chocolate. Sift together flour, baking powder, baking soda and salt. Add to chocolate mixture alternately with milk, beating well after each addition. Beat egg whites until stiff and fold into mixture. Bake 15 to 18 minutes. Cool for 10 minutes on a wire rack and remove.

• For filling, melt chocolate chips and cool. Whip the cream until fluffy. Add the chocolate and continue beating until stiff. Place cake on the serving dish, spread truffle filling on top and top with second layer of cake.

• For glaze, melt chocolate with butter and stir in confectioners' sugar and vanilla. Gradually add boiling water, beating until smooth. Spread over the cake top and garnish the sides with toasted sliced almonds. (Glaze should be somewhat thin to smoothly cover the entire cake top).

Serves 8-12

Pumpkin Patch Cheesecake

Crust:

1 ¹/₂ cups ground gingersnap cookies

*1 ¹/₂ cups toasted pecans
(about 6 ounces)*

¹/₄ cup firmly packed brown sugar

¹/₄ cup unsalted butter, melted

Filling:

*32 ounces cream cheese, room
temperature*

1 ²/₃ cups sugar

*1 ¹/₂ cups canned solid pack
pumpkin*

9 tablespoons whipping cream

1 teaspoon ground cinnamon

1 teaspoon ground allspice

4 large eggs

*1 tablespoon Caramel Sauce
(recipe follows)*

1 cup sour cream

• Preheat oven to 350°.

• To make crust, finely grind cookies, pecans
  and sugar in food processor. Add melted
  butter and blend until combined. Press crust
  mixture onto bottom and up sides of 9-inch
  springform pan.

• Using electric mixer, beat cream cheese and
  sugar in large bowl until light. Transfer ³/₄
  cup mixture to small bowl; cover tightly and
  refrigerate for later use.

• In a large bowl, add pumpkin, 4 tablespoons
  whipping cream, cinnamon and allspice to
  mixture and beat until well combined. Add
  eggs 1 at a time, beating just until combined.

• Pour filling into crust (filling will almost fill
  pan). Bake until cheesecake puffs, top
  browns and center moves only slightly when
  pan is shaken, about 1 hour 15 minutes.

• Transfer cheesecake to rack and cool 10
  minutes. Run small sharp knife around cake
  pan sides to loosen cheesecake. Cool. Cover
  tightly and refrigerate overnight.

Caramel Sauce

½ cup butter
1 ¼ cups brown sugar
2 tablespoons light corn syrup
½ cup heavy cream

In a heavy saucepan over low heat melt butter, brown sugar and corn syrup. Bring to a slow boil, stirring constantly until sugar dissolves. Gradually add cream and return to boil. Remove from heat.

Yields 2 cups

• Remove cheesecake from refrigerator. Bring remaining ¾ cup cream cheese mixture to room temperature. Add remaining 5 tablespoons whipping cream and stir to combine. Pour cream cheese mixture over cheesecake, spreading evenly. Spoon caramel sauce in lines over cream cheese mixture. Using tip of knife, swirl caramel sauce into cream cheese mixture. Cover and refrigerate.

• When ready to serve, release pan sides from cheesecake. Spoon sour cream into pastry bag fitted with small star tip. Pipe decorative border around cheesecake.

Serves 10

Heavenly Hazelnut Chocolate Cheesecake

³/4 cup finely ground hazelnuts

*three 8-ounce packages cream
cheese, softened*

1 cup sugar

2 tablespoons flour

¹/8 teaspoon salt

4 eggs

4 ounces semisweet chocolate, melted

¹/4 cup hazelnut or coffee liqueur

1 teaspoon vanilla extract

• Preheat oven to 325°. Generously grease the
bottom and sides of a 9-inch springform pan.
Press hazelnuts onto bottom and 1³/4 inches
up the sides of the pan.

• For filling, in a large bowl, beat the cream
cheese until creamy. Stir together the sugar,
flour and salt; add to the cream cheese
mixture and beat until blended. Add the eggs
and beat just until blended. Do not overbeat.
Stir in melted chocolate, liqueur and vanilla
until blended. Turn into prepared pan.

• Bake for 45 to 55 minutes or until the center
appears nearly set. Remove cheesecake from
oven; cool on a wire rack for 10 minutes.

• Carefully loosen the sides of the cheesecake.
Cool 30 minutes more; remove sides of the
pan. Cover and chill at least 2 hours.

Serves 12 to 14

Mocha Madness

1 cup butter

2 cups confectioners sugar

1/4 teaspoon salt

1/2 teaspoon cinnamon

2 ounces unsweetened chocolate,
    melted

4 tablespoons strong brewed coffee

2 eggs, beaten

1 package lady finger sponge cookies

whipped cream, for garnish

• With an electric mixer, cream together butter, sugar, salt and cinnamon. Add next three ingredients, beating after each addition.

• Crumble half of lady fingers (about 1½ cups). Line a 7½ x 2-inch round mold with waxed paper. (May also be prepared in a glass flat-bottomed trifle bowl.) Place whole lady fingers standing up around inside wall of mold for edging. Sprinkle crumbled lady fingers on bottom. Fill mold with alternating layers of mocha mixture and crumbled lady fingers, finishing with lady fingers.

• Chill, covered, in refrigerator, overnight. Flip mold onto cake plate. Remove waxed paper and serve with whipped cream.

Serves 8

Silky Smooth Chocolate Tart
with Raspberry Purée

Crust:

8 tablespoons unsalted butter, chilled

*1 cup plus 2 tablespoons
confectioners sugar*

2 1/2 cups flour

1 egg

ice water

"Rawzbree" - the true way older
Mainers pronounce raspberry.

• For the crust, combine butter, sugar and flour in the bowl of a food processor fitted with a plastic blade. Process until it resembles coarse meal. Add egg and process until blended. With motor running, add 1 to 2 tablespoons of ice water, processing until mixture just forms a ball. Remove dough from food processor bowl, press into a flat round and wrap in plastic. Refrigerate 1 hour.

• Preheat oven to 375°. Lightly flour both sides of dough and place between 2 pieces of waxed paper. Roll out dough to a thickness of 1/4 inch. Carefully fit dough into a 9-inch tart pan, preferably one with a removable bottom. Refrigerate 10 minutes. Line pastry with foil and fill with pie weights or dried beans. Bake for 5 to 6 minutes. Remove weights and foil, prick tart bottom with a fork and continue baking 8 to 10 minutes longer or until pastry is pale brown and has slightly withdrawn from side of pan.

Tart:

1 pound bittersweet chocolate

10 ounces unsalted butter

6 egg yolks

3 whole eggs

7 1/2 tablespoons sugar

1/2 pint heavy cream, whipped

10 sprigs fresh mint

- For the tart, reduce oven to 350°. In a double boiler over low heat, melt together chocolate and butter.

- In a large mixing bowl, beat the egg yolks and whole eggs until foamy. Add sugar and beat until pale and thick. Add melted chocolate mixture and stir until it is thick and shiny.

- Pour into prepared crust and bake for 15 minutes. Remove from oven. Chill overnight or at least 2 to 3 hours.

- Return to room temperature before serving. Serve each serving with a dollop of whipped cream and a sprig of mint, surrounded by a plate of *Raspberry Purée* (recipe follows).

Serves 8 to 10

Raspberry Purée

10 ounce package frozen raspberries in a light syrup, thawed and drained well

1/3 cup raspberry liqueur

1/3 cup unsweetened orange juice

2 teaspoons cornstarch

- Purée raspberries in a food processor until smooth. Strain out seeds. In a saucepan, combine purée with raspberry liqueur and bring to a boil. Reduce heat and simmer uncovered 5 minutes.

- Combine orange juice and cornstarch. Stir well and add to raspberry mixture. Over low heat cook until thickened, stirring constantly. Let cool. Refrigerate.

Yields 1 cup

Whipped Cream Nut Cake

¹/4 cup butter

1 ¹/2 cup sugar

4 eggs, separated

4 tablespoons milk

¹/2 cup plus 2 tablespoons flour

1 teaspoon baking powder

1 teaspoon vanilla

pinch of salt

1 cup chopped pecans or hazelnuts

1 pint heavy cream, whipped

• Preheat oven to 325°. Grease two 8 or 9-inch cake pans.

• Cream butter and ¹/2 cup sugar. Add egg yolks, milk, flour and baking powder and beat until well blended. Pour mixture into cake pans.

• Beat egg whites until stiff but not dry. Add 1 cup sugar, vanilla and salt. Spread over batter. Sprinkle both pans with nuts. Bake for 30 minutes or until cake tester comes out clean.

• Let cool completely on cake racks before removing carefully from the pans. When cool, put the two layers together with ¹/2 of the whipped cream between the layers and the other half on top. Refrigerate leftover cake.

Serves 8-10

Make sure oven is fully heated before baking — preheat at least 15 minutes. Using an oven thermometer can be helpful, as the precise temperature is crucial when baking.

Blueberry Burgundy Ice

2 1/2 cups sugar

2 cups water

4 cups blueberries

2 cups dry red wine

• Combine sugar and water in a large saucepan and stir well. Bring to a boil and cook until all sugar is dissolved, approximately 1 minute, stirring constantly. Set aside.

• Place blueberries in a food processor with a metal blade. Process until smooth. Strain blueberry mixture into a large saucepan and discard solids. Add sugar water and wine to blueberry juice and bring to a boil. Reduce heat and simmer, uncovered, 3 to 4 minutes. Remove from heat and cool thoroughly.

• Pour mixture into an 8-inch square baking dish. Cover and freeze overnight. To serve, scrape entire mixture with tines of a fork. Spoon into wine glasses and serve immediately.

• This ice can be kept frozen in a container for up to one month.

Serves 8 to 10

Blackberry & Lime Phyllo Tulips

Curd:

¹/₃ cup sugar

1 teaspoon cornstarch

*¹/₃ cup dessert wine, such as
    Essensia, or a sweet white wine*

¹/₃ cup fresh lime juice

1 teaspoon lime zest

¹/₂ cup egg substitute

Tulips:

4 sheets phyllo dough

2 tablespoons unsalted butter, melted

4 teaspoons (generous) sugar

• To make curd, mix sugar and cornstarch in heavy medium saucepan until no lumps remain. Mix in wine, lime juice and lime zest. Whisk in egg substitute (mixture may appear curdled) over medium heat until thick and just beginning to boil, about 7 minutes. Transfer curd to small bowl; cool. Cover and refrigerate overnight.

• To assemble phyllo tulips, lightly butter four ³/₄-cup custard cups or ramekins. Trim phyllo to 12-inch square. Cut 12-inch square into four 6-inch-square stacks.

• Lightly butter 1 phyllo square. Sprinkle with generous ¹/₄ teaspoon sugar. Repeat with 3 more phyllo squares, placing each at a different angle on top of others so that corners point in different directions.

• Gently press stack of phyllo squares into 1 prepared custard cup, forming pastry tulip. Repeat process forming 3 more pastry tulips.

• Preheat oven to 350°. Place custard cups on baking sheet. Bake until pastries are golden brown, about 20 minutes. Cool.

Berry sauce:

2 cups fresh or frozen blackberries

3 tablespoons sugar

¹/₄ cup raspberry flavored liqueur

2 cups fresh blackberries

• Purée 2 cups berries and 3 tablespoons sugar in blender, then strain. Add liqueur. Mix in 2 cups fresh berries. Chill.

• To serve, spoon curd into pastry cups, dividing equally. Top with berry sauce.

Serves 4

Working with Phyllo dough

To keep phyllo dough from drying out, cover dough with plastic wrap or waxed paper then top with a damp kitchen towel. Use one sheet at a time and you should have good results.

Blueberry Parfait with Lemon Custard

Blueberry sauce:

2 ¹/₂ cups fresh blueberries

³/₄ cup sugar

¹/₄ cup lemon juice

Lemon custard:

6 egg yolks

³/₄ cup sugar

1 cup Champagne or extra dry
   sparkling wine

2 tablespoons lemon juice

1 cup whipping cream

Other layers:

1 pint fresh blueberries

1 cup crumbled graham crackers

• For the sauce, purée berries in food processor. Transfer to medium saucepan. Add
sugar and lemon juice. Bring to boil, stirring
frequently. Reduce heat and simmer for 3
minutes. Pour into bowl. Chill.

• For the custard, whisk yolks and sugar in top
of double boiler. Set over bottom pan of
simmering water and whisk until foamy
(approximately 5 minutes). Add Champagne
and lemon juice and whisk until mixture
triples in volume and reaches 160° on candy
thermometer (4 minutes). Let stand until
cool, whisking occasionally for 30 minutes.
Chill. Whip cream until medium-stiff peaks
form then fold into chilled mixture.

• To assemble, use 8 wine or champagne
glasses. Spoon 1 tablespoon blueberry sauce
into each glass. Top with fresh blueberries.
Add ¹/₄ cup custard. Sprinkle with 1¹/₂
tablespoons graham crackers. Repeat
layering 1 to 2 more times, finish with a
blueberry layer. Refrigerate 3 to 8 hours.

Serves 8

Strawberries Flambé in Chocolate Lace Cups

Chocolate Lace Cups

12 ounces semisweet chocolate

Strawberries:

¹/₂ cup unsalted butter

4 cups sliced strawberries

²/₃ cup sugar

¹/₄ cup raspberry liqueur

¹/₂ cup dark rum

vanilla ice cream

- For chocolate lace cups, melt chocolate in saucepan. Pour into pastry bag or squeeze bottle. Line 6 small bowls with aluminum foil. Drizzle melted chocolate over aluminum foil bowls in criss-cross pattern (or random patter for a lacier appearance). Chill in freezer for at least 15 minutes.

- Carefully tear away aluminum foil from chocolate. Return to freezer until ready to serve.

- For strawberries flambé melt butter in skillet. Add strawberries and sugar. Add liqueur and rum. Light to flame.

- Fill cups with vanilla ice cream and top with strawberries flambe.

Serves 6

May be prepared in dessert bowls in place of chocolate cups.

Wild Berry Tart

Crust:

1 ⅓ cups flour

2 tablespoons sugar

8 tablespoons cold butter

1 egg yolk

ice water

Filling:

2 tablespoons cornstarch,
    dissolved in orange juice

¼ cup sugar

2 cups blueberries

1 cup raspberries

1 cup blackberries

1 egg yolk, lightly beaten

whipped cream (optional)

- Preheat oven to 400°

- To prepare crust, mix flour and sugar in a medium bowl. Cut butter into pieces and add to flour. Mix with fingers or pastry knife until butter is evenly distributed and mixture resembles coarse meal. Blend in yolk. Add water (approximately 2 tablespoons) until mixture can form a ball. Shape dough into a disk, wrap in waxed paper and refrigerate until ready to use.

- To prepare filling, in saucepan over medium heat, cook cornstarch, sugar and blueberries until mixture starts to thicken. Add ½ cup raspberries and ½ cup blackberries and continue to cook until fully thickened. Remove from heat and cool completely.

- Bring dough to room temperature. Place between two sheets of wax paper and roll out to ¼ " thickness. Peel off wax paper and place crust on 12"-14" tart or round flat pan. Spread filling evenly over center of crust leaving 1" at edges. Fold edges of crust up over filling, allowing crust to overlap. Brush crust with egg yolk and sprinkle with sugar.

- Bake tart 20 to 25 minutes until golden brown. Remove from oven and cool. Top with whipped cream if desired and decorate with remaining berries.

Serves 8-12

Nubble Light Nut Bars

2 cups flour

2 teaspoons baking powder

1 teaspoon baking soda

$^1/_2$ teaspoon salt

$^1/_2$ cup shortening
 (do not use butter)

$^1/_2$ cup sugar

1 $^1/_2$ cups firmly packed brown sugar

2 eggs, separated

1 teaspoon vanilla extract

3 tablespoons ice cold water

12 ounces semi-sweet chocolate bits

$^3/_4$ cup salted peanuts

• Preheat oven to 350°. Grease and flour
9 x 13-inch pan. Sift together flour, baking
powder, baking soda and salt.

• In a large bowl, cream the shortening. Add
$^1/_2$ cup each white and brown sugar. Mix
well. Blend in egg yolks and vanilla. Alternately, add the sifted dry ingredients and ice
cold water to the shortening mixture. Dough
will be stiff.

• Press dough into prepared pan. Sprinkle
semi-sweet chocolate bits over dough and
press gently.

• In a small bowl, beat the egg whites until
foamy. Add remaining brown sugar and beat
until stiff. Spread the egg whites over
chocolate bits. Sprinkle peanuts on top of
egg whites.

• Reduce oven temperature to 325° and bake
for 30 to 35 minutes. Remove from oven and
cut into bars while still warm.

Yields 12 to 18 bars

Toasted Coconut Chiffon Cup Cakes

2 ¹/4 cups flour

1 ¹/2 cups sugar

1 tablespoon baking powder

1 teaspoon salt

¹/3 cup salad oil

1 cup milk

1 ¹/2 teaspoons vanilla

2 eggs, separated

1 ¹/4 cups flaked coconut

• Preheat oven to 400°.

• Sift together flour, 1 cup sugar, baking powder and salt in a mixing bowl. Make a well in dry ingredients. Add salad oil, half of milk and vanilla. With electric mixer, mix until smooth. Add remaining milk and egg yolks. Beat one minute.

• In a separate bowl, beat egg whites until soft peaks form; gradually add remaining sugar and beat until stiff peaks form. Fold into batter. Fold in ¹/4 cup flaked coconut to batter.

• Fill paper muffin cups ³/4 full. Sprinkle remaining coconut on top.

• Bake 12 to 15 minutes or until light golden.

*Yields approximately 2 dozen regular size or
3 ¹/2 dozen mini muffins*

Chocolate Nut Meringue Drops

3 large egg whites

1/4 teaspoon cream of tartar

pinch of salt

3/4 cup sugar

1/2 cup cocoa

2 teaspoons vanilla extract

1 cup chopped pecans

• Preheat oven to 275°. In a large bowl, combine egg whites, cream of tartar and salt. Beat until soft peaks form. Add sugar, about 2 to 3 tablespoons at a time, and beat until peaks are firm. Fold in cocoa, vanilla and nuts.

• Line a cookie sheet with brown paper. Drop by rounded teaspoonfuls. Bake about 45 minutes.

Yields 3 dozen

"Wicked Awesome" Cookies

1/2 cup butter

1 1/2 cups white sugar

1 1/2 cups brown sugar

4 eggs

2 1/2 teaspoons baking soda

2 teaspoons vanilla extract

18-ounce jar peanut butter

6 cups oatmeal

12 ounces chocolate chips

• Preheat oven to 350°.

• Cream butter and sugars together in a large bowl. Add eggs and mix well. Add the remaining ingredients and combine well with a spoon. (Do not use a mixer). The batter should be very stiff and sticky.

• Drop by large spoonfuls onto a greased cookie sheet. Bake 12 to 15 minutes.

• Cool on a wire rack.

Yields 6 to 8 dozen

Sugar & Spice Cookies

¹/2 cup unsalted butter

1 cup sugar

1 egg, well beaten

1 ³/4 cups flour

2 teaspoons baking powder

Topping:

1 teaspoon cinnamon

2 tablespoons sugar

1 egg white

*2 ounces semisweet chocolate, melted
  (optional)*

• In large mixing bowl, cream butter and sugar. Add the egg and beat until smooth. Add the flour ¹/2 cup at a time and blend well after each addition. Add the baking powder and mix until fully incorporated. Form dough into a ball and chill for half an hour. Flour a cutting board. Roll dough out very thin, approximately ¹/8-inch in thickness. Use cookie cutters to cut dough. Place cookies on greased baking sheet.

• Preheat oven to 350°. To decorate, combine sugar and cinnamon in a small bowl. Coat cookie with egg white and sprinkle with cinnamon/sugar mixture. Bake for 10 to 12 minutes until edges are lightly browned. Do not overcook. Remove to wire racks to cool.

• For optional chocolate topping, do not coat cookie with egg, cinnamon and sugar. Instead, place cookies on waxed paper and drizzle with melted chocolate or dip one half into chocolate. Let chocolate harden and enjoy!

Yields 3 dozen

Banana Pecan Cookies

2 cups flour

1 1/2 teaspoons baking powder

1/2 teaspoon cinnamon

1/4 teaspoon salt

1/4 teaspoon ground cloves

1/2 cup butter

1 cup sugar

2 eggs

1/2 teaspoon vanilla

1 banana, mashed

1/2 cup chopped pecans or walnuts

whole pecans for topping

Glaze:

1 cup confectioners sugar

1 tablespoon butter

4 teaspoons milk

1/2 teaspoon vanilla

• Preheat oven to 375°. Sift together dry ingredients. Set aside. Cream butter and sugar. Add eggs and vanilla. Add dry ingredients, then banana and chopped nuts. Drop by teaspoons onto greased cookie sheets. Bake for 10 to 12 minutes.

• Combine glaze ingredients until smooth. Drizzle glaze on warm cookies and top with pecan halves.

Yields 2 1/2 dozen

Sesame-Anise Melt Cookies

2 cups flour

¹/4 teaspoon baking soda

³/4 cup unsalted butter, softened

³/4 cup granulated sugar

1 tablespoon anise seed, crushed

¹/4 teaspoon salt

1 egg

³/4 cup sesame seeds, toasted

• Preheat oven to 400°. Grease 4 large baking sheets.

• In a medium bowl, combine flour and baking soda. Set aside.

• In a large mixing bowl, beat butter, sugar, anise seed and salt until light and fluffy. Beat in egg. Stir in flour mixture ¹/2 cup at a time, blending well after each addition.

• Place sesame seeds in a bowl. With well floured hands, roll heaping teaspoons of dough into 1-inch balls. Roll balls in sesame seeds. Place on a baking sheet and flatten to ¹/4 inch thickness with the bottom of a glass. Bake 6 to 9 minutes, until lightly browned on edges. Cool on racks.

Yields 3 ¹/2 dozen cookies

Maple Curls

½ cup maple syrup

4 tablespoons unsalted butter

½ cup sifted flour

¼ teaspoon salt

¼ teaspoon ground ginger

chopped candied ginger for garnish

- Preheat oven to 400°. Grease a baking sheet and set aside.

- In a small saucepan over medium-high heat, combine maple syrup and butter. Boil for 30 seconds. Remove from heat and add dry ingredients. Mix well.

- Drop batter onto prepared sheet, leaving 3 inches between cookies. Bake for 4 to 6 minutes, until cookies begin to brown.

- Cool slightly and remove from sheet. Wrap warm cookies around a wooden spoon handle to form curls. (If they harden before being shaped, put back in oven to warm a bit). Garnish cookies with a little chopped candied ginger.

Yields 2 dozen

Doubly Decadent Raspberry Brownies

10 ounces bittersweet chocolate

3 ounces semi-sweet chocolate

2 1/2 ounces unsweetened chocolate

1 cup butter

1 cup sugar

3/4 cup packed brown sugar

3 large eggs

3/4 cup raspberry liqueur

2 teaspoons vanilla

1 1/2 cups flour

1/4 teaspoon salt

2 tablespoons confectioners sugar

• Preheat oven to 350°. Butter a 9x13-inch baking pan. Coarsely chop chocolates. In top of a double boiler, melt chocolates with butter, stirring occasionally, until smooth. Remove top portion of double boiler and cool mixture to lukewarm, about 10 minutes.

• In a large bowl, beat sugars and eggs with an electric mixer at high speed until thick and light colored, about 5 minutes. Beat in liqueur and vanilla. Add chocolate mixture and mix until well blended. With mixer on low speed, beat in flour and salt just until combined.

• Pour batter into prepared pan and smooth surface with rubber spatula. Bake 25 to 30 minutes or until toothpick inserted 2 inches from center comes out slightly moist. Cool brownies in pan on a wire rack. When completely cool, cut brownies into squares. Place powdered sugar in a sieve and dust brownies with sugar after cutting.

Yields 20 brownies

Almond Butter Strips

1 ³/4 cups flour

¹/2 cup granulated sugar

¹/4 teaspoon salt

¹/2 cup sweet butter, at room
   temperature

1 large egg, lightly beaten

Glaze:

¹/3 cup sweet butter

1 cup sliced almonds

¹/4 cup granulated sugar

¹/4 cup brandy or ¹/4 cup water and
   1 teaspoon brandy extract

3 tablespoons honey

1 teaspoon almond extract

• Heat oven to 350°. Lightly grease a 15x10-inch jelly-roll pan.

• Meanwhile, in a large bowl, mix flour, sugar and salt. Cut in butter with pastry blender or 2 knives until mixture resembles fine crumbs. Stir in egg until blended. Press dough evenly over bottom of prepared pan.

• To prepare glaze, melt butter in a small saucepan over medium-low heat. Add almonds, sugar, brandy, honey and almond extract. Stir over medium-high heat until mixture comes to a boil. Remove from heat and let glaze cool slightly. Pour glaze over the top of dough and spread evenly.

• Bake 20 to 25 minutes until light brown. Cool in pan on wire rack. Cut into 2x1-inch strips. Store airtight up to 2 weeks.

Yields 5 to 6 dozen

Sunset Sangria

1 ¹/₂ liters dry red wine

3 cups orange juice

1 quart club soda

juice of 4 limes

juice of 3 lemons

¹/₂ cup sugar

¹/₂ cup brandy

1 lemon, sliced, for garnish

1 orange, sliced, for garnish

• Mix all ingredients, except garnishes. Chill. Serve over ice with lemon and orange garnish.

Yields 16 cups

Zingy Iced Tea Slush

2 ¹/₂ cups water

6 lemon flavored tea bags

1 ¹/₂ tablespoons chopped fresh mint

2 tablespoons sugar

³/₄ cup unsweetened orange juice

2 tablespoons undiluted frozen lemonade concentrate

3 cups chilled club soda

• Bring water to a boil; pour over tea bags and mint. Cover and let stand 5 minutes; discard tea bags. Strain mixture; discard mint. Add sugar and stir well. Add orange juice and lemonade and stir well. Pour mixture into an 8-inch square baking pan; cover and freeze 2 hours. Spoon mixture into a pitcher; stir in club soda. Stir gently until mixture becomes slushy, breaking up frozen pieces with a spoon. Serve immediately.

Yields 6 cups

Citrus Wine Punch

2 bottles dry white wine

two 12-ounce cans frozen pineapple
  juice, thawed

6-ounce can frozen lemonade,
  thawed

6-ounce can frozen orange juice,
  thawed

10-ounce jar maraschino cherries

2 oranges, sliced

• Combine all ingredients except for orange
slices, in large container. Cover and chill for
8 hours. Serve chilled garnished with orange
slices.

Yields 10 cups

Ginger Almond Iced Tea

1 cup boiling water

5 regular-size tea bags

1 cup sugar

4 cups water

1/2 cup lemon juice

1 teaspoon vanilla extract

1 teaspoon almond extract

1 quart ginger ale, chilled

• Pour boiling water over tea bags; cover and
steep 5 minutes. Remove tea bags, squeezing
gently. Stir in sugar and next 4 ingredients;
chill. Stir in ginger ale just before serving.
Serve tea over ice.

Yields 3 quarts

Chilled Spiked Coffee

4 cups strong brewed coffee

2 tablespoons sugar

4 cups skim milk

1/2 cup brandy or 1 tablespoon
    brandy extract

1/2 teaspoon vanilla extract

• Combine coffee and sugar in a pitcher. Chill
thoroughly. Stir in milk and remaining
ingredients. Serve over ice.

Yields 2 quarts

Mulled Apple Cider

2 quarts apple cider

1 teaspoon whole allspice

1 teaspoon whole cloves

3-inch cinnamon stick

dash of nutmeg

whole cinnamon sticks, for garnish

• Combine all ingredients and bring to a boil.
Reduce and simmer 20 minutes. Remove the
spices. Serve in mugs with whole cinnamon
sticks.

Yields 2 quarts

Berry Good Eggnog

10-ounce package frozen raspberries
in syrup, thawed

1 quart cold prepared eggnog

1 cup raspberry liqueur

• Purée the raspberries and strain through a
fine sieve to remove the seeds. Transfer the
purée to a pitcher. Stir the eggnog and
liqueur into the purée . Cover and refrigerate
for at least 4 hours to blend flavors.

Serves 10

Brown Sugar Hot Chocolate

¹/₃ cup firmly packed brown sugar

¹/₃ cup unsweetened cocoa

1 cup water

5 cups milk

1 teaspoon vanilla or almond extract

• Combine brown sugar and cocoa in a
saucepan; stir in water. Bring to a boil over
medium heat, stirring occasionally; reduce
heat and slowly stir in milk. Cook until
thoroughly heated, stirring constantly.
Remove from heat; stir in extract. Serve
immediately.

Yields 6 cups

The *Maine Ingredients* Committee would like to express our appreciation to the
following members, families and friends of the Junior League of Portland, Maine who
shared their ideas and recipes with us. We regret that we were unable to include
all recipes submitted due to similarity or availability of space.

Judy Adams
Rhonda Ainsworth
Carla Akalarian
Suzy Andrews
Kelly Ann Johnson
Betts Armstrong
Carol I. Austin
Cecelia Austin
Rachel Avery
Sandy Barner
Barbara Bates
Pam Bates
Sandy Bennett
Abigail Bernard
Mary Beth Kwityn
Anne Bosworth
Denise Bowers
Susie Canon
Cyndy Chaney
Barbara Chellis
Pricilla Cianchette
Carolyn Cianchette
Peter Cianchette
Marilyn Cianchette
Elizabeth Colgan
Jane Collins
Mary Cook
Nan Corcoran
Catie Costello
Sylvia Costlow
Lesley P. Craig
Kathy Cramer-Howe
Beth Currier
Jane Dann
Steve DiCicco
Ellie Duley
Stephen Eddy
Terri Eddy
Jeri Edgar
Debbie Edwards
Sandy Enck
Mary Nash Flagg
Judy Flaker
Patti Foden
Ann Foden
Joy Foster

Beth Franklin
Katie Freilinger
Peggy Frongillo
Kim Gallagher
Leslie Gibbons
Janet Gibson
Cynthia Orr Gillis
Ethel Faulkner Gillis
Patricia Gleason
Barbara Goodbody
Jean Gorman
Audrey Gough
Mike Graef
Elaine Graef
Patti Grennon
Mary Gresge
Barbara Hadlock
Jenny Hall
Amy Happ
Jean Harrison
Jennifer Hayden
Fran Haywood
Ann Heald
Maureen Healy
Michelle Hedrich
Christina Heldenbrand
Laura Lennon Hertz
Margaret C. Hewes
Betsey Hewes
Nan Higgins
Susan Hobbs
Molly Horn
Joan Houghton
Flo Houston
Margaret Hudman
Laurie Hyndman
Michelle Ibarguen
Beverly Intravaia
Peter Johnson
Barbara Johnson
Kim Joyce
Peggy Keach
Katie Keith
Julie Lake
Elizabeth Lakeman
Jeanne F. Langsdorf

Sara Laprade
N. Richmond Leach
Sally Leach
Susan Leach
Rho Leavitt
Cindy LeFevre
Ann Leighton
Catharine Pilling Lennon
Mary E. P. Lewis
Nancy Libbey
Cotheal Linnell
Marcia Livada
Nancy Machesney
Peg MacVane
Alicia Lewis Manter
Mary Martin
Donna Martin
Anne Mason
Ginny McGinley
Joan McGorrill
Rabecca McKelvey
Beryl McPherson
Sonya Messer
Alison Metsker
Mary Michals
Joyce Miller
Bette Milley
Hope Mitchell
Tricia Mitchell
Margaret Mixon
Sally Morrison
Julie Myers
Mamie Ney
Sally Nichols
Pauline Noyes
Linda Nye
Jane Parker
Shelly Paules
Mary Pederson
Joan Pendexter
Ann Perrino
Philip Perrino
Janet Philbrick
Laurie Piasio
Steve Picocco
Alison Prawer

Elizabeth Preti
Martha Proulx
Ginny Ray
Mary Jane Reevy
Mary Alice Reilley
Cay Reiman
Rachel Resnick
Gail Rice
Mary Rickert
Karen Rickley
Janet Gillis Rivard
Julie C. Rourke
Judy Rowe
Libby Rust
John Rust
Mary Rutherford
Phil Scavotto
Linda Schrader
Anita Scott
Barbara Seelen
Mary Jane Shaw
Katie Shisler
Joan Smith
Barbara Smith
Sheila Sneider
Courtney Spencer
Jane Sperlazzi
Elizabeth Stageman
Pam Straw
Nancy Thompson
Martha Timothy
Nancy Tobin
Mary Trace
Alice Kane Tucker
Daniel J. Tucker
Lucy Lennon Tucker
Janet Tunis
Regina Murray
 Vanasdale
India Weatherill
Valerie Webster
Lee Wilson
Victoria W. Wright
Winston Case Wright
Robert Zolendjuski

Maine Ingredients acknowledges with great appreciation, the generous
contributions and support received from the following
individuals and businesses.

Patron
Cotheal Linnell, Mrs. John R.

Donors
Linwood & Carol Austin	Gail M. Liberty
Mrs. Elizabeth Costello	The Liberty Group
Mr. & Mrs. "Bud" Cianchette	Maine Financial Trust, Inc.
Bill & Chris Dewhurst	Mr. & Mrs. Robert Ney
Sharon A. Dunlap	Mrs. H.D. Penley
Jeri D. Edgar	Smith Barney, Portland, ME
John & Amy Happ	The Travelers

Contributors
Anonymous	Elizabeth L. Knowles
Dr. & Mrs. David Andrews	Susan Koch
Deborah A. Barnes	Margaret O. MacVane
Jane V. Berry	Priscilla H. McCarty
Eveline Cianchette	Mrs. James E. McCullum
Peggy Cianchette	Beryl Reid McPherson
Frank & Ruth Coffin	Mr. & Mrs. Michael S. Paules
Dave & Catie Costello	Mary Morse Reevy, Mrs. John H.
Cornelia A. Greaves	Pia Mary Rice
Nan & Jim Higgins	Richard & Mary Walker
Doris Homer	Ann M. Washburn
Laurie & Tom Hyndman	Nickey Wilson
Inplan Group	Mr. & Mrs. John H. Wright, Jr.

Friends
Cecelia L. Austin	Mrs. William K. Hadlock
Rob & Nancy Craig	Pamela S. Howard
Jane J. Dann	Mr. & Mrs. Richard Intravaia
Mary Nash Flagg	Harry Leach
Katie Freilinger, Mrs. James E.	Catharine P. Lennon
Mrs. Eli Forsley	Judy Wright Mathews
Dorothea B. Foss	Cathy-Ann Wirth

Special Thank You:
Hannaford Brothers Company, Whip & Spoon, Omni Press, Thyra & John Porter,
Shop'n Save Supermarkets, Frontier Communications of New England,
Notes of Distinction, and Bookland of Maine

Betty Ann Maynard Handpainted Originals

Individual handpainted New England and Christmas designs are available in boxed and unboxed notecards with envelopes as well as signed and matted single designs in three popular sizes. Signed original art in watercolor and tempera is offered in two special series of affordable high quality notes. Custom work is invited. Information and orders:
P.O. Box 225
East Boothbay, ME 04544
(207) 633-2399

Turner's Garlic Sauces

Friends' demands for their old-fashioned garlic dressing got to be too much. So in 1991, the Turner family created Hybrid Vigor Kitchen to commercially bottle their recipes. Still made by hand! Using only fresh garlic! Turner's has developed a following around New England among those who appreciate the benefits of a real garlic sauce. There are six types.
P.O. Box 245
Georgetown, IL 61846
(217) 662-2799

Kibco

From the woods near "Golden Pond" comes this satisfying blend of fruits and spices. PIQUANT SAUCES combine the subtle spicy essence of the Maine woods with the zest of Texas-style hot flavors to create uncommonly refined sauces. Use as a spread, dip, marinade or barbecue sauce on meats, fish, poultry, vegetables and sandwiches. No fat, no cholesterol. Six flavors.
P.O. Box 565
Belgrade Lakes, ME 04918-0565
(207) 495-7749

Maine Wild Blueberry Company

The Maine Wild Blueberry Company located in Machias is involved in growing, buying and processing (freezing, canning and dehydrating) wild blueberries. The company has state-of-the-art facilities and in the 11 years since its inception has seen phenomenal growth. Maine Wild® excels in research and development, customer service, problem solving and quality products. Maine Wild® is a leading supplier of wild blueberries and wild blueberry products to major users in the U.S. and overseas. For a supplier nearest you:
P.O. Box 278
Machias, ME 04654
(207) 255-8364

Maine Balsam Fir Products

Balsam pillows from the Maine woods. Our beautiful and fragrant balsam filled pillows and sachets are a wonderful reminder of Christmas or of a walk in the woods. They feature original wildlife designs and continue to delight people of all ages. Our new draft stoppers, trivets and tapestry pillows are especially pleasing and practical. In our fourteenth year, we can ship most orders within two weeks. Call or write for a free color catalogue.
P.O. Box 9
West Paris, ME 04289
(800) 522-5726 • (207) 674-5094

River Music

To soothe, cheer, or simply amuse—the music of composer and pianist Paul Sullivan. A blending of classical and jazz styles that has earned national awards and recognition worldwide comes from Blue Hill Falls, Maine. For tapes, CDs or concerts call or write:
Route 175
Blue Hill Falls, ME 04615
(207) 374-2208
FAX (207) 374-2082

Maine's Own Treats

We offer over 30 varieties of homemade jams and fruit syrups including Blueberry, Strawberry-Rhubarb, and Yummy Toast Spread (tastes like apple pie). Visit our year-round gift shop and factory outlet, sample our products

and select from the large assortment of gift packages. Bus tours welcome. Free mail order brochure available. Wholesale inquiries welcome. All major credit cards accepted.
Bar Harbor Road
Trenton, ME 04605
(207) 667-8888

Wilbur's of Maine Chocolate Confections

Award winning homemade confections. Wilbur's produces a full line of high quality chocolates from blueberry creams made with real Maine blueberries to grant turtles oozing with homemade caramel and smooth silk chocolate. All forms of molded chocolates are available for every occasion. Wilbur's has a mail order catalogue which we would gladly send upon request.
11 Independence Drive
Freeport, ME 04032
(207) 865-4071
FAX (207) 865-4650

Spruce Mountain Blueberries

An authentic Maine cottage industry. From our own wild Maine blueberries, Spruce Mountain Blueberries makes: wild Blueberry Chutney (hot and spicy, adapted from a North Indian recipe); Chutney with Almonds and Raisins; Blueberry Conserve (a spicy but not hot preserve); reduced sugar Blueberry

Jam; wholeberry Blueberry Syrup; and Blueberry Vinegar.
Box 68
West Rockport, ME 04865
(207) 236-3538
FAX (207) 236-8545

Great Eastern Mussel Farms, Inc.

Great Eastern Mussel Farms has been farming mussels on the coast of Maine since 1978. Sweeter, richer, and less expensive than clams, our mussels are pre-soaked so they are grit-free. Great Eastern Mussels are available in supermarkets throughout North America. Call for free recipe cards or to find a supplier near you.
P.O. Box 141
Tenants Harbor, ME 04860
(207) 372-6317
FAX (207) 372-8256

Canterbury's Crack and Peel, Inc.

For the true garlic lover! Canterbury's Crack and Peel is a kitchen utensil used to open garlic fast and easy. It is 2⅞" high and 3" in diameter made of solid maple in the shape of a mushroom. Canterbury's Crack and Peel can also be used as a pestle by turning it upside down to crush herbs and crackers. Gentle, safe, fast, and easy.
109½ Pleasant Street
Claremont, NH 03743
(603) 543-0191 • (800) 551-0496
e-mail Bob at crackandpeel.com

D.J.C. Design Studio, Inc.

Woven throw blankets, decorative pillows, and distinctive women's apparel and accessory items. Colors and textures inspired by the landscapes of Maine and woven in natural fibers - chenille, mohair, cotton, silk, wool, rayon. Each item is hand-crafted on antique looms with unusual novelty yarns. Great for gift giving! Mail order shipped world-wide, or visit our factory outlet store. Call for color catalogue or directions to visit.
9 Grove Street,
Kennebunk, ME 04043
(mail only)
227 Sheep Davis Road,
Concord, NH 03301
(store and mail)
(800) 554-7890

Decorating Den by Kim Connell, Owner & Interior Decorator

Unique window treatments, bed ensembles, accessories and wallcoverings, etc. Kim is experienced and trained to work within your style and budget to help you create the look you want for your home or office. Call for a convenient complimentary consultation.
196 Prince's Point Road
Yarmouth, ME 04096
(207) 846-3745

Mulberry Cottage

Mulberry Cottage, a warehouse and showroom full of English Country Pine furniture and antiques, accessories for the home and wonderful, unusual gift ideas. We also carry a full line of doll house miniatures and we can deliver anywhere for you. On the premises we hand cast concrete garden ornaments and statuary and mix it with other garden items, both new and old. It's worth a trip to see us, but allow a few hours—there's lots to see!
45 Western Ave.
South Portland, Maine 04106
(207) 775-5011
FAX (207) 775-0321

Eggemoggin Reach Bed & Breakfast

Every room enjoys a waterfront panorama of the "Reach," Pumpkin Light, and Penobscot Bay. Private dock, moorings, acres of shorefront privacy. Charming "farm-house" from which to explore Castine, Deer Isle, Blue Hill, and Acadia National Park.
Herrick Road
Brooksville, ME 04617
(207) 359-5073

The Whip & Spoon

Maine's extraordinary resource for cooking implements, kitchen accessories, specialty foods, fine wines and beer making supplies. A vast assortment of cookware, knives, bakeware, small appliances, cookbooks, linens, glassware is complimented by an extensive wine selection, imported cheeses, pâtés, caviar, smoked salmon and other delicacies, and, by our famous collection of Maine-made products. We specialize in gift baskets. Call about cooking classes.
161 Commercial Street,
Portland, ME 04101
(207) 774-6262
FAX (207) 774-6261
198 Maine Mall Road,
South Portland, ME 04106
(207) 774-7191
Monday–Saturday 10–8
Sunday 12–5

Federal Jack's Brew Pub

Federal Jack's Brew Pub invites you to join us for a brew with a view! Healthy affordable dining, fantastic daily specials, world class ale, and a breathtaking view of Kennebunkport Harbor await you. Federal Jack's also features live acoustic music every Friday and Saturday, daily happy hour 4–6 p.m., and a huge game room (pool, darts, shuffle board.) In addition, brewery tours may be arranged. Come experience Federal Jack's. Cheers!!
8 Western Avenue
Kennebunk, ME 04043
(207) 967-4322
FAX (207) 967-4903

Good Clean Food

Love good food? Don't always have time to prepare it? Try our fresh simmer sauces for fish...for a delicious, one-step gourmet meal in 10 minutes. Fresh, natural ingredients, full of flavor yet respectful of excellent seafood, offer tastes, textures and smells to please your senses and your spirit. Just add fish or seafood, simmer, and enjoy! We've made it from scratch, so you don't have to. Available in three distinctive flavors: Mediterranean, Scandinavian Dill and Japanese.
21 Summit Road
Cape Elizabeth, ME 04107
(800) 4U-ENJOY

TREATS

Located in the old Masonic Hall in Yarmouth, TREATS is a specialty gourmet food store that promises "something for everyone." From savory cheese & pâtés to specialty groceries to penny candies for the kids, TREATS has it all. And, for the wine enthusiast, TREATS also has one of the finest selections of imported and domestic wines, champagnes, dessert wines, and imported beers available in Maine. And, with the recent addition of a full cafe to the store, TREATS also offers unsurpassed lunches, takeout, and catering. Above all else, the owners strive to bring

their customers the best and most unique gourmet products available in a fun and casual environment.
106 Main Street
Yarmouth, ME 04096
(207) 846-1117
FAX (207) 846-6950

Pleasant Valley Sugarhouse

On waffles or ice cream, in cookies or black-peppered maple cream pie, live the maple experience whenever you taste our product. We offer maple products and honey at the sugarhouse or via mail. Recipes are included with every order.
35 Sturbridge Lane
Cumberland, ME 04021
(207) 829-4596

McMillen's Gourmet Foods

Try our Prize-Winning, salt-free Champagne Mustard Sauce, Jalapeño Jelly and assorted preserves. All natural ingredients make these handmade products a treat for you or great for gifts. Also, don't forget our line of Mid-Life Crisis Spices for that special cook. Daily shipment—please call for retail mail order and wholesale information.
Deborah J. McMillen, Proprietor
P.O. Box 63
Eliot, ME 03903
(207) 439-2481
FAX (207) 439-6755

Harbor Fish Market

Located on Portland's waterfront since 1969. A family owned and operated seafood business specializing in high quality seafood and wide varieties from Maine to Florida to the West Coast. Harbor Fish Market will ship throughout the USA. Voted Portland's best for years.
9 Custom House Wharf
Portland, Maine
(207) 775-0251

Mother's Mountain

Feel extra good about offering your family and friends the finest, tastiest, all natural Specialty Sauces! Handmade in small batches, most are: No Salt – No Sugar – No Preservatives – Gluten-Free. Mother's Mountain is celebrating their 15th year in business. Using family recipes that Grandmother and Mother made to enhance the good food they served to their family, Mother's Mountain shares them with you today! Product line includes: Mustards (Classic Honey, Zesty Honey, Beer, Peppercorn Dijon), Sauces (Dijon Dill, Creamy Horseradish, Honey Hickory BBQ, Catchup, New England Chili Salsa), Pepper Sauces (Habañero Heaven, Fire Eater), and Natural Trail Mixes. Kosher Certified.

Available in assorted sizes and gift packaging, too! Please write or call the mustard makers:
Carol Tanner & Dennis Proctor
110 Woodville Road
Falmouth, Maine 04105
(800) 440-9891

DAIRY

"On this 75th anniversary of the Junior League of Portland, all of us at Oakhurst Dairy salute the volunteers who make such a difference in our community.

"We also salute the *Maine Ingredients* cookbook, which captures the essence of Maine cooking. We invite you to savor this culinary trip through our state—and to choose fresh, native ingredients like Oakhurst Milk, Buttermilk, Creams, and Sour Cream."

Stanley T. Bennett II   Althea Bennett Allen   William P. Bennett

Index

Index

Junior League of Portland Cookbooks

Quantity	Book		Total
_____	**RSVP** (our first cookbook)	@ $14.95 each	_____
_____	MAINE *Ingredients*	@ 19.95 each	_____
	Shipping & Handling @	4.50 each	_____
	Maine residents add 6% sales tax		_____
	Total enclosed		_____

Please send the above cookbooks to:

Name _____

Address _____

City _____ State _____ Zip _____

Telephone (_____) _____

Please make checks payable to the Junior League of Portland, Maine, Inc. Please do not send cash. Sorry no C.O.D.'s

Mail to: The Junior League of Portland, Maine, Inc.
107 Elm Street, Suite 100R
Portland, Maine 04101

- -

Junior League of Portland Cookbooks

Quantity	Book		Total
_____	**RSVP** (our first cookbook)	@ $14.95 each	_____
_____	MAINE *Ingredients*	@ 19.95 each	_____
	Shipping & Handling @	4.50 each	_____
	Maine residents add 6% sales tax		_____
	Total enclosed		_____

Please send the above cookbooks to:

Name _____

Address _____

City _____ State _____ Zip _____

Telephone (_____) _____

Please make checks payable to the Junior League of Portland, Maine, Inc. Please do not send cash. Sorry no C.O.D.'s

Mail to: The Junior League of Portland, Maine, Inc.
107 Elm Street, Suite 100R
Portland, Maine 04101